# Rave Reviews for the First Edition of PLAYING SMART:

"The beauty of this guide is that most games call for nothing
more than two people and two brains."
—*Working Mother*

"Full of interactive ideas."
—*Child*

W9-AUK-311

"There's enough stuff in this book that you wouldn't get
through it all by the time you were 104. . . . It's a very
creative amalgamation of ideas that families can use for
play and relating. . . . Any family would want it on
the shelf—and then make it a point to use."
—*Youth Ministry Bulletin*

"The best family activity book we have seen. Period."
—*Minnesota Parent*

"Parents and teachers have a marvelous opportunity to
recreate the planet through the tools we give our children.
I really think this book can help."
—*Whole Life Times*

"Perry has come up with a list of excellent activities that do a
good job of defining quality time for parents and children."
—**Jane Crosby, "ABC's for Parents" syndicated column**

"The real joy of *Playing Smart* is seeing how various mundane activities . . . can be given new twists that give
them depth and richness."
—*L.A. Weekly*

"A one-volume shelf of original ideas."
—*L.A. Parent Magazine*

"A treasure chest of activities that sharpen the senses,
hone skills, and encourage creativity."
—*San Diego Family Press*

# Playing Smart

The Family Guide
to Enriching, Offbeat
Learning Activities
for Ages 4–14

SUSAN K. PERRY, Ph.D.

free spirit
PUBLiSHiNG®

Works
for kids®

**Library of Congress Cataloging-in-Publication Data**
Perry, Susan K.
    Playing smart : the family guide to enriching, offbeat learning activities for ages 4 to 14 / Susan K. Perry.
        p. cm.
    Includes bibliographical references and index.
    ISBN 1-57542-095-3
    1. Family recreation. 2. Creative activities and seat work. 3. Creative thinking. I. Title.

GV182.8 .P38 2001
649'.51—dc21                                                                                           00-053570
                                                  CIP

At the time of this book's publication, all facts and figures cited are the most current available; all telephone numbers, addresses, and Web site URLs are accurate and active; all publications, organizations, Web sites, and other resources exist as described in this book; and all have been verified. The author and Free Spirit Publishing make no warranty or guarantee concerning the information and materials given out by organizations or content found at Web sites, and we are not responsible for any changes that occur after this book's publication. If you find an error or believe that a resource listed here is not as described, please contact Free Spirit Publishing. Parents, teachers, and other adults: We strongly urge you to monitor children's use of the Internet.

Edited by Pamela Espeland, Bonnie Z. Goldsmith, and KaTrina Wentzel
Cover design by Percolator
Interior design by Percolator and Marieka Heinlen
Illustrations by Eyewire, Marieka Heinlen, and Kristin Verby
Index compiled by Pamela Van Huss

10 9 8 7 6 5 4 3 2 1
Printed in the United States of America

**Free Spirit Publishing Inc.**
217 Fifth Avenue North, Suite 200
Minneapolis, MN 55401-1299
(612) 338-2068
help4kids@freespirit.com
*www.freespirit.com*

For Simon John Lakkis and Kevin Michael Lakkis, still my creative kids.

Thanks beyond words go to Stephen Perry for introducing
me to deeper levels of creativity and for helping me
see the infinite possibilities of just plain fun.

> *"The quality of a life is determined by its activities."*
> **—Aristotle**

# CONTENTS

**CHAPTER 4**

# Brain Benders . . . . . . . . . . . . . . . . . . . . . . . . . . . . . . . . . . . . . . 48

**CHAPTER 5**

# Adventures in Ordinary Places . . . . . . . . . . . . . . . . . . . 66

**CHAPTER 6**

# Learning Comes Alive at the Cemetery . . . . . . . . . . . . . 79

# Introduction

In the decade since the first edition of this book came out, the world and I have changed a lot. For one thing, the Internet has profoundly affected our lives, from the ways we find out things to the ways we shop. For another, I went back to school for a doctorate, studying creativity in particular. My longtime interest in how children and adults learn and achieve their potential has intensified.

While I consider most of the activities and suggestions in the original edition to be timeless, I've continued to think about the topic of "playing smart" over the years. Thus, my file folders thickened with new games, tips, insights, and resources to the point where it was clearly time for an updated and expanded edition of *Playing Smart*.

*Playing Smart* offers hundreds of unusual ways for you to enrich your child's days by spending creative time together. It's about the fun people can have while learning, and the learning that goes on while you're having fun.

It's not about glitter and eggshells, nor is it specifically about getting your child to read more, write better, or score higher in math and science. But children who experiment with the activities described here will find their reading, writing, calculating, and thinking skills enhanced as a natural by-product of their explorations.

Using this book as a guide, you and your child will survey new subjects ranging from cultural relativity to photography, journal keeping, psychology, geography, and the mental side of physical education. You'll learn how to learn wherever you are: in the health clinic, the kitchen, the garden, the car. You'll visit places you may not have thought of visiting before, including the cemetery.

The activities in *Playing Smart* stress creative thinking. Very few require complicated preparations or equipment; you and your child can do most of them in small bits of time on ordinary days, without making a big deal about it. Many involve nothing more than mental interactions between parent and child. All are meant to feel like play. The time you spend together should be time you enjoy. It should flow.

## Encourage Your Child to "Flow"

"Flow" is an intriguing and useful concept that may be new to you, though it's been studied by psychologists for a couple of decades now. Watch closely the next time your child is deeply involved in playing. If she's so focused on what she's doing that she doesn't come when you call her, she's probably not simply ignoring you to be ornery.* There's a good chance she's in flow.

Flow is a highly gratifying state of mind. According to research, everyone experiences flow at least now and then. Athletes call it being "in the zone." It happens whenever you're so absorbed in a task, whether alone or with someone else, that you forget yourself. It happens all the time when you're playing a game or engrossed in conversation. Nothing else matters but what you're doing. Such intense focus is most likely to happen when there's enough challenge in the activity to keep you interested but not so much that you get frustrated.

The activities in *Playing Smart* aim for that happy balance. In flow, you want to keep right on doing whatever you're doing, because it's fun.

But flow isn't only fun. When your child is focused this intently, he's more likely to be creative, because he's pursuing his own intrinsic interests. He's self-motivated, and research indicates that self-motivation aids creative production. Also, children who have learned the knack of concentrating fully in a variety of activities tend to be happier, healthier, and more involved in life. Follow some of the suggestions in this book and your child may become more fully engaged in everything else, including schoolwork.

# Be Mindful

Another aspect of a creativity-enhancing approach to life is mindfulness. While all healthy children begin life alert and questioning everything, parents often don't realize how crucial it is to encourage such open-mindedness. If you or your child's teachers give the impression that questions have only one right answer, mindfulness may soon diminish. The mindful child pays attention, notices differences, looks at everything from more than one angle. According to Harvard psychology professor Ellen J. Langer, such a child knows that what he's been taught is not necessarily the whole truth or the only truth.

For instance, teach your child to see things in new ways. Next time you pass a garden, ask your child to imagine seeing it from underneath, as though he were a mole, or from above, as if from an airplane. When you read your child his favorite story day after day, help him tune into it fully by asking questions about it as you read, or by changing some detail to wake up his interest. Paying such close attention, of course, may often lead your child to flow.

And always seek out the offbeat and amusing angle—as so many of the activities in *Playing Smart* aim to do. Humor is a wonderful way to expand people's mindsets and get them to think creatively. According to Langer, "If

---

* I mix the pronouns "she" and "he," "him" and "her" throughout this book. I've done this to keep the tone friendly and straightforward. The activities are meant for boys and girls alike. You know your child best. If an activity looks like it might fit, try it.

you're a mindful thinker in the first place, you're always walking around with a playful hat on, looking at things as new. They call it creativity, but it should simply be life."

# Tips for Raising a Child Who "Plays Smart"

▶ **Talk with your child about flow, focus, and challenge.** Learn your child's signs of flow when he's deeply engaged in an activity and point them out to him. For instance, when your child is playing with his friends so intently that he forgets to stop for lunch, you might say, "You were really involved just now, having fun with your friends. When you're in flow like that, it's hard to get back to ordinary stuff, isn't it?"

Discuss the difference between focusing on something wholeheartedly, such as a favorite hobby, and only giving it distracted attention, such as drying the dishes when you'd rather be doing something else. Ask your child to name some times when he's genuinely focused on tasks. Is that usually an enjoyable state for your child?

Make a point of commenting on your child's reaction to challenges. Since modeling is the best way to teach, if you really enjoy tough challenges, express your feelings by saying something like, "Wow! That was really hard! I think that's why I enjoyed it so much. It feels great to stick with something long enough to see results!"

▶ **Offer time and space to concentrate.** Make a point of not filling every moment of your child's day. Allow your child time to follow her own interests. If she's focused intently on reading or doing a puzzle, let her finish. When it's time for school or bed, acknowledge her frustration at the need to stop. Encourage a longer attention span by not having the TV on during reading or homework time. Make it a family habit to put away one thing (or place it out of sight) before beginning another.

▶ **Learn and teach self-monitoring.** Show your child how to monitor his own attention by becoming more aware of what you yourself need to concentrate fully. For instance, say, "I'll have to read this later. I'm so tired right now that I don't know what I'm reading." Help your child see that it's a good idea to stop when his focus flags. Perhaps all that's needed is a change of pace or a rest break. Or does he need some help to get over a difficult spot? Suggest that your child note his daily energy levels. At what times of day does he feel most energetic? Is doing his homework the moment he comes home from school the best use of his energy?

▶ **Offer challenging pastimes.** Encourage hobbies that grow more complex the more your child works on them, such as drawing, story writing, photography, cooking, and kite making—all activities with infinite options. (Most everything in this book fills the bill.)

▶ **Encourage activities for their own sake.** Encourage your child to do things because she enjoys them, not because you want her to do them well. Rather than, "You did a good job," say, "You certainly are having a lot of fun learning about dinosaurs, aren't you?"

According to Alfie Kohn, well-respected author of books on psychology and education, at least seventy-five studies have shown that the primary effect of offering rewards for creative activities is that kids lose interest in whatever they've had to do to get the reward. "If they have been bribed with pizza or candy to read, reading becomes less interesting in itself," notes Kohn. Resist saying, "If you draw a picture for me now, I'll play with you later." A better phrasing might be, "If you draw a picture or play by yourself while I finish paying these bills, I'll have more time to play with you later."

▶ **Experiment and find the novelty.** Teach your child to experiment with tasks in order to add novelty and interest. For instance, ask your child to choose the simplest everyday chore and find a way to make it more enjoyable. How might your child make straightening his room more interesting? He could put music on, dance from location to location, try to beat the clock, decorate storage boxes, and so on. When something new doesn't work as well as you'd hoped, point out that it was, at least, a learning experience.

# Towards Better Brainstorming

Many activities in *Playing Smart* suggest brainstorming. The purpose of brainstorming is to free the mind to think up as many answers to a question or solutions to a problem as possible.

Brainstorming isn't appropriate for questions with a single correct answer, such as, "What's the capital of California?" But it's wonderful for questions like, "What are all the ways you can think of to get your teacher's attention?" Creative thinkers come up with lots of responses: "Throw something. Shout. Tap her on the shoulder. Break a window. Pass a note. Pretend to be sick. Bang on your desk. Sing. Wink at him. Pop a balloon. Play an instrument. Steal her chalk." And so on.

Brainstorming is a skill that can be taught, practiced, and developed. The more children use this skill, the more creative they'll be. Here are some tips for helping your child become a better brainstormer:

▶ **Anything goes.** When you present a question or problem, encourage your child to give any and every response that comes to mind. There are no "right" or "wrong" answers. It's not wrong even if it's illegal or physically impossible—not at the brainstorming stage.

▶ **Banish the critic.** All of us have resident "internal critics," voices inside our minds that say, "But that's too silly, too impractical, too expensive, too bizarre. . . ." Tell your child that brainstorming is a time when that voice should pipe down! If your child has a habit of negative self-talk ("I can't do that," "My idea's too dumb"), this is your chance to do something about it.

▶ **Judge not.** Brainstorming tends to generate a lot of ideas. Naturally, some are better than others. But the purpose of brainstorming isn't to judge or eliminate ideas. The only time you should select some ideas and not others is when there's a compelling reason to do so—and when all possible ideas have been brought out into the open.

# Playing Smart on the Internet

The Internet has made it easier than ever before for your child to find information of all kinds. Yet along with that exciting potential come risks: questionable advertising, exposure to sexually explicit or violent material, contact with predatory strangers. It's the responsibility of parents to monitor children's computer use. To keep your child's Web-surfing a safe, positive experience, consider the following guidelines:

▶ Put the computer in a well-traveled area of your home where you can easily observe how your child is using it.

▶ Stay involved in your child's use of the Internet so that she knows YOU know what she's doing.

▶ When your child begins using the Internet for homework help, show him how to do so without plagiarizing the work of others. Help him find credible sources of information (see the sites that conclude this section, for example).

▸ Establish a few basic rules for using the Internet, depending on your child's age. For example: Your child must always check with you before giving out her name, address, phone number, or email address; she must not buy anything without asking you first; she must check with you before participating in any chat room. Add any rules specific to your own family's values. (For more on this topic, see Robert Maynard's book, *GoodParents.com: What Every Good Parent Should Know About the Internet,* Amherst, NY: Prometheus, 2000.)

▸ Provide your child with some kid-friendly search engines and online sources of information. Here are a few to get you started (and most have valuable information for adults, too):

**Ask Jeeves for Kids,** *www.ajkids.com.* Type in a question ("Is the electoral college fair?") and this site offers several choices for related questions to which it can supply a full answer ("What is the difference between the electoral vote and the popular vote?"). It also relates the question to current events and provides additional links. Young children will need help formulating questions suitable for a search engine like this.

**The Copernicus Education Gateway,** *www.edgate.com.* This site features pages for K–12 educators, parents, and students, and includes daily links to other interesting and fun sites. Students can find information using the Research Center, get creative in the Creative Zone, or explore Fact Monster. Sign up for free newsletters with articles, activities, and sites for your child's age group.

**FamilyEducation.com,** *www.familyeducation.com.* This site features parenting advice and family reference resources, including activities, school help, an atlas and encyclopedia, and pages for students.

**Homeworkspot,** *www.homeworkspot.com.* This site simplifies the search for free, online K–12 homework resources. Your child will find resources for specific subjects, a reference center (with links to museums, libraries, experts, and more), current events, virtual field trips, and activities—plus a free newsletter about new and relevant sites.

**Searchopolis,** *www.searchopolis.com.* Your child can choose a topic by word, phrase, or subject area, along with grade level (or "all"), and search for links among a selection of educational Web sites.

**Yahooligans,** *www.yahooligans.com*. This is Yahoo's "Web Guide for Kids," featuring sections called Around the World, Arts & Entertainment, School Bell, Science & Nature, and Sports & Recreation. (It's PG-rated, so no matches are found when you search for "sex," for instance.)

# How to Use This Book

I have not suggested an age range for most of the activities in *Playing Smart*. Most are adaptable for any age, right through adulthood. A good approach is to read the introductory material in each chapter and then skim the activities. Then, at dinner, after breakfast on weekends, at bedtime, or whenever, flip open the book to whatever looks like fun and suggest an activity to try or an idea to talk about.

When you introduce new concepts to a young child, simplify the language as much as you need to. The same imagination-sparker will bring about entirely different results when you use it again a year or two later. You'll notice that many activities offer examples and variations, and that suggestions are richly varied: art projects, games, "field trips," dramatics, discussion starters, experiments, wordplay, and puzzlers.

What if your child becomes bored with an activity, or would rather do something else? Let go! There's nothing more deadening to a child's interest than insisting on continuing or completing some activity because it's supposed to be fun.

At the end of each chapter is an annotated list of resources for further exploration: books, games, materials, organizations, and Web sites. All the books are in print as of this writing, unless noted. To find them, try your library or support your local independent new or used bookstore. (To connect to independent bookstores in your area, visit *www.booksense.com* or call 1-888-BOOKSENSE, 1-888-266-5736.) Consult *www.abebooks.com* for books that may be hard to find. Suggested age ranges are provided for all children's books and for children's materials, when appropriate—but you're the one who knows the most about your child's reading ability and attention span. Many children will gladly look through books or other materials far above their reading level, if they're interested in the subject.

Now, begin playing smart . . .

# CHAPTER 1

# INSTANT FUN

**T**he year my son Kevin was eight, one of our car pool drivers was often delayed picking the kids up from school. One afternoon, when Kevin was dropped off at home particularly late, I asked him what had happened. He said that school personnel had told him to wait for his ride in the room next to the principal's office. Hadn't he been awfully bored for that half-hour? "No," he said, "I kept busy finding pictures in the wallpaper."

That's what "instant fun" is all about: keeping creatively occupied when a wait is unavoidable. Your child won't be bored for long if you teach him how easy it is to keep himself entertained and amused.

Here's a multitude of ideas you and your child can use when the doctor or dentist makes you wait, when a car trip seems endless, or whenever you have minutes to spare. For many of these activities, a group can play as well as two.

## Waiting Games

▶ Make up stories about the people around you. You can either take turns— one sentence or idea each—or improvise together. See where the story goes and who wants to contribute the next bit of information or plot turn.

*Example:* Let's say there's a man with a briefcase seated across the room. Perhaps he's a spy or a counter-spy. Maybe he's got secret plans in his briefcase for a new type of weapon, one that causes people's shoes to untie so they trip on them. Maybe he's a movie star traveling in disguise or a software inventor who's just developed an "instant book report" program.

▶  One of you chooses a person or an object (a sofa, a cluttered desk) that both of you look hard at for a short time. Then you close your eyes or look away and take turns telling everything you can remember about the person or object.

   This is more than a memory game—it sharpens visual perception. You'll find yourselves improving with repeated play.

▶  Play a version of "I Spy." Think of something in the room and have the other person guess what it is by asking five yes-or-no questions about it. Or think of something not in the room and allow ten or twenty questions.

   *Example:* You're thinking of a frying pan. Your child asks questions like, "Is it bigger than a salt shaker?" "Is it hard?" "Is it in our home?" "Do I ever use it?" "Do we have more than one?"

▶  Look for evidence of artists at work. When you're waiting outside, notice and talk about billboards, signs, the architecture of buildings and other structures, store window displays, and landscaping. Inside, notice and discuss furniture, room decoration, book illustrations, corporate logos, stamps, Web pages, and newspapers (photographs, ads, page layout).

   Expand on this by discussing which examples each of you thinks are the most creative.

▶  Play "Opposites." You say a word, and your child comes up with an opposite. After you've done some common opposites, try some offbeat or unusual ones. It's fine if your opposites only "oppose" each other in one way, such as shape or size.

   *Examples:* Light, dark; happy, sad; angelic, devilish; compete, cooperate; circle, square; oil, vinegar; honey, lemon juice; whale, minnow; railroad track, ball of string.

▶  Play "Connections." You say a word and your child tries to think of a word that's related to your word in some way, however far-fetched. Then your child has to explain the relationship or connection.

   *Examples:* If you say "brain," she might say "walk," explaining that you use your brain to command your legs to walk. If you say "toenail," she might say "nosebleed," explaining that if your toenail catches on a loose carpet thread, you might fall on your nose and get a nosebleed.

   *Variation:* Play a more complex version. This time, your child says a word, such as "book," and you say a word that seems to be completely unrelated, such as "squirrel." Her task is to *make* a connection. In this case, she might say, "When you cut down trees to make paper for books, squirrels lose their homes."

▶   Make up New Year's resolutions for animals.

   *Examples:* A porcupine might resolve to "stick to it from now on." A penguin might decide to "dress casually."

▶   Play "I Packed My Stepcousin's Trunk." The first person says, "I packed my stepcousin's trunk, and in it I put an artichoke" (or anything else starting with "A"). Each person then adds something new and creative to the line-up, in alphabetical order. The hard part is repeating everything that has been said before.

   *Example:* "I packed my stepcousin's trunk, and in it I put an artichoke, a beanbag, a canary, a daisy . . ."

▶   If you're stuck waiting in line, closely investigate the passing people parade. See what you notice about the way people look, walk, or carry things.

   *Examples:* What is each person's most outstanding quality? One may be dressed fashionably, another may look unusually happy, and another may be talking on a cell phone. Assess trends: How do most of the men wear their hair? What kind of earrings do most people wear: dangly, large, tiny, colorful? How many people are carrying shoulder bags? Backpacks? Briefcases? Suitcases? Shopping bags? How many people are wearing glasses? Wearing boots? Riding bikes? Riding skateboards?

▶   Play "Firsts and Lasts." Choose a category, such as geography, people, animals, foods, or plants. (With an older child, you can choose a more limited, challenging category such as nongreen plants or countries in Africa.) One of you names an item in the category. The other names an item in the category that begins with the last letter of the item named by the previous player.

   *Example:* If the category is "animals" and you say "dog," your child might respond with "goat." "Turkey" might be next.

▶   If you know a foreign language, even just a little of one, teach your child a couple of words while you wait.

▶   Look around, pick out a common object, and invent new ways to use it. Then imagine that it's many times larger or smaller and think of more ways to use it. Could its parts be rearranged to multiply its uses? What might a visitor from another planet do with it?

▶ Make up your own Sniglets. Invented by comedian Rich Hall, A Sniglet is defined as "any word that doesn't appear in the dictionary, but should."

   *Examples:* From Hall's book, *Sniglets* (now out of print): "Memnants: The chipped or broken m & m's at the bottom of the bag." "Conagraphs: The raised relief squares on an ice-cream cone."

▶ Take turns humming familiar songs and have the other person guess the title.

▶ Make up a haiku about your surroundings or your mood. Haiku is a Japanese verse form of three unrhymed lines that add up to seventeen syllables, arranged 5-7-5. What counts here are originality and fun, not artistic durability!

   *Examples:*

Green-leafed plant in the
still air of a waiting room—
When is it my turn?

Waiting in the room,
doctors' offices aren't fun.
Time goes so slowly.

▶ Take turns coming up with thought provokers like, "List ten ways to complete the statement, 'I am . . .'" or "What would you do if you had only six months to live, or six months with no responsibilities at all?" or "The ten CDs I would take for a month on an island would be. . . ."

▶ Make up a perky advertising slogan for a dull product.
   *Example:* To sell plain white shoelaces, "If the shoe fits, it's laced by Ace."

▶ Ask your child to choose a year in your life (say, when you were five or ten years old). Try to remember everything you can about that year, from your friends, to what you wore, to what your room looked like. Then choose a year in your child's life and see what he can remember about it. Add your memories to his for a more complete picture.

▶ Even if you don't have paper or pencils with you, you can still play tic-tac-toe. Imagine (or take a look at) the number pad on a telephone, with 1-2-3 across the top row, 4-5-6 across the second row, and 7-8-9 across the third row. Now take turns mentally placing your X or O in one space at a time, naming that space by its number on the pad ("I put an X in 3," "I put an O in 6"). It takes a bit of concentration, but it works.

▶ Think of a variety of things you could never be or do: "I could never be a pirate." "I could never ride a dinosaur." "I could never write a book and build a house at the same time." "I could never fly." Then talk about how you could be or do those things in one way or another.

   *Examples:* "I could be a pirate in a play." "I could 'ride' a dinosaur skeleton in a museum." "I could hire someone to build a house. While it's being built, I could write a book about it." "I could fly in an airplane."

▶ Play "What's the Question?" Someone says a sentence or phrase that answers an unknown question, and the other person tries to find a question that fits. Encourage creativity and humor.

   *Examples:* Answer: "Play marbles in the rain." Question: "What should a child made of sugar never do?" Answer: "Rusty screws." Question: "What did you eat for breakfast?" Answer: "A sheep with a wig." Question?

▶ Play "Kid Improv." Describe something, such as a particular moment in history, that can be acted out (but not easily). Have your child see if she can bring it to life.

   *Examples:* It's ten minutes before the invention of the paper clip, and you're trying to get two pieces of paper to stay together. You're the first person ever to try riding a bicycle.

## Catch This!

Children enjoy testing their reaction times. Here are two activities your child can try on the fly:

1. Hold your arm out, palm down. Put a penny on the back of your hand. Tilt your hand until the penny slides off and then try to catch the penny with the same hand. Keep track of your successes and see if your rate improves with practice.

2. Hold your hand out with the thumb and forefinger separated and ready to catch something. Curl your other fingers in. Another person holds a yardstick by the top edge, resting the bottom edge between your thumb and forefinger. When he drops the yardstick, see how long it takes you to catch it. Did you catch it at the 6-inch mark? The 8-inch mark? (If you don't have a yardstick, try this with a piece of paper, a pencil, a magazine, or a tissue.)

▸ Turn your hand into a puppet: Make a fist with your thumb inside. Use a pen to draw eyes, a nose, and hair on the outside of the bottom joint of your forefinger. Move your thumb to make your puppet "talk."

*Variations:* Draw on your child's hand instead. Draw on both yours and his, so your two "hand puppets" can have a conversation.

▸ Together, design physical exercises you can do while you wait, wherever you are.

*Examples:* Show your child what isometrics are (tensing various parts of the body, holding them for a brief count, then relaxing them). Create exercises for parts of your body, from head to toes. See if you can wiggle one eyebrow or one ear.

This activity is especially recommended for longer waits, when most children get squirmy or cranky.

▸ While waiting for your meal in a restaurant, encourage your child to use straws, sugar packets, napkins, spoons, closed ketchup bottles, or anything else on your table to build something or to act out a scene.

*Examples:* Your child can easily build a see-saw by placing a straw on a pile of two or three sugar packets. It may not see-saw gracefully, but the idea is simply to evoke scenes. Straws can be laid end to end to represent fences, or held upright to act as tall, thin play people. A packet of sugar might be a 50-pound sack of sand that a straw person is trying to move.

▸ While waiting with a younger child in a restaurant or anywhere else with a table (unless you don't mind getting down on the floor with your child), line up a series of nine pennies or other coins of the same denomination. Each penny should be touching the one next to it. Put a tenth penny a few inches behind the others. Now shove the tenth penny quickly so that it knocks against the row. Your child will enjoy seeing how the first penny in the row jumps forward when the row is hit from behind.

*Variations:* Experiment a little. What happens when your child pushes the tenth penny hard? Lightly? What happens when he uses a larger coin, such as a quarter, as the tenth coin? Try lining up eight pennies and then pushing two others so they slide into the row.

▸ Make up an instant mystery and see if your child can figure out what really happened.

*Example:* When John comes home from school, he finds no one there. He notices a grocery list on the floor near the dresser where his father keeps his wallet. The wallet is gone. What happened?

▸ Ask your child to search the magazines in a waiting room for pictures of, say, animals or cars, or for a particular word, such as *global* or *buy*. How many pictures can she find? How many appearances of the word?

▸ Take a tape measure with you the next time you know you'll be spending time waiting. Have your child estimate, then measure, the distance between two objects, such as the reception desk and the door. (A large tape measure would be helpful for measuring such distances, or you can limit the estimates to much closer objects, such as "this magazine" and "that plant.")

   *Variation:* Have your child estimate how many steps it will take him to get from the door to the reception desk (or wherever), using the length of his foot as the unit of measurement. He can check his guess by walking the distance heel-to-toe, heel-to-toe, counting steps.

## Pack an Emergency Fun Bag

An Emergency Fun Bag has saved many a parent's sanity and many a child's mood. Always carry one with you, especially if your child is young. Then you'll have it for appointments that might otherwise leave you sitting toyless and bookless in a waiting room. Pack your "emergency fun" in a tote bag, a small nylon carry-on, a lunchbox, or a backpack. Here are some things to put in the bag:

- a ball (either a tennis ball or a tiny rubber one if your child is beyond the age of putting things in his mouth)
- paper, pencils, pens, crayons
- finger puppets
- a deck of cards
- magnets
- a yo-yo
- a mirror (preferably metal and unbreakable)
- wax or clay for modeling
- travel versions of games like Yahtzee, Othello, Memory, Hi-Q, or checkers
- a favorite book or two

- Have your child experiment with her writing or drawing style. How many different ways can she write her first name? How many different ways can she draw the sun or a flower?

# On the Road Again

Creative kids will be able to come up with lots of ways to keep busy while cruising the highways. Help out in duller moments with ideas like these:

- Look for distinguishing characteristics of cars (or trucks, RVs, SUVs, minivans, or motorcycles).
   *Examples:* How many cars have whitewalls? Are most of the cars old or new? (In some states, you can tell relative age by the sequence of numbers on the license plates.) How many different car makes can you identify? How many things can you find wrong with the cars you see, such as wheel wobble, dented fenders, broken trunk locks, cracked windows, or bent antennas?

- Play the oldest on-the-road game of all: Count things! The possibilities are endless, from train cars to horses, barns, fire hydrants, and billboards. Narrow your category down further—say, to billboards with pictures of women, or of women selling cars. As you drive through towns or cities, count people with briefcases, people carrying paper bags, or people wearing blue shirts. Or count everything you pass that begins with a "B."

- Notice unusual bumper-sticker slogans. Then make up some of your own.

- Notice and count custom license plates. Come up with ideas for custom plates for people you know.
   *Examples:* NML-DR ("Animal Doctor") for a veterinarian, DR-NML ("Doctor Enamel") for a dentist, or 2X2S4 for a math teacher.

- Make predictions and see whose are most accurate. Begin by choosing a target area, such as a town you're approaching. Either have each person write down his or her predictions about what you'll see there, or have one person write down everyone's predictions so even the youngest can play. Decide on the time you'll allow for looking (try ten minutes). Once you reach the target area everyone looks closely for the allotted period of time.

When you see something you've predicted, you announce it aloud and someone puts a mark next to that item on the list. The person who predicts most accurately "wins."

*Examples:* You might predict you'll see a post office, a giant warehouse store, a dalmatian, a school, a house with a porch, or a bait shop.

---

### Fun with Tongue Twisters

Try saying these quickly, three times in a row:

- Cows graze in groves on grass which grows in grooves in groves.
- Six slippery seals slipped silently ashore.
- Barbara burned the brown bread badly.
- A regal rural ruler ruled regally.

*Variations:* Make up your own tongue twisters. Take turns choosing a letter of the alphabet for the other person to work with. Or take turns coming up with hard-to-pronounce phrases for each letter of the alphabet, starting with "A." Or begin with one-syllable words and then try to trip the tongue with words of two or more syllables.

Twisters that combine two or more sounds, particularly those that mix blends such as "th," "sh," or "ch," are super hard to say. Try, "Shave a cedar shingle thin," or:

Theophilus Thistle, the thistle sifter,
sifted a sieve of unsifted thistles.
If Theophilus Thistle, the thistle sifter,
sifted a sieve of unsifted thistles,
where is the sieve of unsifted thistles Theophilus Thistle,
the thistle sifter, sifted?

---

# Paper-and-Pencil Quickies

▶ One of you draws a squiggle or part of a picture. Then you take turns adding to it. The final drawing will probably look entirely different from what the first drawer had in mind.

▶ Write a letter together. Both of you compose it; either one of you can write it. Your letter might be a suggestion or complaint directed to your local council member or the President of the United States, a friendly missive to a relative or pen pal, or anything else you choose.

- Teach your child to make lists. Brainstorm different kinds.

  *Examples:* A "Why Not?" list of things to do next summer, when your school-age child has more free time. "Why not milk a cow?" "Why not watch a sunset?" "Why not learn to swim?" Other lists might include healthy snack foods, friends to invite to a birthday party, or chores that can be done to earn extra money.

- Have your child begin a "Wish List" of things she'd like for her birthday or holidays. (Of course, let her know she won't necessarily get what's on the list, but that you'll pick and choose from it when you need inspiration.)

  A "Wish List" can go beyond the merely personal to include wishes for world peace, an end to hunger, and other altruistic hopes and dreams. Talk about what each of you could do to help make such fantasies come true. (See "Get Involved" in Chapter 5, pages 70–71.)

- Invite your child to write up a "report card" for you. (If you're lucky, you'll get an "A" for Effort.) Ask your child to grade you on such abilities and achievements as Treats Me Fairly, Has a Good Sense of Humor, Spends Time with Me, Learns from Mistakes, Generous with Allowance, Cooks What I Like to Eat, and Helps with Homework.

- Play "Dot-to-Dot." Fill a few square inches with evenly spaced dots. You and your child take turns drawing a line connecting any two adjoining dots, either up and down or across. The object is to complete as many boxes as possible. Whenever a player completes a box, he gets to place his first initial inside it and take another turn. When all the boxes are completed, the player with the most boxes wins.

  *Variation:* Play it with triangles. Begin by drawing a large triangle made of unconnected, evenly spaced dots. Take turns connecting lines to form small triangles.

- Make paper airplanes. See whose flies the farthest or does the most nosedives.

- Play "Finger Pool." Sit at opposite ends of a table. Fold a piece of paper into a compact chunk and take turns flicking your fingers at it to make it cross the table to your partner.

▶ Borrow from the game *Mad Libs* (for the book, see Resources, page 20) and make up silly sentences. One of you writes a sentence (don't show the other person), leaving one word out. The other person has to supply a word in the needed part of speech.

    *Example:* Your sentence is, "The hungry _____ nibbled at the little boy's toe." You ask your child for a noun (or "a word that names something"), or perhaps for a specific noun like the name of an animal or vehicle. He fills in the blank with "helicopter," "dinosaur," "platypus," or anything he chooses. Read the completed sentence aloud. Is it silly?

▶ Try your own homemade version of "Droodles," a game introduced by Roger Price in his book of the same name (newly reissued—see Resources, page 20). Draw something simple that looks like what you say it is, but only when you stretch your imagination.

    *Examples:* A single straight line could be "what you see through a closed elevator door." Several straight lines could be "your food's view of your fork."

▶ Play "Scrambled Sentences." Make up and write down a really silly sentence, such as "Three blue aardvarks danced by the light of the moon." Now cut or tear the sentence into three or more parts. Move the parts out of order. Challenge your child to replace the parts in correct order and read the sentence aloud. Now have your child write down a silly sentence, cut it into three or more parts, and scramble the order. You try to piece it back together.

    *Variation:* Add a couple of slips of blank paper, called "wild cards." Wild cards can represent any word your child chooses. Have your child make up a new sentence using the original cut-up parts and the wild cards. For example, "Three blue aardvarks danced THE TANGO by the light of the moon" or "Three blue GIRAFFES AND aardvarks danced by the light of the moon."

▶ Play "Word Detective." Cut or tear out part of a newspaper or magazine page (a whole page may contain too many words). Now choose a word that appears on the page, without telling your child what it is. Give your child clues about the word. For example, if you chose the word car, you might say, "It's large, comes in different colors, and is made out of metal." Then give your child the page and have him try to find the word. Once he guesses and finds the word, it's his turn to choose a word from the page and give you clues.

▶ An anagram is a word or phrase you make up by transposing the letters of some other word or phrase. For example, an online anagram creator (see Resources below) came up with *waste runoff* by rearranging the letters of *fun software*. Have your child take a common word and see how many other words she can find in it by rearranging the letters.

---

## The "What If" Game

Explore hypothetical situations, brainstorming as many imaginative responses as possible. These can be personal, such as:

- What if you had a million dollars? A hundred million dollars? What would you do with it?

- What if you could never leave your home again? What five objects, and what one person, would you choose to have there with you?

- What if you could change your name—what new name would you choose?

- What if you could choose to have another sense—something besides sight, hearing, touch, smell, and taste? What would you choose?

- What if you could be reborn at another time, past or future? When would you choose, and why?

- What if you could clone yourself? What if you could tell scientists which creature to clone next? What would you suggest, and why?

These pretend situations can also go beyond the personal, as in:

- What if gravity were twice as strong? Half as strong?

- What if nobody had to work for a living?

- What if people could change their sex (or appearance) as often as they wanted to?

Make up your own "What Ifs" to brainstorm and discuss.

---

# Resources

**Arrak Anagrams,** *www.arrak.fi/ag/index_en.html.* Stuck on an anagram? Type in the jumbled word and Arrak Anagrams will help you figure it out. Or, type in your name, a silly word, or even a phrase, and this site will rearrange the letters to form another word or phrase. (Susan Perry, for example, can turn into "raspy nurse.")

*The Best Card Games in the Galaxy* by the Editors at Klutz (Palo Alto, CA: Klutz, 1989). Ages 8–12. This book comes packaged with a deck of cards, instructions for popular card games, and complete plans for an architecturally sound house of cards. A good item for an emergency fun bag.

**Blibs.com,** *www.blibs.com.* This site offers word games similar to the ones in *Mad Libs* (below). Find one you like and print it, or email it to a favorite friend.

*Droodles* by Roger Price (Kansas City, MO: Andrews McMeel, 2000). All ages. Dozens of simple, odd drawings with unexpected titles and explanations. Highly recommended to get creative juices flowing.

*Finger Skateboard Tricks and Tips* by Susan Buntrock (New York: Scholastic, 2000). Ages 8 and up. This illustrated guide teaches eight tricks that can be performed by using the included 4-inch fingerboard (a mini-mini-skateboard). No helmet needed!

*Glove Compartment Games* by the Editors at Klutz (Palo Alto, CA: Klutz, 1997). Ages 8–12. These classic games are designed to keep kids so entertained that questions like "Are we there yet?" never come to mind.

**HearthSong.** P.O. Box B, Sebastopol, CA 95473-0601; 1-800-382-6779; *www.hearthsong.com/.* Request a catalog from this distributor of toys, books, games, and kits for imaginative play. You can also search online by age and price to find all kinds of instant fun, from pattern blocks to a paint-a-mug kit.

*Mad Libs* by Roger Price and Leonard Stern (New York: Price Stern Sloan, many editions). Ages 8 and up. This party game in the form of a book can be played by any number of people, anywhere, anytime. Each version consists of a tablet of one-page stories with blank spaces where key words have been omitted. Without knowing the title or theme of the story, the reader asks players to come up with adjectives, nouns, verbs, or other parts of speech, as specified under each blank. Later, the reader reads the silly story aloud.

**Pocket Etch A Sketch** (Ohio Art). All ages. The classic toy in a pocket version. Also check out *The Etch A Sketch Book* (Palo Alto, CA: Klutz, 1996), which includes the mini-toy attached to a book with ideas and patterns to copy.

*Science Is . . . A Source Book of Fascinating Facts, Projects and Activities* by Susan V. Bosak (Buffalo, NY: Firefly Books, 2000). For parents to use with kids ages 5 and up, or for ages 8 and up to use alone. This book includes lots of quick, clearly laid out activities, as well as fun and interesting factual tidbits. The activities, each with many variations, represent a wide range of science topics.

*Sheep Trick or Treat* by Nancy Shaw (Boston: Houghton Mifflin, 1997). Ages 4–10. Part of a series that includes *Sheep in a Jeep, Sheep in a Shop,* and others, this delightful read-aloud picture book is appealing to those of any age who still get a kick out of clever and funny tongue twisters ("Sheep shape wool in pointy clumps/To make a dinosaur with bumps").

*Six Sick Sheep: 101 Tongue Twisters* by Joanna Cole and Stephanie Calmenson (New York: Beech Tree, 1993). Ages 5 and up. Open this book to find old and new tongue twisters, from one-liners to short stories.

*World's Toughest Tongue Twisters* by Joseph Rosenbloom (New York: Sterling, 1987). Ages 7–12. Try tripping over these definitely difficult, yet daringly delightful tanglers of tongues.

# CHAPTER 2

# JOURNAL JOURNEYS

**Y**ou'll be repaid a hundredfold if you take the time to introduce your child to the adventure of self-exploration. "Know thyself" is still terrific advice, and one of the best ways to gain self-knowledge is by keeping a diary or journal (terms used interchangeably in this chapter). The younger your child is when you get her started, the more extensive the benefits. When my older son, Simon, was in his teens, he reread the diary entries he'd dictated as a four- and five-year-old and mourned that he hadn't begun when he was two or three!

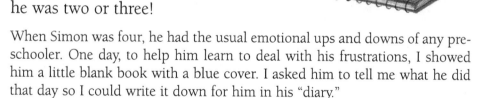

When Simon was four, he had the usual emotional ups and downs of any preschooler. One day, to help him learn to deal with his frustrations, I showed him a little blank book with a blue cover. I asked him to tell me what he did that day so I could write it down for him in his "diary."

Here is his first entry:

*Today I got my new diary and it even has a lock, and it is little. Mommy is nice. The day after tomorrow I am going to a new school. And in the class I know only two of my friends.*

I asked him if he had more to say. He added,

*I was bad to Mommy but now I am nice to Mommy. And she didn't even punish me. And now I feel good because Mommy wrote for me.*

From this first entry, I could see that Simon was concerned about starting a new preschool where he hardly knew anyone. He also had mixed feelings about his own behavior and my reactions to it. The phrase "and now I feel good" showed me that by expressing his troubled feelings he'd helped himself feel better. Children's feelings are often stronger and more complex than is their ability to deal with them. Once negative emotion is put down in words, in a safe place, the sting is lessened. Like adults, children need to feel validated, need to know that their feelings are real and okay.

Forget the outdated notion that males aren't very good at expressing feelings. If you show your boys, as well as your girls, how to record their feelings on a regular basis, they'll all get a head start in dealing confidently with emotional issues.

# Eight Good Reasons for Your Child to Keep a Diary

Depending on your child's personality and the type of diary she chooses (see "Six Kinds of Diaries to Try," pages 27–32), the process of committing to paper a permanent history of daily life provides countless benefits. Here are eight:

1. **Catharsis.** There's no safer place to express difficult feelings. School-age kids, even preschoolers, have lots of emotions to cope with. If your child is in her turbulent preteens, she's at a particularly suitable time for starting a diary. A personal journal can help fulfill the strong need for self-expression and privacy children experience at this stage. As a young teenager, I read and reread my own diary entries almost daily. Such self-absorption is normal at that age, as is the teen's desire to gain perspective during a tumultuous period.

2. **Insight into growing up and help in dealing with change.** Struggling to put her feelings into words—working to figure out what she actually does feel when it isn't always obvious—adds to your child's self-knowledge and self-esteem. She'll also learn a lot about herself by rereading her entries as time goes by.

3. **Better powers of observation and sharpened senses.** The diarist turns not only inward to record feelings, but outward to record actual happenings. Once your child gets in the habit of recording experiences, she'll begin to notice much more—smells, colors, changing seasons.

4. **Capture of early memories before they fade.** Nearly everyone sooner or later thinks about recording his or her life in the form of a memoir. How lovely to have a record of the early years!

5. **Development of a writing style and language skills.** In a journal, your child can experiment with language in an unpressured way, without worrying about grammar and spelling.

6. **A more active imagination.** Keeping a diary may inspire your child to try other nonfiction or fiction writing and creative projects.

7. **Pleasure in the act itself.** There's no age limit on the sheer fun of having a safe place to explore ME! ME! ME! Writing a diary can be an art form in itself, providing pleasure in the writing and greater joy in simply living, since details are more deeply seen and felt when one is considering every experience as a potential diary entry.

8. **Improved communication, bonding, and trust between you and your child**—as long as you never belittle anything your child writes or invade his privacy without invitation.

# What to Write In?

Almost any notebook will do for a child's diary. Though tiny notebooks are cute and portable, a larger format encourages experimentation and ease. A medium-sized bound book with blank pages works best for many people. Your child can choose his own, or you might provide one as a gift. An attractive cover may be appreciated, and a lock can be reassuring.

A notebook with undated pages is best, because if your child skips dated pages he may feel he's "not doing it right," which can cause him to lose motivation. The worst case is when a diarist feels he has to apologize to his own notebook for "not writing for so long." You can encourage your child to date each entry himself instead. Many calendar diaries, especially the five-year kind with only a few lines provided per day, don't allow enough space to be creative.

What to write with? Pencil smears, but some kids demand erasability. Others like to use different-colored pens. If the aesthetics of crossing out aren't pleasing, you might offer your child correction fluid for errors—or, since correctness isn't important in a diary, suggest that your child make a clever design or picture out of an error.

Then there's the computer diary. Your child may or may not respond to this format—some don't find it "organic" enough. Yet, if your child is a good typist, keeping a journal on a word processor can actually be very freeing. With certain kinds of diaries, such as a writer's journal (see page 31), a child may relish the chance to move entries around from section to section. Make the suggestion and let your child decide. But be sure to provide some kind of backup program for those irreplaceable pages, even if it's only printing out each day's entry. There's nothing sadder than losing an electronic journal when your hard drive crashes (and most do, sooner or later).

# How to Begin, Age by Age

Starting with the very young, here are some guidelines for helping your child keep a journal:

**Ages 4–7.** Until your child can write comfortably herself, have her dictate her entries to you. A line or two a day is fine for teaching the value of writing regularly, but a voluble child may dictate pages at a time. Allow complete freedom for entries that may range from the mundane to the highly charged. Read back any and all entries as often as your child asks.

If nothing seems to come to your child's mind at first, ask leading questions. "What was the most fun you had today?" "Did anything make you angry?" "What did you play with your friend?" "What was the best new thing you learned at school?" Zero in on a moment of special happiness. Or focus on a moment of sadness and suggest, "Let's write that feeling down. It might help you feel better." The rereading is its own reward for your child—and a new diarist will have been born.

Encourage your child to immortalize "big" events, such as when her friend moved away, when she learned to ride a bike, or when her sister was born. But remember that even something as seemingly inconsequential as the day she lost a piece of her favorite puzzle can be worth recording.

Every so often, suggest that your child look back to what she wrote on the same day (or week) the previous year (or even month). Talk about how much she's grown and changed.

Don't pressure the child who finds it difficult to express feelings. For instance, my second son, Kevin, liked to talk about what *happened* in his journal. At four-and-a-half, he dictated,

> We got a typewriter that's broken. I held the mouse at school and I put it back in the cage.

> Today we drove around and they wouldn't let people get in the snow unless they lived there. And we tried to go to Mt. Wilson but the road was blocked by a sign that said "Road Closed."

Even in those simple entries, you can detect more complete stories, with emotional undertones.

By age five, Kevin's entries were a bit more elaborate:

*I went camping for four days. It was very fun. I saw a movie there. I had campfires there. I made some friends there. I saw a cave there. The ocean used to be over the whole mountain. I walked through a tree. We walked up a trail. It's going to start all over again: the ocean is going to go over the mountains again, in about a million years. We went on a long walk and I found a little daisy flower. I dug an ant hole. I climbed a high tree. I flew a play plane. I got it stuck in a tree lots of times.*

Notice that he's talking about things that gave him pleasure and, occasionally, caused him frustration, as well as going over conversations we'd had that particularly struck him.

# Ages 8–12. Let your child know there are no rules about how much or how often to write. He can skip a day or two, write only a line some days, or write two pages at once if he chooses. Keeping a journal shouldn't ever be a chore. You may find that your child is more faithful about journal writing at particular times, such as during a school break or when some big change has stirred up feelings.

At this age, your child may enjoy reading the real or fictional diaries of other children for inspiration (see Resources, pages 33–34, for suggestions).

Help build your child's self-concept by suggesting topics like, "Some things I feel good about are . . ." or "The best thing I've done lately is . . ." or "Something I know now that I didn't know last week is. . . ."

Your child may be comfortable with you reading what he's written, or he may take pleasure in reading entries aloud. Let him take the lead, though. Most children need privacy, and you can quash your child's drive to keep a journal if he doesn't feel it's safe from others' eyes. He may well go from recording homework assignments and describing his irritation at a friend's behavior to sharing his innermost thoughts and desires with his journal. It's hard for some parents to let go—but when you're longing to read what your child's written, your best bet may be to go write in your own journal about the challenge of separating from your child as he matures.

And don't forget to help your child keep his journal safe from siblings. One woman told me that as a child she loved her journal until she caught her younger sister drawing pictures in it.

When I was ten and eleven, I tended to downplay my emotions in my diary, possibly because it only had space for a few daily lines:

*It is freezing today. Mom ran over my scooter while she was backing the car in the driveway.*

*The dentist was fun! It was a new one that we had not gone to before. I have only 3 or 4 cavities.*

*I am on the top line in the spelling chart. We had words from a sixth grade speller.*

However, I also wrote:

*For the past few days I have been having strange emotional phases. I guess it's just signs of maturity. I was seemingly going mad over the fact I was alone. I was dying to be with boys.*

Then, one week later:

*I started menstruating today. One more sign that I'm becoming a young lady.*

**Ages 13 and up.** Tumultuous changes make the teen years a perfect time for your child to learn to record emotional events. Privacy is top priority here (though, of course, respecting your child's privacy is good advice at any age). *Never* read your child's journal unless invited. The trust you'd lose cannot be measured.

At around fourteen, I began a diary in which I explored feelings in depth. I felt I would have died if my parents had peeked at those journals. I recorded every passing mood, the highs and the lows that often changed places within hours on the same day. My journal, which I kept in a series of inexpensive steno notebooks, was a lifeline through the hard parts of high school. No matter how close I felt to my parents or how many friends I had, my journal was the one place I could be completely honest. Whenever I'd read over what I wrote—say, about the beginnings of a crush I had on some boy—I learned so much from my "former" self.

I kept this up for decades, eventually switching to a computerized version. Also in my teens, I started keeping track of the many books I read by listing them in a notebook. When I was fifteen, I kept a "date diary" for rating boys. From age sixteen and into my twenties, I had a "moving diary," in which I recorded the major life changes that occurred each time I packed to move (we moved every few years, for one reason or another). At age seventeen, I kept a travel diary during a trip to Europe.

The teen years are when a lot of people start lifelong journaling habits. Help your child develop the practice and reap the benefits.

# Six Kinds of Diaries to Try

Here are some journals to explore with your child:

1. **The Personal Feelings Diary.** "I want to write, but more than that, I want to bring out all kinds of things that lie buried deep in my heart," wrote Anne Frank in *The Diary of a Young Girl.*

In a personal feelings diary—the kind that comes to mind when most people think of a "diary"—intermittent entries are as appropriate as daily ones. When your child records and perhaps analyzes her emotions, she may feel calmer.

When your child keeps a diary of her feelings, she's writing to her future self. When novelist Gail Godwin rereads old diaries, she jots down a word or two to her former self as a way of setting the record straight.

The youthful diaries of many famous people have been published, whether they planned it that way or not: Theodore Roosevelt, Louisa May Alcott, Karen Horney, and Margaret O'Brien are just a few that come to mind. (Of course, some people write with an eye to posterity.)

Some starting suggestions for a feelings diary are:

- Record your emotions about some problem in your life.

- Imagine, in writing, what would happen if you made one decision as opposed to another.

- Write about your friends or parents and what they mean to you.

- Write about what makes you happy or sad.

Family interactions were a prime source of inspiration for some of Simon's early entries. Once he dictated:

*Sometimes I get ashamed of myself from Kevin* (little brother) *because he fights with me, and sometimes Daddy makes me feel ashamed because sometimes he bothers me too much when I'm doing something.*

Another time his entry read:

*I am mad at Daddy and I am also mad at me because I didn't want to do such a bad thing and I don't know if I did.* (The "bad thing" was taking Daddy's wrench.)

In this kind of diary, a younger child might be writing to the parent taking the dictation. When I look back at Simon's early entries, I realize that he was, in a way, writing to me rather than to himself. Sometimes what started as distress on both sides ended in mutual warm feelings.

It was especially satisfying when I realized that Simon trusted me enough to dictate his angry feelings about me. For instance, he dictated:

*My Mommy forces me to take a bath in the morning and it's crazy to do that.*

Another time I wrote this down for him:

*Today I'm mad. Mommy went to the store and I wanted her to get a present for me, but she said I have too much toys and too much books.*

Your child may enjoy being able to criticize his teacher without repercussions. Here is Simon at four-and-a-half:

*Even my teacher is dumb and no one can tell her that, because she didn't let me go up the stairs by myself today.*

You can use such dictated revelations to open up a simple conversation with your child about what's happening at school.

**2. The Dream Journal.** Here, the child dictates or writes down her dreams each morning while they're still vivid. Some tips for this type of journaling are:

- Your child should keep a pen and paper, or a tape recorder, within easy reach of his bed.

- Before your child goes to sleep, he needs to tell himself, "Tonight I will remember what I dream." (You can remind him to do this at first.)

- Some dream journalists set alarms to wake themselves up at odd hours, the better to interrupt dreams-in-progress. I think it's best for a child to wake up naturally and recall the last dream he had, which is usually the longest and most detailed.

- The more details your child records, the better. He can include moods, colors, and any ideas about what the dream might refer to or mean. For more about dreams, see "Dreamwork" in Chapter 13 (pages 182–186).

At five-and-a-half, Simon enjoyed sharing his dreams:

*Hello. What I dreamed about was my girlfriend. My girlfriend was talking Martian talk. We were saying, "Poomp, doomp, dingerp." It was really a nice dream, very nice and sweet and lovable.*

**3.  The Activities Diary.** Ordinary-seeming, "what-I-did-today" accounts may eventually lead to expression of feelings. But don't pressure the child who keeps feelings out. Activities diaries are often kept every day, always with dated entries. Suggest that your child write at least three or four sentences daily. Sometimes this kind of diary is kept for a certain length of time to record a particular event, such as a family vacation. Or your child might describe a new puppy's early growth and antics.

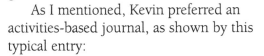

As I mentioned, Kevin preferred an activities-based journal, as shown by this typical entry:

*I rided my bike today. We went to a party and we got little hats.*

You might focus the activity-minded child's attention with a journal devoted to discoveries. Have your child record (or dictate) whatever discoveries (scientific or otherwise) he made that day or week: "Daddy is sometimes not very attentive when he's working hard to finish a project."

**4.  The Scrapbook Journal.** When presented with a blank book, some children, especially younger ones, feel more comfortable expressing themselves with drawings. If this sounds like your child, you might dub her book an "art journal." Photographs can be included, too. In fact, this kind of journal can become a more inclusive album in which your child keeps a variety of small souvenirs: movie stubs, fortune-cookie slips, party invitations, birthday cards, or favorite jokes.

## Time in a Capsule

A time capsule, in which children capture an ordinary day, is a variation on the scrapbook journal. Help your child think of everyday details and items she could include in a time capsule, ones guaranteed to bring back memories a year, five years, or twenty years from now. The time capsule's form can vary from a book to slips of paper tucked into a large envelope to items placed in a box.

Here are some questions you can use to start your child thinking about an ordinary day:

- What time do you get up? Go to bed? Do you read in bed at night?
- What are you reading today? What's your all-time favorite book?
- What do you eat on a typical day, including snacks? Do you watch TV or read while you eat?
- How much TV do you watch each day? Do you have a favorite show?
- What chores are you supposed to do around the house? Which ones do you do without being reminded?
- Did you buy a toy, something for a hobby, or a sports item recently?
- What was the last movie you saw? How much did it cost? Who starred in it? What was it about?
- What do you do with your friends when they come over?
- How much is your allowance? What did you do with it this week? Are you saving up for something special?
- Did you argue with someone today? About what?
- What do you collect?
- What's your height? Your weight?

Here are some items you might suggest your child include in a time capsule:

- the front page, a few ads, and movie and TV listings from today's newspaper
- a gum wrapper, trading card, or homework paper
- drawings or photographs of herself, the family, her pet, her bedroom, her school, or a favorite place

Finally, encourage your child to write a message to herself to be read a year from today—and perhaps another to be read a long time from now.

**5. The Writer's Journal.** This type of journal, with its detailed observations, is particularly suitable for verbally adept children. A writer's journal may include all kinds of fodder for future writing, such as ideas, plans, feelings, notes about projects, overheard dialogue, a favorite poem, or a line or two of original poetry. Some children enjoy writing lists, which can be inventories of gripes, wishes, resolutions, even books read. These materials are then available to be reprocessed, if the child desires, into stories, poems, or other literary forms.

Instead of "Today I went to the doctor," a writer's journal might contain a description of the receptionist, the doctor, or the office itself; a word picture of the writer sitting on the paper-covered examining table; details about patient-doctor chatter; feelings about the experience.

Should you be concerned if your child fictionalizes reality in his diary entries? Presuming he knows fantasy from reality, there's no harm in embroidering the truth or in making up entire scenes. In fact, these stories could free your child's creativity, allowing him to explore the delights of fiction writing in a completely safe context.

Here are some ideas to share with a child who's starting a writer's journal:

- Take a walk. When you get back, describe everything you heard (saw, smelled, or touched).

- Describe your classroom.

- Listen to a conversation between two people (such as students on the playground at recess). Then try to reconstruct what they said in your journal.

- To anchor your entries in historical time, include what you paid for things like movies, candy, or clothes.

- Choose someone you know well and describe the person as completely as you can. Include both personality and physical traits. (What does the person look like? How does he or she act? Describe the person's laugh.)

- Make lists of all kinds: what you like best about yourself, your best friend, your school, your life; what you would like to do this year, next year, ten years from now.

- Imagine you're someone else, or an animal. Write an entry describing your feelings and actions as though you were that other being.

- Choose an event from your past. Begin by recalling and writing down every detail you can remember about it. Then go on to analyze how this event has affected you in the present.

**6.   The Family Journal.** All family members contribute to this chronicle of day-to-day activities and feelings. It's an open book for all to write in and read, though at times the children's experiences may predominate. Everyone feels free to include details of what's going on in their life or in the life of the family. Maybe the family went to the park and the kids learned how to slide down a hill on a piece of cardboard. Maybe Mom got angry but caught herself before she raised her voice. Even what seems dull and ordinary at the time will bring pleasure when it's reread years later. Everyday events take on a special quality when you reminisce about them as a family.

For example: "Our family had an old-fashioned Thanksgiving get-together at the home of Aunt Em and Uncle Hubert. Aunt Em showed everyone how to dance the polka. . . ." "We picked our our own apples at an apple farm, and then we drank hot cider. . . ." "We enjoyed a winter's day outside, and the baby tasted snow for the first time. . . ."

An alternative version of the family journal is a dialogue journal. Here, two (or more) family members write interactively, putting on paper what they might be reluctant to say to each other. For some families, this is a good way to deal with problem situations.

# Diary Rules

When it comes to your child's diary, there *are* no rules. There are no teachers, no grades, no exams. It's absolutely okay to mix formats within a single book—for one day to be a "dream day," the next a "feelings day."

If your child seems to have the perfectionist (or revisionist) urge to go back over entries and edit or rewrite them, you might explain that a big part of the value of keeping a diary is capturing reality as it's experienced. You lose some of that immediacy if you go back and rewrite. Also, you might add, no one is judging or grading the diary, so there's no need for it to be "perfect." (Of course, a writer's journal is a bit different. One of its purposes is to rework material into something more "artistic.")

All topics are acceptable. For some people, writing about happiness is easier than writing about pain. Others only feel the urge to write when they're depressed or upset. If your child finds it difficult to open up to others, or if she isn't ready to entrust deep, personal feelings to parents or anyone else, suggest using a diary as a "friend" who wants to be kept informed. Never imply any sort of obligation to write.

If your child shares his journal with you, the one and only rule for *you* is to never criticize anything he writes, no matter what. No nitpicking about her writing style or grammar, and no negativity about the content, even if his feelings surprise you. If you don't understand something, gently ask, "I'm not sure I get what you mean here." A child's journal should be where he learns to go with the flow, writing freely with absolutely no fear of criticism. On the other hand, feel free to express your delight at a particularly evocative or amusing section.

As mentioned earlier, reading the real and fictional diaries of other people, especially of other children, may be the best inspiration for your child to begin his own journal journey. Start by checking the following resources.

# Resources

*The Absolutely True, Positively Awesome Book About . . . ME!!!* by Jessica Wilber (Minneapolis: Free Spirit Publishing, 1999). Ages 6–10. This book for younger diarists shares creative ideas for starting and keeping a journal, seasonal activities, and more.

*The Adrian Mole Diaries* by Sue Townsend (New York: Avon, 1997). Ages 8 and up. This first book of a highly popular British series features fictional teenager Adrian Mole as he details every bit of his adolescence in his secret diary.

*All About Me: A Keepsake Journal for Kids* by Linda Kranz (Flagstaff, AZ: Rising Moon, 1996). Ages 7–12. Kids who complain they have nothing to write about will like the fact that each page of this journal contains thought-starters to help them begin.

*Anne of Green Gables Journal* by L. M. Montgomery and Donna Green (New York: Smithmark Publishing, 1997). Ages 9–12. Each page in this journal contains an excerpt from one of the *Anne of Green Gables* novels. Illustrations depict Anne, her friends, and her environment.

*Charlotte in Giverny* by Joan MacPhail Knight (San Francisco: Chronicle Books, 2000). Ages 6–12. The fictional travel diary of a young American girl who visits Monet's artist colony in 1892.

*The Diary of a Young Girl: The Definitive Edition* by Anne Frank (New York: Bantam Books, 1997). Ages 8 and up. A beloved classic since its initial publication in 1947, this vivid, insightful journal is a fitting memorial to the Jewish teenager who died in a Nazi concentration camp in 1945. Anne's diary covers the twenty-five months she and her family were in hiding in Nazi-occupied Amsterdam. This particular edition includes entries omitted from the original publication.

*Hannah's Journal: The Story of an Immigrant Girl* by Marissa Moss (Orlando, FL: Harcourt, 2000). Ages 8–12. This fictional journal concerns a girl's life during America's peak immigration years in the early 1900s. Also by the same author and publisher: *Rachel's Journal: The Story of a Pioneer Girl* and *Emma's Journal: The Story of a Colonial Girl*.

*Jazzimagination: A Journal to Read and Write* by Sharon M. Draper (New York: Scholastic Trade, 2000). Ages 9–12. A combination of fictional entries by a thirteen-year-old girl and space for the reader to write his or her own entries.

*Jorah's Journal* by Judith Caseley (New York: Greenwillow, 1997). Ages 4–8. This read-aloud chapter book is presented in the form of diary entries written by a young girl who has to move and hates the idea.

*Lights Out: A Nighttime Diary* by Robie Rogge (San Francisco: Chronicle Books, 1998). Ages 7–13. This diary full of writing prompts also includes a pen that lights up for private nighttime journaling.

*Mostly Michael* by Robert Kimmel Smith (New York: Yearling Books, 1988). Ages 9–12. An eleven-year-old boy is given a diary and learns to enjoy writing about his growing pains. This warm-hearted story could motivate other boys to seek out the solace of their own private journals.

*Only Opal: The Diary of a Young Girl* by Opal Whiteley (New York: Paperstar, 1997). Ages 5–9. This book uses a combination of actual journal entries by a very young pioneer girl in the early 1900s and watercolor paintings by a modern-day illustrator.

*Personal Journaling,* a bimonthly magazine from the editors of *Writer's Digest.* Contains ideas to inspire all kinds of journals. Available on newsstands or visit *www.writersdigest.com/journaling.*

*Rainbow Writing: A Journal with Activities for Budding Young Writers* by Mary Euretig and Darlene Kreisberg (Carmichael, CA: Dream Tree Press, 1992). Ages 4–8. This book was created specifically for the beginning writer and includes developmentally appropriate prompts, vibrant illustrations, and heavy-bond pages that allow the use of markers without bleed-through.

*Speaking of Journals: Children's Book Writers Talk About Their Diaries, Notebooks, and Sketchbooks,* edited by Paula W. Graham (Honesday, PA: Boyds Mills Press, 1999). All ages. This book is exactly what its title states. It provides a unique source of inspiration for the entire family.

*Totally Private & Personal: Journaling Ideas for Girls and Young Women* by Jessica Wilber (Minneapolis: Free Spirit Publishing, 1996). Ages 8 and up. The savvy fourteen-year-old author offers creative journaling tips, advice about growing up, and more.

*Through My Eyes: A Journal for Teens* by Linda Kranz (Flagstaff, AZ: Rising Moon, 1998). Ages 12 and up. This book gives teens a place to express themselves—and the inspiration to begin. Each lined page includes a thought-starter that encourages teen writers to explore their relationships with parents, friends, and themselves.

*Write Where You Are: How to Use Writing to Make Sense of Your Life* by Caryn Mirriam-Goldberg (Minneapolis: Free Spirit Publishing, 1999). Ages 12 and up. Written by a creative writing teacher, this book is full of writing ideas for teens, including getting started, discovering what's important to them, honing their craft, revising their writing, and connecting with other readers and writers.

*Writing Down the Days: 365 Creative Journaling Ideas for Young People* by Lorraine M. Dahlstrom (Minneapolis: Free Spirit Publishing, 2000). Ages 12 and up. Creative suggestions for journal entries based on interesting things that happened in the past on that day, week, or month. Topics include celebrations, hobbies, science, sports, famous people, and more.

**Your Notebook with Help from Amelia** (Pleasant Company). This American Girl® CD-ROM allows young diarists to password-protect entries and add sound effects and pictures. Find it at a local store, call 1-800-845-0005, or visit *www.americangirlstore.com.*

*Zlata's Diary: A Child's Life in Sarajevo* by Zlata Filipovic (New York: Penguin, 1995). Ages 11 and up. A true wartime diary that the author began when she was eleven years old.

# CHAPTER 3

# (ELEBRATE THE SENSES

**O**ur five senses are capable of giving us so much pleasure, even beyond their major role in helping us learn about the big, wonderful world out there. Yet few of us were shown, as children, how to fully appreciate what our senses have to offer. You can help your child, beginning in his earliest years and continuing throughout childhood, celebrate his senses.

There's no need to take on your child's sensory life as a structured project, of course. I'm talking about playful learning, about teaching your child to tune in to what is usually taken for granted, about appreciating the awesomeness of the ordinary.

For instance, when my friend Linda's daughter, Sharra, was only a few months old, Linda would dance around with her to a tape of the hokey-pokey. Sharra loved having her hands and feet moved in and out in time to the music. "She thought it was a hoot," recalls Linda.

We've all probably done something similar with our babies, without thinking much about it. Playful games like these help babies learn to relish several of their senses—for Sharra, sight, sound, and touch. And while the familiar is comforting, kids—like all of us—pay closest attention to what is new. Brains enjoy and *need* interesting, varied sensory stimulation to grow and keep developing (and research has recently shown that our brains are capable of making new connections throughout our lives). And when something new is absorbed through more than one sense, both learning and memory are enhanced.

## Sensory Beginnings

Some background: Even in the first few months, an infant's sensory systems are surprisingly mature. Throughout the first year, different regions of the brain continue to develop rapidly. During the period from about four to eighteen months, sensory and motor functions become linked. At that point, a baby starts pushing away a food that smells yucky and grabbing a shiny toy.

By about eight or nine months, a baby's brain can make associations. She can go beyond simply hearing a sound; a baby can *interpret* what she's heard. Now she "gets" that the sound of a buzzer by the door means the babysitter has arrived or that the smell of cooking means the family will be eating soon.

Before and after your child can talk, help her tune into the particular properties of an object by using lots of adjectives. For instance, point out the *fuzzy* coat, the *tiny* ant, the *huge* tree, the *smooth* nightgown. "By combining words with sensory stimulation, you begin a long process," explains Martha Arterberry, associate professor of psychology and coordinator of the Infant and Child Study Research Center at Gettysburg College in Pennsylvania. "Someday when you talk about the subtleties of the light on the water, it's going to sink in and make real sense to your child, and she'll start noticing it herself."

Don't be surprised if your own capacity for wonder increases as well. If some of your senses are weaker than others—maybe, like me, you're simply not a "visual" person—make a special point of exposing your child to experiences appealing to these less developed senses. If nothing else, such activities are a wonderful excuse to linger, to savor the small, everyday delights it's so easy to rush past.

# Use Them All

Here are a few activities that make use of ALL the senses, even if only in your child's imagination:

▶ Have your child close his eyes and imagine he's inside a spaceship, a tent, a castle, a hot-dog factory, or a barn. Ask him what he can see, hear, smell, taste, and touch in the place he's imagining. Encourage him to describe in detail everything he experiences through his senses there. With practice, such exercises will strengthen your child's powers of both imagination and observation.

▶ Describe something to your child using every sense but sight. See if he can guess what it is.

   *Example:* "I'm thinking of something that's hard on the outside, less hard on the inside, smells a certain way when it's new, feels smooth, and makes very little noise until you shut it." The answer is "a book."

▶ Your preschooler may like to play a game called "Mystery Box." Put a food item—say, a piece of broccoli—in a box and have him (without looking) stick his hand in and feel it. Can he guess what it is? What color it is? Now take the broccoli out and talk with your child about the way it looks and smells. See if he'll taste a little, maybe if you dip it in something he likes. Ask him to be your assistant as you prepare a kid-friendly recipe using cooked broccoli. When it's done, again see if he'll taste a little. Which texture does he prefer: raw or cooked? Which taste? Which smell?

For convenience, the rest of the activities in this chapter are organized by sense, though in real life more than one sense is often involved in whatever we experience. Feel free to adapt any activity as your child grows older and more sophisticated.

# Vision: Shades of Meaning

As your child grows beyond babyhood, her vision doesn't actually get any sharper than it was in late infancy. What does develop is her ability to notice and appreciate finer distinctions. Ask your child to bring you the *bigger* cup, or to put the *tiniest* car in the toy garage. The more observant you are, the more you can share new ways of seeing with your child. It's not so much a matter of stimulating your child's visual sense as it is of helping her appreciate and discriminate among various sights.

▶ To help your child appreciate the world around her, direct her attention to how sunlight makes shadows on the furniture. Point out the way light reflects on shiny surfaces, such as glass, and on dull surfaces, such as carpet.

▶ Outdoors, point out the varying shades of green things, such as leaves, grasses, and flower stems. Show your child the sparkle of a lake and the skittery little shadows leaves make on the ground on a windy day.

▶ Have your child collect five blue things from a room, or to point to everything brown in your home.

▶ With you nearby, let your child use a flashlight to explore the play of light across a dark landscape, both indoors and out.

▶ To increase your child's observational skills, take a walk and seek out repeating shape patterns—say, Xs or squares—in sidewalks, fences, and buildings. At home, look for repeating shapes in such things as napkins, linoleum, and baskets.

▶ Buy your child a small prism so he can experiment with the interplay of color and light. A prism hanging at my own bedroom window provides dancing rainbows all around the room at certain times of the day.

You and your child can make a prism by placing a clear plastic glass filled with water so that it overhangs the edge of a windowsill by one-quarter to one-half inch. When the sun shines in, the glass will make rainbows on the floor, especially if you place a large white sheet of paper there. (White light is a combination of all the colored light waves, and they all travel at different speeds. The water bends and separates the sunlight into colors.)

▶ Get your child an inexpensive kaleidoscope for more wonderful light and color displays.

▶ To introduce the idea that things look different depending on how close or far away you are, have your child look through a magnifying glass and a telescope. Line up several items on a table and have him examine each closely through a magnifier. How does each look different from the others? How does each look through the magnifying glass, compared with the way it looks through the naked eye? Now compare how things look through a telescope to how they look when vision is unaided. For example, notice how you may only see a portion of a huge object, such as the moon, when you use a telescope.

▶ When you go grocery shopping, point out to your child how colors are used in packaging to get our attention. While shopping for clothes, observe the predominant colors in the men's, women's, teens', and children's departments.

▶ Introduce your child to works of art at a museum or in books. Certain artists, such as Picasso, are more likely to appeal to kids (but, of course, use your child's tastes and your own as your best guide). Seek out art that features broad brushstrokes, child-related themes, or silly juxtapositions. Back home, provide art materials and talk about how different colors make your child feel. Ask her to draw a line that looks "happy" or "nervous," or a picture that looks "sad" or "excited." How does what we see affect our emotions?

# Hearing: The World in a Seashell

Even a very young child can let you know quite definitely what he enjoys hearing and what bores or irritates him. One night when I was singing to my toddler son, he said, "No more singing, Mommy." (I tried to absorb this as mere "information" and not feel rejected.) Your child can also interact with sound and music, move to it, and create it himself.

▶ To increase your child's awareness of sounds, whether indoors or out, ask him to be totally silent for a few moments. Now have him tell you everything he hears, from the hum of a refrigerator to birds tweeting. Try this in your kitchen or basement, in a park or forest or desert, in a busy city setting, in the middle of a frozen lake, on a hill, or on a beach (check out that seashell—can you hear a "whoosh"?). An older child can be asked to listen quietly for five full minutes to pick up all possible sounds.

▶ To help your child learn to discriminate among different sounds, gather three noisy things (like a bell, rattle, and set of keys). Show him each item, put them in separate paper bags, and shake each bag to reveal the item's sound. Then mix up the three bags, shake one, and see if he can tell what's in it.

▶ Turn your child on to the joy of moving rhythmically. When my sons were little, one of their favorite activities was bouncing on a bed to the rhythm of a tambourine I hit. Sometimes I'd suggest, "Now pretend you're roadrunners," or "You're lions chasing a mouse." (You don't have to allow bed bouncing—any resilient surface will work.)

▶ Share with your child the enjoyment of making her own sounds and music. Show her how to produce a pleasing rhythm by rubbing a piece of wood on sandpaper, shaking a set of keys, and banging on a pot. Provide her with simple musical instruments, such as bells, a drum, a toy horn, or a harmonica.

    How many different sounds can your child make using only her voice? What happens when two children, or you and your child, make sounds together?

▶ To broaden your child's musical tastes, expose him to different kinds of music, such as choral music, Indian music, folk music, chamber music, jazz, show tunes, or a violin, flute, or drum solo.

▶ Make a tape recording of sounds in and around your home (such as a flushing toilet, vacuum cleaner, doorbell, telephone, slamming door, barking dog, car horn, siren, or running or dripping water). Play it for your child and see how many sounds she can identify.

*Variation:* An older child can make her own tape of sounds, such as someone walking, wind or rain, or a newspaper being thrown against the house—with or without a story line.

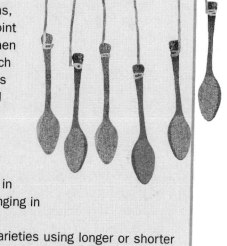

### Make a Wind Chime

Your child might enjoy making and putting up a wind chime. First, let him fool around with various jingly-jangly items (such as spoons, aluminum pie plates, even pencils or ballpoint pens) that will create different sounds when the wind makes them bump against each other. He'll learn he can control the sounds by making simple changes in the items and their positions. To make the actual chime, knot a variety of simple metallic objects, such as different-sized spoons, to pieces of cord. Hang the pieces of cord by tying them to two pieces of wood nailed together in an "X" shape, with a hook at the top for hanging in the wind.

Wind chimes can be made in limitless varieties using longer or shorter cord, strings made of different materials, lighter or heavier objects, and more or fewer objects. Hang your homemade wind chime inside near a window or outside in the wind for different results. Hang it where your child can reach it and make it jingle with a puff of breath.

▶ Explore how music makes your child feel. Share some of your favorite music (all kinds) and talk about the emotion or mood conveyed by each piece or type of music.

Also ask your child to notice how music can *change* her mood. What was she feeling before listening? After? Is there a kind of music she finds particularly relaxing? Particularly energizing? Can she explain why?

▶ Have your child put together a musical autobiography by choosing various selections to represent certain stages of her life so far. She might also enjoy making a musical diary of one particular day.

# Taste: From Picky to Appreciative

The way to help your child develop his sense of taste has more to do with what he eats than anything else. From toddlerhood on, talk about the different flavors you're feeding him: "This is spicy," or "This is tomato-y."

As kids mature, they may reject foods they ate as babies. As their senses develop, their awareness of texture changes, and they may react to foods in quite an individual way. A friend of ours has a nine-month-old girl who will try anything. I've seen her suck on a slice of lemon and reach for another one. When she's older, she'll probably be pickier. On the other hand, the pickiest child when it comes to food (I had one) might turn out to be the most adventurous eater as an adult.

Kids are often very influenced by what the people around them are eating. If an older child is eating green beans, your younger one is more inclined to want some. When *you* eat with your child, talk about the food: what it looks like, what color it is, and whether it's crunchy or soft. Say, "This banana is really sweet and it's kind of mushy."

▶ Blindfold your child and offer him several different foods he's tasted before, such as applesauce, banana, and cooked carrot. Can he identify them? Now try this again with another set of foods when he's both blindfolded and holding his nose. Can he identify foods without the help of his sense of smell?

▶ Let your child explore the tastes of sweet, salty, bitter, and sour by placing samples of each of the following on paper towels and having him taste them in turn: sugar, salt, unsweetened cocoa, lemon juice.

▶ Explore how a food can change its flavor when you prepare it differently. Potatoes and apples, for example, can be dished up in a multitude of ways, changing flavor a little or a lot.

▶ Make use of the appeal of appetizers and finger foods. Have a tasting party: set out tiny bits of many kinds of foods for your child to try, such as pickle slices, cubes of cheese, radish roses, pitted olives, and orange sections.

▶ Make dining a pleasurable event. Have your child decorate plates with different foods. She can make a ketchup smiley face on a grilled cheese sandwich. She might enjoy creating a green bean maze and eating her way through it. Children are attracted to foods that appeal to all their senses. If a food looks nice, is colorful, feels appealing, and smells okay, they're more likely to taste it.

# Smell: The Nose Knows

As far as the experts can determine, the sense of smell is fully functioning at birth. Having the physical ability to smell, though, doesn't mean there's nothing more to learn. Your child will continue to learn the *meaning* of smells throughout infancy and the early years, including which smells are good, which are unpleasant, and which go with food.

Exercise your child's sense of smell to help her learn to appreciate some of the thousands of odor combinations. Memories of odors are particularly powerful—what she learns about smells as a child may last forever.

▶ Put a few pinches of aromatic stuff—perfume, mint, vanilla, lemon or orange peel, onion, garlic, banana, coconut, or cinnamon—in empty baby food jars or film canisters. Completely cover the jars with foil and poke small holes in the top. Play a simple game in which your child sniffs and tries to guess what's in each jar.

▶ Most kids love sniffing and talking about yuckier smells like dirty socks, spoiled milk, an untidy public restroom you happen to find yourself in, skunk fumes along the road, or a due-for-cleaning pet cage or litterbox.

▶ Go on a "smell walk" around your home. Sniff all kinds of things: leather, wood, rugs, painted objects, dishes, and books.

▶ Visit a public garden, an arboretum, or a nursery and have your child sniff all the different kinds of flowers.

With an older child, you can talk about how certain smells appeal to or repulse us depending, to a certain extent, on society's dictates. Point out that in many countries, deodorant is not used, nor is it considered necessary. You can help a preteen or teen observe how many products seek to cover up natural odors around the house or on the body.

# Touch: Rough, Fluffy, Squishy, Scruffy

As early as possible in your child's life, encourage him to take an active role in his own explorations of touch. Touch something silky yourself and say, "I like the smooth, silky way that feels." Then encourage him to express his own ideas about the way things feel.

- Let your child play with material like mud, clay, piecrust dough, papier-mâché. Does he love or hate putting his hands in goopy textures? Can he tell you why?

- Lightly touch your child's skin with a variety of textured items, such as a feather, plastic wrap or foil, tape, a brush, a cotton ball, or a nail file. Help him get to know the feel of nature by going on a walk together to touch leaves, twigs, moss, rocks, and ferns.

- Make a point of exploring textures everywhere. In a health clinic, for example, your child might feel the smoothness of a plastic or metal chair, the woolliness of a carpet, the patchy roughness of a plastered wall, or the veins of a plant's leaf.

- To increase awareness of the texture of everyday items, show your child how to make rubbings (place a large sheet of paper on an item and rub the side of an unwrapped crayon over it). Anything with a raised surface works well, including linoleum, fireplace tile, or the base of a lamp.

- Have your child close her eyes. Then pull something out of your purse, pocket, or briefcase and ask her to figure out what it is by touch. Can she distinguish a penny from a dime, an apartment key from a car key?

- Together, make a texture book, using scraps of silk, corduroy, fur, wool, sandpaper, or cotton. Or make a texture board. Glue string onto a large piece of cardboard to make several separate "boxes." In each box, glue objects with varying textures, such as sand, feathers, leaves, and rice.

- Make a tactile finger maze. Apply white glue (let one coat dry and add another for thickness) in a zig-zaggy pattern on a piece of cardboard. Then have your child close her eyes and follow the maze with her finger.

- With your finger, trace a design on your child's back. See if he can tell what you've drawn. Start with letters of the alphabet and move to faces, animals, tables, chairs, and trees. "Draw" slowly. Take turns.

▸ Collect some old socks. Put a small object in each one and see if your child can figure out what it is by feeling it through the sock. Good choices are a coin, golf ball, thread spool, spoon, rock, marker from a board game, chess piece, or pair of dice.

▸ Buy pieces of sandpaper in several different grades, with the roughness grade noted on the back. Mix them up and place them rough side up. Have your child arrange them from smoothest to roughest.

### Make a Feel-It Box

Decorate a shoebox or a larger box. Cut a hole big enough for a hand in one or two sides or the top of the box. Put something textured inside, such as a stone, twig, or cotton ball. Now have your child reach in and try to determine what the item is by how it feels. Try things with varying textures (rough, smooth, lumpy, scratchy). A younger child can identify the item by name ("a spoon"); an older child can say how it feels ("smooth and cool").

*Variations:* Show your child several items before placing them in the box. Then name one item and ask him to find it by touch alone. Or place several items in the box and ask him to find the smooth one, the tiny one, or the soft one.

Put differently shaped items in the box. Have your child discover what shape a thing is by touch alone.

Make texture blocks to use in your "feel-it box." Take your child on a search for different textures in your home (and, perhaps, in a crafts or fabrics store). Glue fabrics and other materials (sandpaper, ribbon, wool, fur, feathers) onto one or more sides of small wooden blocks, *one texture per block*. Now place three blocks, two having the same texture and one having a different texture, into the box. Ask your child to reach in with both hands and, without looking, try to match the two similar blocks.

# How the Senses Work

A few easy experiments will give your child some idea of the workings of her own senses:

▸ **Optical Illusions.** An optical illusion is a mistake your brain makes in judging the color, shape, size, or distance of an object.

With your right hand, hold an empty toilet paper tube (or a sheet of paper rolled into a tube with a 1-inch opening) against your right eye. Keeping the fingers of your left hand together with your palm toward your face, touch the left edge of the end of the tube.

Keep both eyes open as you look through the tube at the wall across the room. You'll see a "hole" in the palm of your hand.

The reason? While we normally see a composite of the images received by both eyes, here only the right eye can see the hole at the end of the tube, and only the left eye can see your hand holding the tube. Since both images are directly ahead, they overlap to cause the illusion.

- **Right-Eyed or Left-Eyed?** Find out by extending one arm and pointing your index finger at some spot across the room. Keep both eyes open. Then close one eye at a time. You'll see two different views of your pointing finger. If the view you see with your right eye is the same as the one you saw with both eyes, your right eye is the dominant one.

- **Mirror Image.** Hold a mirror perpendicular to a piece of paper on a table. Try to write your name or draw a square while watching only your hand in the mirror.

- **Skin Sensitivity.** Get a ruler and a circle-drawing compass. Ask your child to close his eyes and keep them closed during the experiment. Set the two points of the compass 45 millimeters (1⅞ inches) apart. Lightly touch your child's forearm with both points. She will probably feel both. Now change the distance to 35 millimeters (or 1¼ inches) and lightly touch her forearm again. This time she may feel only one point.

  Try the smaller setting on her cheek. Since the cheek is more sensitive than the forearm, she will probably feel two points there.

  If your child enjoys this exercise, experiment to see how sensitive a fingertip is, the back of the hand, the chest, and the lips.

- **Tongue Sensitivity.** Have your child map how sensitive her tongue is to different kinds of tastes. Ask her to place each of the following (one at a time) on the tip, side, and back of her tongue: a bit of salt, sugar, lemon juice, and instant coffee. She'll find that the tip of the tongue is more sensitive to salty and sweet tastes, the sides to salty and sour, and the back to bitter.

‣ **Hot or Cold?** Find out whether lukewarm feels hot or cold. Fill three pans—one with very warm water, one with cold water, and one with luke-warm water (put this one in the middle). Have your child place her left-hand fingertips in the pan on the left side, her right-hand fingertips in the pan on the right side. After you count to sixty, have her put both hands in the middle (lukewarm) pan. One hand will "think" the water is hot; the other will "think" it's cold.

‣ **Scents Galore.** Aphelion, a British perfume maker who has designed cus-tom perfumes for royalty and other famous people, is able to distinguish perhaps 2,500 different scents. He uses this unusual ability to capture the unique individual fragrance, or "odor signature," of each of his clients.

How many separate scents can you and your child distinguish in a single day?

# Resources

*Art Fraud Detective* by Anna Nilsen (New York: Kingfisher, 2000). Ages 7–12. This colorful book comes with a small magnifying glass. Readers are given clues to enable them to detect which of the famous illustrated paintings are genuine and which are fakes. A good way to fine-tune the visual sense.

**BrainPop,** *www.brainpop.com.* This site features animated versions of how the ear and the eye work, along with other kid-pleasing science, health, and technology information and activities.

*Come Look with Me: Enjoying Art with Children* by Gladys Blizzard (Charlottesville, VA: Thomasson-Grant, 1990). All ages. This first in a series of art appreciation books for children intro-duces twelve paintings, each featuring children as the main subject. Includes questions about each work, brief biographies of the artists, and information for adults.

*Head to Toe Science: Over 40 Eye-Popping, Spine-Tingling, Heart-Pounding Activities That Teach Kids About the Human Body* by Jim Wiese (New York: John Wiley & Sons, 2000). Ages 7–12. One chapter in this book focuses on the senses and the nervous system, providing a good introduction to the physiology behind our five senses. Each project introduces the topic, provides a list of materi-als and guidelines, and explains the science involved. Lots of sidebars and illustrations.

*Looking at Pictures: An Introduction to Art for Young People* by Joy Richardson (New York: Harry N. Abrams, 1997). Ages 9–14. Neither intimidating nor condescending, this book makes art appre-ciation accessible to middle-grade readers. Full-color reproductions of famous paintings in London's National Gallery, informative sections on themes and techniques of art, and information on art museums and on each painting make this book especially valuable.

*National Gallery of Art Activity Book* by Maura A. Clarkin (New York: Harry N. Abrams, 1994). Ages 4–8. This book introduces young readers to more than forty masterpieces from Washington's National Gallery of Art, using a series of "adventures" to help children understand the elements of art. A creative art-making activity follows each adventure.

**Neuroscience for Kids: The Senses,** *faculty.washington.edu/chudler/chsense.html.* This extensive site offers information, experiments, and activities about the five senses, as well as links to other relevant sites.

**Seeing, Hearing, and Smelling the World,** *www.hhmi.org/senses.* This site, sponsored by the Howard Hughes Medical Institute, features a vast amount of fascinating information about the brain and the senses.

*Sense-Abilities: Fun Ways to Explore the Senses* by Michelle O'Brien-Palmer (Chicago: Chicago Review Press, 1998). Ages 4–8. Amusing, instructive science activities to introduce and explain the workings of the five senses to young children.

*Show Time: Music, Dance, and Drama Activities for Kids* by Lisa Bany-Winters (Chicago: Chicago Review Press, 2000). Ages 6–12. With the aid of this book, children will explore their musical and kinesthetic selves by putting on shows. They'll find more than eighty activities, such as creating a mirror dance, making puppets, acting out a song, and imitating a musical instrument. Several play scripts are included.

*Smelly Old History* series by Mary Dobson (New York: Oxford University Press, 1997, 1998). Ages 6–12. These Scratch 'n' Sniff paperbacks are delightfully original: Kids can learn first-hand (or first-nose) that life stank in the "old days." Nasty smells were apparently rampant when, instead of good public sanitation, there were "night pots," raw sewage, and no refrigerators. The series includes such titles as *Mouldy Mummies, Greek Grime, Vile Vikings, Reeking Royals, Medieval Muck,* and *Wartime Whiffs.* The scratchable smells don't last very long and aren't really strong enough to upset the delicate, but the illustrations and explanations (disgusting details about the jobs of scavenger and manure raker, ratcatcher, and fishmonger, for instance) remain fascinating. Smelly examples include rotten fish, sewage in the River Thames, cotton factory fumes, gazelle dung, and the diseased, sweating foot of Henry VIII. Good smells, too: aromatic bath oils, yummy banquet food, and Victorian roses.

*Sounds All Around* by Wendy Pfeffer (New York: HarperCollins, 1999). Ages 4–8. This book contains simple explanations of sounds and the sense of hearing. The author describes how sound waves vibrate through the air and cause the tiny bones in our ears to vibrate as well. Readers also learn how various animals hear, from bats to whales. Includes suggestions for activities.

**Spotlight on Science: The Senses Kit** (Learning Resources). Ages 8 and up. Twenty-four experiments focusing on sensory illusions. Call 1-888-800-7893 or visit the company's educational catalog online at *www.learningresources.com.*

*You Can Make a Collage: A Very Simple How-To Book* by Eric Carle (Palo Alto, CA: Klutz, 1998). All ages. This book includes seventy-two pages of lovely printed tissue created by famous children's author and artist Eric Carle. Easy instructions make creating collages a pleasant means of enriching the visual sense in a hands-on way.

*The Young Person's Guide to the Orchestra* by Anita Ganeri (Orlando, FL: Harcourt Brace, 1996). Ages 7 and up. Kids get an overview of the orchestra followed by information on how various groups of instruments make their unique sounds, with some history thrown in. The book includes a CD of music by Benjamin Britten, narrated by Ben Kingsley. A good introduction to classical music and a fun way to explore and enrich a child's sense of hearing.

# CHAPTER 4

# BRAIN BENDERS

It's pretty amazing when you stop to think about it: the human brain is capable of designing computers that can perform tasks unimaginably faster than humans could, unaided. But even more telling, it seems to me, is that the brain can imagine all kinds of things that humans can't do yet. It's the power of imagination that helps make us what we are.

If you're like most parents, you want your child to develop her brainpower as fully as possible. You can help extend your child's mental reach by teaching her to think both creatively and logically—and by discussing the differences between the two. This chapter contains lots of exercises for young brains.

## Paradoxes for Kids

**Don't read this sentence.**

For you to have followed that instruction, you must *not* have followed it.

Paradoxes like this one are fun to share with kids. A dictionary definition of a paradox is "an argument that apparently derives self-contradictory conclusions by making valid deductions from acceptable premises." In other words, the information you're working with seems reasonable and your logic is correct, but what you end up with just doesn't make sense.

▶  Here are some more paradoxes to explore with your child:

  • In the sixth century B.C., Epimenides the Cretan said: "All Cretans are liars." Is he telling the truth? If so, he's lying . . . and so on.

  • A modern version: Say, "I'm lying." Are you? Then you aren't Or are you?

  • Say to a friend, "Answer yes or no: Will the next word you speak be 'no'?"

  • Am I asleep, or just dreaming I am?

  • There are no errors on this page except this one.

  • This sentence is false.

  • The only people I cannot tolerate are intolerant people.

  • Jason was disappointed that his club meeting room had no suggestion box, because he wanted to put a suggestion in it about having one.

  • My son Kevin once left the following outgoing message on a friend's answering machine, with her permission: "This is Kevin. I can't answer your call because I'm at home right now. . . ."

  • A creative friend of ours named Will Smith, constantly mistaken for the many other Will Smiths in the world, got tired of feeling anonymous. He eventually changed his name legally to Anonymous Will Smith: Paradoxically, he never felt anonymous again.

▶  Try this with your child. Then have your child try it with a friend: Place a marble in one of two boxes, labeled #1 and #2. Say, "In one of these boxes, there is an unexpected marble. You may open the boxes only in the order of their numbers. Which box contains the unexpected marble?"

  If the friend opens box #1 and the marble isn't in it, then it must be in box #2, so it's not unexpected there. But by realizing that a marble won't be expected if it's in box #2, then it can *only* be expected in box #1—which makes it expected. So where is it? Perhaps in #1, perhaps in #2. Either way, it will be expected. Or will it? It's logically impossible to expect, at the same time, that the marble will be in both boxes.

▶ Can you imagine a map of the country drawn on a scale of 1 mile = 1 mile? Where would you spread it out to look at it?

▶ Print on one side of a card, "The statement on the other side of this card is true." Then print on the other side, "The statement on the other side of this card is false." The problem is, if you believe the first side to be true, then it must be false. If you assume it's false, it turns out to be true. This is called a self-reference paradox.

▶ Another kind of self-reference paradox is the endless sequence. This is what you get when you look into a mirror with another mirror.
   Here's an endless sequence that's popular with young children: "Pete and Repeat are on a boat. Pete falls off. Who's left?" At the obvious answer, "Repeat," the first part is repeated. (Caution: This can go on for quite a while.)

▶ The concept of traveling through time offers a multitude of paradoxes, as anyone knows who has seen the movie *Back to the Future* and its sequels. For example: One reason you can't possibly travel back in time is that if you met your grandfather and accidentally kept him from meeting your grandmother, you would never have been born. Can your child think of other complications of time travel?

▶ An oxymoron is a short paradox expressed in words that seem to contradict each other. The word comes from the Greek *oxys* (sharp, keen) and *moros* (foolish).
   *Examples:* Soft rock, loud whisper, sad smile, living doll, mighty mouse, permanent loan. Can your child think of others?

▶ Come up with oxymorons that only make sense in your own family. For instance, I recently realized that to my book-collecting husband, the phrase "having too many books" is an oxymoron. In other words, he believes it's impossible to have too many books.
   I once conceived of an article about teaching cooperative values in the family with the following title: "Who Can Cooperate the Best?"

▶ Have you seen the bumper sticker that says, "Honk if you hate noise pollution"? Or heard the sentence, "I used to be indecisive, but now I'm not so sure"? Can you and your child think of similar paradoxes?

▶ A magazine once awarded a prize in its "New Laws" competition to the originator of the so-called Hofstadter's Law, which states, "It always takes longer than you expect, even when you take into account Hofstadter's Law."

- Some instruction manuals contain pages marked "This page left intentionally blank," or "This page is blank." Can your child find other unintentional paradoxes of this type? (Or are they intentional?!)

- The drawings of Dutch artist M.C. Escher, including the famous one in which he shows hands drawing and being drawn by themselves, illustrate the notion of visual paradox. Many children enjoy Escher's drawings, most of which have been reproduced in books and magazines. Consider visiting your local library to explore some of these with your child. You might also check out the following Web sites:

  **IprojectOnline,** *www.iproject.com/escher/teaching/teaching.html.* This site has lesson plans and suggestions for using Escher in the classroom, some of which can also be used at home.

  **M.C. Escher Web site,** *www.mcescher.com.* This official site offers a biography, a free interactive game to download, and a 3-D multimedia section that takes viewers through three famous works.

  **World of Escher,** *www.worldofescher.com.* Here you'll find an Escher gallery, quotations, essays by and about the artist, items for sale, and contests for students.

---

### The Möbius Strip: A Visual Paradox in 3-D

The Möbius strip is an example of a "vicious circle"—a visual self-reference paradox. Your child can make a Möbius strip by taking a strip of paper, giving it a half-twist, and taping or gluing the ends together.

When you follow its edge, the Möbius strip seems to have only one edge and one side, even though that's impossible.

Draw a line down the middle of the outside of the Möbius strip. What happens?

Now cut the Möbius strip along the line. The result isn't two strips, but a single larger band.

# Tough Questions, Alibis, and More Mind Stretchers

*Parade* magazine has a long-running question-and-answer column called "Ask Marilyn." Readers direct questions to Marilyn vos Savant, who is listed in the *Guinness Book of World Records* under "Highest I.Q." Here's a question that ran in one of her columns: "If given an opportunity to choose, what is the most important choice that could be made in anyone's life? I think it would be to choose our parents, because they determine our environment." Marilyn's answer: "It might be even better if we could choose our children."

Other questions from the column: "What do you think was the first word to be spoken?" (Marilyn believes it might have been "no.") "How come a psychic never wins a lottery?" (Marilyn's response: "Why don't psychics *always* win lotteries?")

Think up some challenging questions to send in. Write to "Ask Marilyn," *Parade*, 711 Third Avenue, New York, NY 10017. Or send an email to marilyn@parade.com. (Note that she doesn't give personal replies.)

▶ Do the younger members of your family seem to use their most creative energies coming up with excuses for why they didn't do their homework or chores? Just for fun, suggest they devise a series of clever, far-fetched alibis. They can carry this further by making up excuses for historical figures or fictional characters.

*Examples:* "I didn't wash the dishes because there were sharks in the sink." "My dog buried my hard drive in the backyard." "George Washington chopped down the cherry tree because he saw termites in it."

## Your Family Book of World Records

Immortalize each of your children's successes, however minute, subtle, or outrageous, by inscribing them in this unusual book. In a simple notebook, write the name of the child, his or her noteworthy feat, and the date.

*Examples:* Louis ate nineteen lima beans, 9/3/00. Kelly did homework three days in a row without being reminded, 9/15/99. Samantha built a tower out of a hundred and twenty dominoes, 1/7/01. Jorge thought up fifty-two uses for an old sponge, 2/28/01.

Virtually anything you or your child can imagine qualifies for inclusion.

- Imagine and list things you'd want to know about a person you were considering for a specific role or task.

  *Examples:* If you were planning to hire someone to work for you, you might want to ask about his work history, grades in school, hobbies, favorite activities, and eventual career plans. But if you wanted to find out if someone would make good company on a trip around the world, you might ask completely different questions—about his favorite book, movie, and TV show; how neat he likes things; his sleep habits; how much quiet he prefers; or which games he knows and enjoys.

  Other information you might seek for this kind of inventory include age; favorite ice cream flavor, color, song, video game, and snack; brothers or sisters; and pets.

- Brainstorm a list of mistaken beliefs and carelessly held assumptions. Begin with the question, "Do you have to_____ to_____ ?"

  *Examples:* Do you have to go to school to be smart? Do you have to be a girl to play with dolls? Do you have to be sad to cry? Do you have to work hard to be rich? Do you have to get caught to be a thief?

- Educator and author Herb Kohl has found that asking students to list "Ten Ways Not to _____" frees their creativity and helps them learn to do a particular task.

  *Example:* Your son wants to learn to bake cookies. You teach him the basics and then ask him to come up with "Ten Ways Not to Bake Cookies." These might include: Be sure the oven is cold. Wrap yourself in foil. Stir the dough with a banana. Throw away half the dough before spooning onto the baking sheet.

- Divide the world into "Two Kinds of People."

  *Examples:* There are two kinds of people: Those who spit out their gum, and those who swallow it. Those who fold their toilet tissue into neat squares before using it, and those who crumple it first. Those who put their stuff (toys, work materials) away every day, and those who only straighten up when they can't find something. Those who back up their hard drives regularly, and those who trust theirs will never crash. Those who divide the world up into two kinds of people, and those who don't.

- Give (or imagine) a party in which guests are asked to come as oxymorons, contradictions, anachronisms, or something equally unexpected.

  *Examples:* Dress as a New Year's baby with a cane, a cactus with an umbrella, or an ancient Greek with a laptop computer.

### An Exercise in Bad Taste

Work with your child to create a "Book of Kitsch" filled with examples of bad or questionable taste. These can be cut from magazines or catalogs, or gathered from any other source.

*Examples:* A vinyl purse in the shape of a banana, a brain gelatin mold, or an outdoor plastic flower garden.

Of course, not everyone will agree on what is and isn't kitschy. (One person's kitsch is another person's treasure.) For a variety of objects that many people would probably put in this category, request a copy of the Archie McPhee mail-order catalog, which features oddball items like Fred Flintstone popsicle molds, fake rotten teeth, rubber chickens, big plastic feet, wind-up walking ears, and much more. Some items may be offensive, but you'll find a wealth of ideas. Write, call, or visit the Web site: Archie McPhee & Co., P.O. Box 30852, Seattle, WA 98103; (425) 745-0711; *www.mcphee.com.*

▶ TV shows sometimes ask guests to perform incredible or silly stunts. Brainstorm some stunts you'd like to see—the more outrageous, the better.

*Examples:* Fold a pretzel and carry it to Guam. Do a backwards double flip. Toss a car across a creek.

▶ Challenge your child to draw a "What's Wrong with This Picture?" picture. Choose a place or scene—bedroom, living room, classroom, grocery store—and imagine everything that could be wrong.

*Examples:* A cat in the fish tank, a TV remote control in the baby's crib, books with their titles spelled wrong or with the wrong authors' names, a computer with the keys in an odd order, a pig opening the refrigerator.

▶ An ordinary balloon can lead to a number of creative insights in the hands of an imaginative child (past the age when choking on a broken piece of balloon is a possibility).

*Examples:* Draw a design on a deflated balloon with a marker and see if you can predict what it will look like when the balloon is inflated. Find out which of two balloons, one larger and one smaller, will make a louder noise when popped. (You might be surprised.)

Kevin once pushed a penny into a balloon before blowing it up. It was interesting to see how it moved erratically around inside the balloon as he tossed it. Another time, he placed one balloon inside another. He blew the inside balloon up first and tied it, then the outside balloon.

▶ Fill a large, clear jar with jelly beans, chocolate chips, or popcorn. Get everyone in the family to guess how many jelly beans (or whatever) are in the jar. Then count them. Work on learning to estimate accurately.

# Change It, Finish It, Make It Up

▶ Remember the old "Believe It or Not!" columns and books? Some years ago, a magazine called *New West* ran a humorous takeoff on that idea called "McColly's Take It or Leave It!" These consisted of "Amazing Frauds" (like a clown who disguised himself as a regular human being) and "Astonishing Feats" (like a kid who could go 53 miles per hour on a playground slide). Create your own versions of Amazing Frauds and Astonishing Feats.

▶ *New York* magazine once ran a weekly competition challenging readers to fill in the blanks in the sentence, "_____ was so _____ that _____ ." Here are two of the responses: "That tie was so loud that when I put it on, the neighbors banged on the pipes," and "That building is so tall that they show movies in the elevator." See if your child can think of more examples.

▶ Assemble a collection of cartoons (those from *The New Yorker* are especially good for this) and cut off or fold under the captions. Then devise your own captions.

▶ Devise new endings for familiar proverbs. First graders came up with these: Don't bite the hand that . . . is dirty. Eat, drink, and . . . go to the bathroom. If at first you don't succeed . . . go play.
   *Other possibilities:* All work and no play . . . Don't put all your eggs . . . Don't count your chickens . . . People who live in glass houses . . . Children should be seen and not . . . You can lead a horse to water but. . . .

▶ Rewrite the endings to common fairy tales.
   *Examples:* Pinocchio might decide to keep telling lies and growing his nose long, so he can cut off parts of it to sell for firewood. Or the wolf in "The Three Little Pigs" might stop bothering the pigs when he realizes that brick houses are a terrific buy. Instead, he buys several brick houses for investment purposes.

▶ Interact with the characters in famous stories and fairy tales. My son Simon, who teaches first grade at a public school, asks his students to write to fictional characters: "I read them 'The Princess and the Pea' and asked them to write letters to either the princess, the prince, or the princesses who didn't get picked by the prince. One child wrote, 'Dear Princesses: I'm sorry you didn't get picked. Maybe there aren't enough princes. I think you should marry someone your own age.'"

▶ Design your own holidays. Start by locating a "book of days." For instance, in the now out-of-print *A Dictionary of Days* by Leslie Dunkling, over 850 days were named. "Daft Days" is a Scottish term for the days of merry-making at the New Year. "Maybe Tuesday" was invented by Peter de Vries in his novel *The Tunnel of Love;* on this day, TV crews would enter homes and take away some article of furniture if the owner answered a quiz question incorrectly. "White Stone Day" was named for the ancient Romans' habit of using a piece of white stone or chalk to mark particularly happy or fortunate days on the calendar. Another interesting example of the "book of days" genre is *Chase's Calendar of Events*, which is updated yearly (Chicago: Contemporary Books, 2000).

Anyone in the family could come up with an apt name for a day of celebration or gloom, along with a particular way to commemorate it.

*Examples:* "Shuffle Shoes Day," when family members trade shoes; "Dead Caterpillar Day," when everyone gives each other "warm fuzzies" (says nurturing things to each other) and crawls around on the floor; or "The Day After Birthday," when any leftover cake may be eaten for breakfast.

▶ Invent a silly game. You don't need rules or equipment—unless you want them. Feel free to make up games that would be impossible to play.

*Examples:* A silly, made-up game that could actually be played is "Sardines, Chili Peppers." Two players take turns running across a room and touching the far wall while saying "Sardines, Chili Peppers." No one wins or loses, of course. Impossible-to-play games might require flying, becoming invisible, or turning quarters into dollars.

- ▸ Invent a new machine that does a better job of handling some everyday problem than does any existing gadget. Draw a diagram of your invention. Name it and write an advertisement describing it.

  Your child (girl or boy) might be inspired to invent after reading *Girls Think of Everything: Stories of Ingenious Inventions by Women* by Catherine Thimmesh (Boston: Houghton Mifflin, 2000), for ages 8 and up, or *Girls & Young Women Inventing: Twenty True Stories About Inventors Plus How You Can Be One Yourself* by Frances A. Karnes and Suzanne M. Bean (Minneapolis: Free Spirit, 1995), for ages 11 and up.

- ▸ Let your imagination run wild. What two things could you put together that just don't go together? How about a game of basketball played by apples and oranges? Or a bed made of rubber bands? Or two birds discussing philosophy? Sketch the results.

- ▸ You may be familiar with the Walk of Fame in Hollywood, California, where stars' names and what they're famous for are embedded in the concrete every few feet along a major street. Other communities and organizations also have commemorative walks.

  Your child might enjoy designing a walk of his own featuring the names of his friends and their greatest accomplishments. For example: "Casey Jordan, biggest spitball, June 2001," or "Marissa Mills, first prize, school basketball tournament."

# Book-Inspired Brainteasers

- ▸ As Edward De Bono did in his book *Children Solve Problems* (now out of print), ask your child to draw solutions to imaginative problems. Encourage lots of detail.

  *Examples:* Invent a machine that washes your dog. How would you go about measuring a giraffe? Design a stove that cooks and then cleans up after itself. Draw a new, improved human body. Design a computer especially for horse trainers.

▶   Robert Fulghum, author of the best-selling books *All I Really Need to Know I Learned in Kindergarten* and *It Was On Fire When I Lay Down On It* (New York: Ballantine, 1993, and New York: Fawcett, 1996, respectively), has developed what he calls "Fulghum's Recommendations." He describes them as being "less ironclad" than the Ten Commandments. They include such tongue-in-cheek suggestions as to always take the scenic route, buy lemonade from any kid who's selling it, and be there when the circus comes to town.

Ask your child to make up her own commandments, laws, recommendations, or rules for living.

*Examples:* "Never sit on a toilet without checking to see if the seat is down." "It's more fun to pay for fun before you have it than after." "If you put off writing a letter to a friend long enough, your friend will think it's her turn."

▶   In *The Kids' Book of Questions* (New York: Workman, 1988), for ages 9–12, Gregory Stock presents a collection of questions especially designed to challenge, provoke, entertain, and expand young minds. Create such a book with your child, adding to it as new questions occur to you.

*Examples:* If you could witness the development of one invention, past or future, which would you choose and why? What are some of the benefits and pitfalls of the long time needed to get approval for new medicines in the United States? If you could have one superhuman power, what would you like it to be and why?

▶   You may have seen books in the genre of 101 Uses for. . . . Try brainstorming ideas for new books about 101 Uses for . . . whatever.

*Examples:* 101 Uses for . . . Empty Coffee Cans, Toothpicks, Dental Floss, Torn Balloons, Dust, Broken Clocks, Brussels Sprouts. . . .

If one or more of the titles is inspiring enough, your child may decide to write the book.

▶   Read and discuss E. A. Abbott's science-fiction classic, *Flatland* (New York: Penguin, 1998), which explores the life of a two-dimensional being in a 3-D world. While the concepts are thoroughly entertaining, it's not a simple book, so if your child is young, you might read it yourself and explain it. The ideas may open your child's mind to all sorts of questions about physics and relativity, even if he isn't scientifically inclined.

▶ At various times, books of lists have been published. Develop your own lists, using questions like these as starting points:

- What are your six favorite foods?

- What are four words with an unpleasant sound?

- What are the five most beautiful words in English?

- Who are the most outrageously dressed rock stars?

- Who are the three people you'd most like to have as weekend guests?

- Which three books would you take with you onto a desert island?

▶ Various authors have published books listing what they believe are the most important facts children of a given age or every adult should know. Work with your child to compile a booklet of "necessary information" for his age group.

▶ Author Dennis Beattie solicited whoppers for a book he was writing, to be called *Liars' Book of World Records and Astonishing Feats*. Among the tall tales he collected are the ones about the woman who ran her car over 641 glass bottles before getting a flat tire, and the man who bowled a 600 game. Have fun with your child inventing some more tall tales.

▶ In Bill Adler's book, *If I Were President: Kids Talk About Running the Country* (New York: Morrow, 2000), kids ages five to twelve explain how they'd improve the nation. Some would make their own birthday a national holiday. Others suggested giving parents five years off of work to raise their kids (but they'd have to work five extra years later on). What would your child do if she were president?

# Your Utopia or Mine?

Your child may be intrigued by the notion of an ideal society—a utopia. Talk together about what the "perfect" world would be like, what your child would like it to contain, how government would work, how such problems as poverty and illness would be handled, and whether any existing societies have come closer to this ideal than our own. Discuss the drawbacks of utopias: One big one is that everyone has a different idea of social perfection.

When I was about twelve, I read Edward Bellamy's famous utopian novel, *Looking Backward: 2000–1887* (most recent edition: New York: Signet, 2000), which led to many impassioned conversations at home. I remember arguing that Bellamy's future world was based on sound logic, since it clearly made sense to have communal umbrellas over all the shops in the shopping district, rather than letting people bump into each other with their small, inadequate, individual ones.

If society at large is too big a concept, have your child design the perfect family, the perfect school, or the perfect neighborhood. What would a perfect neighborhood contain? A kids' food court? An indoor-outdoor park? A library of video games?

A. W. Peller, Inc., sells a variety of educational materials related to designing a future. Visit them online to order a catalog, or see the online version at *www.awpeller.com*. If you click "Bright Ideas for the Gifted and Talented," for instance, and search for "utopia" or "future," you'll find "Create-a-Utopia: Writing an Idealistic Story."

▸ Have your child read a fictional version of the future and then suggest she write her own. Hers might be positive (utopian), negative (dystopian), or mixed in its vision of what the future might hold. I've mentioned Bellamy's book (which is dated, but still thought provoking). Here are a few other futuristic novels with social improvement themes that older children may appreciate:

*The Giver,* by Lowry, Lois (New York: Laurel Leaf, 1994). Ages 10 and up (if you don't mind mention of taking pills to quell "the stirrings," which are intimations of sexuality). Young Jonas lives in a strange new world without war, fear, pain—or choices. When he's twelve, he's singled out to receive special training from The Giver, who alone holds the memories of the true pain and pleasure of life. Winner of many honors, including the Newbery medal.

*Walden Two,* Skinner, B. F. (Needham Heights, MA: Allyn & Bacon, 1976). Ages 12 and up. Skinner's detailed description of a socially engineered commune is quite compelling. The idea is that with proper, scientifically validated planning, a society can work beautifully, with all members functioning happily, productively—even creatively. Citizens aren't committed to a single system, but rather to science (and behaviorism) as a guiding model. Babies are raised in nurseries. No one expresses gratitude to anyone else, since all contribute to and benefit from the common good.

# Imagination Towers

Designing, decorating, and populating an imaginary apartment building will keep your child or several children creatively busy for an hour or longer. All that's needed are a few feet of butcher paper (or several sheets of paper taped together) and some colorful marking pens or crayons. More than one building can be "under construction" simultaneously.

Spread the paper on a table or the floor, or attach it to a wall. Draw the building's outline using a ruler. Make it at least 4 feet long (or high), with plenty of large windows. Extra touches such as a fancy door, front porch, or rooftop garden can be left to the whim of individual child designers.

Say, "Pretend you can get close to each of the windows, so you can see into the entire room. Imagine what you might see in each of these rooms and draw it."

I've used this idea with kids from ages five to thirteen (you can join them when there are leftover windows). Some draw a person asleep on a bed, perhaps adding an alarm clock ringing. In the next room we might glimpse someone preparing breakfast. One child drew a pot overflowing on the stove. Some children delight in expanding pictures, adding kites out windows or message systems (ropes and pulleys, perhaps) that connect two or more tenants. Two tenants could be seen chatting over the Internet.

It's fun to add word balloons, cartoon-style, to give voices to the characters. There might be an argument in progress in one window and a party in another, with each guest making some comment to a birthday child.

What if, through one window, we can see the results of a bathtub faucet left running too long? What if, through a partly open door, we see the surprised face of a tenant returning to face a goldfish swimming in his bubble-filled apartment?

It's also possible to choose a futuristic setting for "Imagination Towers"—say, an apartment building in the year 2025. Or combine this activity with a history lesson and choose a time (and a structure) from the past.

# Raise a Skeptic

Big kids play more sophisticated games with their parents than little ones do. One day, my son, then in junior high, decided to test my gullibility. He said, "A hundred kids followed my friend Dylan up the mountain to Big Bear (a local mountain resort) the other day." "Wow, that's really weird," I said. "Aw, Mom, you believe everything, don't you? Dylan is president of the ski club, and he was riding in the front of the bus."

I'd successfully raised a couple of skeptics, but this didn't mean I was immune to occasional gullibility myself.

A major part of being skeptical is questioning everything. I never objected when my kids wanted reasons for what I said, even though outsiders might sometimes have assumed we were arguing. A skeptical child is actually one who is curious and inquisitive, not one who argues for the sake of arguing.

Many parents are put to the test for the first time when it comes to the Easter Bunny, Santa Claus, or the Tooth Fairy. Up to a certain age, which varies by child, everything a parent says is believed.

Parents have to "read" their own children to decide whether the kids are going to feel betrayed when they find out the truth, says Jonni Kincher, author of *The First Honest Book About Lies* (see Resources, page 64). The moment your child expresses a doubt about the existence of a long-eared, furry creature who delivers candy to every child, or a fairy who deposits cash under pillows in exchange for used teeth, it's best to admit that you've told her these stories just for fun. That way, you're showing your child she can trust her own perceptions. Besides, points out Kincher, "if you go on pretending after that point, then it falls into the area of lying."

Following are a host of activities designed to help you raise a savvy kid:

▶ Try a version of an experiment educator Neil Postman has used on friends. Make up a study that "proves" something highly illogical—a study that *should* be regarded with skepticism. For example, tell your child that a new study has shown a connection between homework and shin muscle development. The "experts" believe the connection has something to do with the way students tense their legs when they concentrate. Encourage your child to question you, or anyone, who comes up with the results of a "study." (Postman found that two-thirds of his friends believed his made-up studies.) Who were the study subjects? What exactly were they asked to say or do? (Try this with a four-year-old: "I'm going to make up a story:

Eating ice cream makes it rain. Can that be true?" Four-year-olds can be pretty gullible, so you might have to add, "That's *not* true. Rain comes from the clouds, and clouds don't have anything to do with ice cream.")

▶ Talk about how advertisements are designed to get people to buy things they don't necessarily need. Point out the silliness of celebrity endorsements—tell your child that famous performers and sports figures are paid millions of dollars to convince us that a particular cola drink is the best, even if they never drink it themselves.

▶ Teach your child how to tell when someone is lying. Kincher lists the following tip-offs: Some people avoid eye contact when they lie. Some use a forced smile, which lasts longer than a real one and doesn't involve any wrinkling below and around the eyes (which happens with a genuine smile). A person's tone of voice may not match the words she's saying, giving another hint that she's not telling the truth. "Trust your gut feelings," suggests Kincher. "Sometimes they're the only 'evidence' you have to go on." But let your child know that most people find it impossible to tell for sure if someone is lying solely by appearance, tone of voice, or body language.

▶ Watch the TV news together. Here are some ways to help kids benefit from the often gritty, sometimes misleading material they'll see there, as suggested by Action for Children's Television:*

- Help your child understand why it's important to be informed about local, national, and world events. Explain that by being informed we can make good choices, and that's the key to a well-functioning democracy.

- Point out some of the ways news is shaped by the *way* it's delivered. Consider those "teasers" the news programs insert at the start of their shows (they tell us what's coming up, but we often have to wait until the end of the show to see it) and the various gimmicks designed to enhance ratings. If you feel some aspect of a story is being left out, say so.

- Use TV news as a springboard for further investigation. Show your child how to compare TV coverage of a news event with coverage in your local newspaper and in a newsmagazine.

- Arrange a visit to a TV news station so your child can see that it's real people who "perform" the news. Just as we often think if something's in print, it must be true, many also believe if it's on TV, it's got to be accurate.

---

* This organization was officially disbanded in 1992. However, the Monroe C. Gutman Library at the Harvard Graduate School of Education houses the ACT collection, which includes publications, videotapes, and more. You can read about the collection at *gseweb.harvard.edu/~library/sc/act.htm*.

By visiting a station and seeing how news shows are put together, kids get a clearer idea of how human—and fallible—the business is.

▶ Read some books on the subject of skepticism with your child:

*Alexander Fox and the Amazing Mind Reader* by John C. Clayton (Amherst, NY: Prometheus Books, 1998). Ages 8–12. An unusual story about a sixth grader who thinks for himself and eventually debunks a fake psychic and his paranormal claims.

*Alice* by Whoopi Goldberg (New York: Bantam, 1992). Ages 7 and up. A little girl dreams of riches and then believes she's won a big prize through a sweepstakes. She learns a lesson some people have to learn the hard way: if it's too good to be true, it isn't true. Although out of print, this book is worth looking for at your local library.

*Maybe Yes, Maybe No: A Guide for Young Skeptics* and *Maybe Right, Maybe Wrong: A Guide for Young Thinkers* by Dan Barker (Amherst, NY: Prometheus Books, 1991 and 1992, respectively). These guides to examining ideas critically can be understood on some levels by a child as young as five, though they're particularly aimed at those ten to eighteen. Barker clearly explains how kids can determine what has a chance of being true and what is based on flawed reasoning. The second book focuses on morality and how we don't need superstition to make moral choices.

# Resources

*Absolutely Mad Inventions* by A.E. Brown and H.A. Jeffcott Jr. (Mineola, NY: Dover, 1976). All ages. Dozens of actual patented inventions, including a hat-tipping device and an edible tiepin.

*American Tall Tales* by Mary Pope Osborne (New York: Knopf, 1991). Ages 5–12. Includes entertaining tales about such real and legendary characters as Davy Crockett, Johnny Appleseed, Paul Bunyan, John Henry, and Pecos Bill.

*Can You Believe Your Eyes: Over 250 Illusions and Other Visual Oddities* by J. Richard Block and Harold E. Yuker (Levittown, PA: Brunner/Mazel, 1992). Ages 8 and up. This book presents visual illusions gathered from around the world to explore the psychology of vision. The authors also discuss the phenomenon of human perception and the use of illusions in society.

*The First Honest Book About Lies* by Jonni Kichner (Minneapolis: Free Spirit, 1992). Ages 13 and up. This book explores the truth about lies and encourages readers to develop honesty as a personal value. Experiments, examples, and games promote active questioning and truth seeking.

*Flat Stanley* by Jeff Brown (New York: Harper Trophy, 1999). Ages 4–8. This classic tale (first published in 1964) is about a young boy who wakes up one morning to find himself two-dimensional. He gets around, however, and even manages to foil some art thieves with his ability to impersonate a painting.

*How to Make Optical Illusion Tricks and Toys* by Richard Churchill (New York: Sterling, 1990). Ages 9–12. More than sixty illusions, including tricks, drawings, and toys that can be assembled.

*101 Amazing Optical Illusions: Fantastic Visual Tricks* by Terry Jennings (New York: Sterling, 1998). Ages 7–12. A variety of illusions illustrated in color, plus brief directions for making some of them.

*Opt: An Illusionary Tale* by Arline and Joseph Baum (New York: Puffin, 1989). Ages 5–12. A royal family and court present a variety of optical illusions that are explained at the end of the book. The authors also include suggestions for making your own illusions.

*The Rumplestiltskin Problem* by Vivian Vande Velde (Boston, MA: Houghton Mifflin, 2000). Ages 7 and up. The author takes an old fairy tale and points out its many logical holes, then utterly reconceives the story in six new and wryly amusing forms. A child reading them may be inspired to do the same with other familiar tales.

*Sasquatches from Outer Space: Exploring the Weirdest Mysteries Ever* by Tim Yule (Amherst, NY: Prometheus, 2000). Ages 8 and up. An elementary school teacher shares smart ways to debunk superstitious claims about UFOs, Bigfoot, astrology, ESP, and vampires. A good way to teach young people about the scientific method, including the sometimes-forgotten fact that you can't prove a negative (meaning that while you can't prove that Bigfoot *doesn't* exist, you can and ought to be appropriately skeptical).

*Short Stories and Tall Tales* by Mark Twain (New York: Courage Books, 1999). All ages. This collection includes the classic tall tale, "The Celebrated Jumping Frog of Calaveras County."

*Skeptic's Dictionary, skepdic.com.* Thorough, fascinating, and comprehensive definitions and essays about occult and supernatural topics (such as déjà vu, the evil eye, and flying saucers). Includes many links.

**Strange Magazine,** *www.strangemag.com.* This online magazine has articles, reports, and facts about topics including UFOs, sea serpents, and more.

*Supposes* by Dick Gackenbach (New York: Harcourt Brace, 1991). Ages 4–8. This picture book imagines and illustrates the improbable. For example, suppose a polar bear had money, or a cow jumped into your bed, or. . . .

*Tatterhood and Other Tales,* edited by Ethel Johnston Phelps (New York: The Feminist Press, 1989). Ages 7–12. The central characters in these traditional tales from Norway, England, China, and many other countries are clever, strong, resourceful females.

*The Young Writer's Companion* by Sarah Ellis (Toronto: Groundwood Books, 1999). Ages 8–12. This book offers inspiration related to words, wordplay, writing, famous writers, and creative "fooling around" with language.

**Zillions,** *www.zillions.org.* This free site, sponsored by *Consumer Reports*, includes trustworthy tests of kid-related products, tips to get the most out of products you buy, a question-and-answer column, and consumer education features designed to help young people make informed (and skeptical) choices in the marketplace. Aimed at ages 8 and older. (A version for children ages 6–12 is available for a monthly fee; find further information at this site.)

# CHAPTER 5

# ADVENTURES IN ORDINARY PLACES

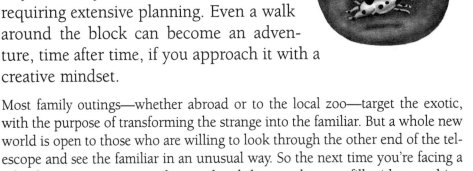

**Y**ou've probably already beaten a path between your home and every nearby museum, park, playground, and playing field. Next time you're feeling stir-crazy and wondering where to take your child for a little adventure, think beyond the obvious. It's easy to pique your child's curiosity in countless free or inexpensive ways, most quite close to home and not requiring extensive planning. Even a walk around the block can become an adventure, time after time, if you approach it with a creative mindset.

Most family outings—whether abroad or to the local zoo—target the exotic, with the purpose of transforming the strange into the familiar. But a whole new world is open to those who are willing to look through the other end of the telescope and see the familiar in an unusual way. So the next time you're facing a school vacation or just another weekend that you hope to fill with something entertaining, consider the benefits of going someplace that *seems* ordinary.

Wherever you go, let your child's curiosity shape the experience. Some children want to look over everything quickly—then zero in on something they find particularly interesting. With a younger child, especially, it's often best to limit yourselves to *thoroughly* exploring only a part of any attraction.

Forget about making each outing self-consciously educational. You don't need to follow up a jaunt with detailed discussion—in fact, doing so risks making your child feel he's "on the spot." Instead, let him take the learning initiative by asking you questions. He may even ask for a return visit. Like many adults, children often get a deeper understanding of something from noticing details that they overlooked the first (or second, or third) time around. And if you're open to learning something new yourself, so much the better: Your own interest will ignite your child's enthusiasm.

# Where to Go and What to Do There

- ▶ Attend an auction. Check the phone book and the classified ads in your newspaper for times and locations. Arrive early so you and your child can rummage through the treasures. Auctioneers really do talk fast, so prepare your child. You might also warn your child to keep her hands down, unless you've decided in advance to bid on an item.

- ▶ Spend a day going to estate, garage, or yard sales (called tag sales in some parts of the country). Often these provide interesting glimpses into people's lives. Think about why various items are being sold. See if you and your child can figure out why the sale is being held at this particular time.

- ▶ Visit an animal shelter or your local branch of The Humane Society. The employees and volunteers will likely be eager to explain their jobs and introduce the animals. It's always a good practice, however, to call ahead. Find out if there are regular tours or whether a personal tour can be arranged. See if your Humane Society has a volunteer dog-walking program—your child might like to participate.

- ▶ Explore the periodicals room of a major library. There you can view microfilms of old newspapers and, for a small charge, photocopy pages to take home. Go prepared to look up specific items, such as the front page of *The New York Times* on the day your child was born or on the day Lincoln was shot.

- ▶ Visit an antique shop or show. Allow your child to look around at her own pace. (For this, as for every adventure with your child, be prepared to spend time differently than you would if you were on your own.)

- ▶ Go to an airport. If possible, arrange for a tour (sometimes smaller airports are more amenable to tours). Notice such things as differences in the angle of takeoff for various sizes and kinds of planes. Stop in a gate area or waiting room to people-watch. Bring along a camera and take pictures from the observation deck.

- ▶ Visit the docks or a pier. Take a boat ride, and notice how the color of the water changes as you leave shore.

▶ Stop by the city or county office where real estate records are kept. Look up the history of your house or apartment building.

▶ Visit a real estate office or the "open house" of a home for sale. Pick up an information sheet. Ask your child to make up a similar—but more imaginative—sheet for your own home. For instance, under "Additional Features," he might write, "seven secret hiding places."

▶ Visit a military base when public tours are offered. Watch for notice of any special events: Air Force bases, for example, often have free air shows. Afterward, discuss the reasons for military organizations and your views about war, peace, draft registration, and military expenditures.

▶ Attend a coin show or browse around a coin shop, where your child may see things like pounds of gold or 2,000-year-old coins. She might want to start checking your loose change for rarities.

▶ Consider doing routine things at unusual times to give your child a fresh perspective on the everyday.
   *Examples:* Visit the beach in the rain. Arrive very early at a supermarket, when the produce is being unloaded. Try serving a hearty breakfast for dinner.

▶ Attend a dog or cat show. Find out how the animals are judged. Your child might like to make up a few categories of his own, such as "Dog Most Likely to Attract Fleas" or "Cat Most Likely to Get Stuck in a Tree."

▶ Visit a beekeeper, jeweler, glass blower, potter, taxidermist, or other artisan who works close by. Phone ahead and ask if the person can show you and your child around briefly and demonstrate some of the things he or she does.

▶ Arrange for a tour of a radio or TV studio. Before you go, have your child watch or listen to a program whose set or performers you might see. Check out procedures for getting tickets to be part of a studio audience.

▶ Whet your child's interest in such activities as judo, yoga, karate, tai chi, drama, or dance by watching a class. Visit such classes even if your child doesn't think she'd want to participate (she may change her mind).

▶ Tour a factory, automobile assembly plant, police department, fire department, newspaper, or courtroom in session. Call to make reservations and find out if there are any age restrictions. Nearby communities may offer what your own does not. (Whenever you go anywhere, ask if your child can go behind the scenes: to see an airplane cockpit, a theater dressing room, or a hospital operating room.)

▶ Walk around the oldest part of your town or neighborhood. See what you and your child can learn about the history of the place by noticing dates on sidewalks and buildings. You might do this in the form of a scavenger hunt: seek out a gargoyle, a column, an arch, a porch, a bay window, or a stained-glass window.

▶ Investigate your area's special resources. If you live near a dam, for example, you might be able to take a tour during which you literally walk under tons of water. Other excursions might include tours of a water filtration center, fish hatchery, milk-bottling plant, bakery, or chocolate factory.

▶ Visit the more offbeat museums and exhibits in your area; don't limit yourself to the usual circuit of children's, science, natural history, and art museums. Check under "Museums" in your local phone book for ideas. Some newspapers' weekend sections and most city magazines list a wide variety of museums.

*Examples:* You may find airplane, railroad, or streetcar museums; firefighters' memorial museums; historical societies; interpretive houses; ethnic museums and societies; childhood homes of famous people and other historic sites; sports halls of fame; museums started by private collectors (of dolls, model trains, baseball cards, old telephones, musical instruments); ongoing special-interest exhibits; and more. A glance through one city's directory turned up this intriguing entry: the "Questionable Medical Devices Museum."

▶ Keep on the alert for opportunities to see and do things you ordinarily wouldn't. Take a close-up look at the searchlight in the parking lot of the new shopping center. Watch workers tear down a neighborhood carnival. Stop to see a bridge being cleaned or a billboard going up. Follow hot-air balloons as they float overhead. Moments like these can be among a child's most memorable experiences.

# Take in the Trash

Find out how waste is disposed of or recycled in your community or region.

▶   Visit a recycling center. You may be able to watch the processing of materials such as glass, newspaper, metal, and plastic.

▶   Get down in the dumps—the city, town, or regional dump. Before or after the trip, discuss with your child what you know about the problems of waste disposal on the local, national, or international levels. Is there a sanitary landfill in your area? An incinerator? Does your area struggle with the problem of toxic or radioactive waste disposal? Watch for news items relating to such issues. Take advantage of the chance to talk with your child about wants, needs, and our "throwaway society."

▶   Visit a place where cars are scrunched into scrap metal (an especially interesting experience after a trip to an automobile assembly plant). Compare the time, technology, and finesse necessary for creation and for destruction. You might also point out that many of the vehicles being scrapped "died" in accidents, not from old age.

# Get Involved

If your child is about eight or older, suggest she start thinking about volunteering in the community as a way of finding adventure. Even younger children can be encouraged to think in these terms, with some help from you. Your support will be crucial to any project a child gets involved in, but be assured that what your child gains—in the short and long run—will far outweigh any efforts expended.

Start by asking your child to consider these two questions:

1.   When you read the newspaper, listen to the news on the radio, or watch TV news, what gets you upset and makes you want to change something?

2.   Have you noticed something in your community that makes you say, "That's not fair! Somebody should do something!"? Maybe *you* could be that somebody.

Volunteering is so much more than just hard work—it's exciting and fulfilling. Young people usually begin to take action after becoming aware of a need around them. They might be encouraged by a school campaign, a program sponsored by a club or religious organization, or a parent who volunteers. Kids who volunteer aren't that different from those who don't, but somehow those who stick with it have come to care deeply about people in need or about some community or environmental issue.

Volunteering does take time away from school activities and social life. But kids who volunteer often find that when they're helping others or contributing to their community, they wish they could do even more. Most manage to keep their grades up, too, finding that community work gives them *more* energy, not less. We've all heard the old saying that the more you have to do, the more you get done.

Your child is also likely to be happier when he participates in volunteer activities. Devoting himself to something outside himself will help give extra meaning to life. Lucky is the child who learns this early.

For more information and inspiration on the topic of young volunteers, see my book *Catch the Spirit: Teen Volunteers Tell How They Made a Difference* (See Resources, page 78).

# 38 Ways to Make Walking Interesting Again

Walking is the simplest, least expensive, and most universally feasible way to stay in shape for a lifetime. It's even been found that physical exercise like walking can enhance mental fitness. But with physical activity in limited supply at most schools, and with the ever-present lures of television, video games, and the Internet, it's up to you as a parent to turn your kids on to walking. You'll be doing their future health a huge favor.

Yet the very simplicity of a daily walk can turn it into something chorelike and tedious—unless you get creative. The spirit may be willing, but if you involve the higher faculties too, you and your child are more likely to get motivated and get moving. And you'll be providing benefits beyond the physical: your child's observational skills will also get a workout, not to mention the opportunities for casual togetherness and conversation between you and your child. So forget the plain vanilla "just put one foot in front of the other" walk and try these fresh ways to make walking more appealing.

1. **Count the Cats Walk.** You'll have to look carefully, as felines have a habit of walking silently, blending in, and relaxing in odd places, such as on roofs and in porch nooks. A "Count the Dogs" walk is easier—they usually

bark as you pass by. Or count *anything:* lampposts, fire hydrants, barns, cactuses, picket fences, different kinds of vehicles, security system signs, swings, broken windows, window bars, or manhole covers.

2.  **Never Before Seen Walk.** As you travel a familiar route, look for ten things you've never noticed before, from the way potted plants are arranged on someone's front porch to cracks in the street that remind you of a cracked eggshell.

3.  **What's Wrong Walk.** Point out things around the neighborhood that need fixing or changing, such as an unmown lawn, a house with peeling paint, overgrown weeds, a sidewalk or street in need of repair, overflowing trash, a broken fence, a roof with missing shingles, graffiti to be removed, or roses in need of pruning.

4.  **What's Right Walk.** Search out pleasing images and scenes. This will enhance your child's sense of aesthetics.

5.  **Camouflage Walk.** Search out what can't be seen readily, such as a rusted toy under a shrub, a dog sleeping in the shade, or a squirrel in a tree.

6.  **Puddle Walk.** Right after a rainfall, notice differences in puddle sizes and make predictions about which will dry up first. Poke a stick into a puddle and measure its depth. Go back later or the next day and check on your predictions. Or try a "Find the Snails (or Worms) After the Rain Walk."

7.  **Rate the Buildings Walk.** Rate the buildings or houses you pass on your walk, giving each a grade based on criteria you determine together, such as attractiveness (or ugliness) of color; loudness (or absence) of barking dogs; amount of unraked (or neatly piled) leaves; landscaping (or its lack); and memorable (or ordinary) doors, windows, decorations, and styles.

8.  **Who Lives Here Walk.** Make some guesses about the people who live in the homes you pass (assuming you don't know them personally). Use clues such as items left near the door, whatever you can notice through the windows as you pass by (without staring), or vehicles parked outside. Does it seem as if children live there? Do you think the people have pets? If you don't notice any real clues, get creative and make up something. Also see if you can figure out what people's priorities are, such as keeping a garden, providing a play area for their children or an exercise area for their dog, feeding the birds, picking up satellite TV stations, or having an artistically pleasing environment.

*Variations:* Use clues to make guesses about other walkers you pass. Where do you think they might be headed? What mood are they in? Are they out for a stroll, or in a hurry?

Collect occupations. Among the people you see, can your child spot a postal carrier, a police officer, a medical worker, a crossing guard, a farmer, a truck driver? What other occupations can be detected by the clothing people wear or the equipment they carry?

9.  **The Time Is Now Walk.** Change the time of day you normally walk. Head out in the moonlight with a couple of flashlights. Notice differences such as streetlights on, people's TV sets visible in windows, and cooler air. Or stroll early in the morning before anyone else is up. At least once, take a walk early enough to catch the sunrise.

10. **Path to a Picnic Walk.** Plan a picnic. Pack a lunch, walk until you're a bit winded, and then sit somewhere and eat.

11. **Go Get Lost Walk.** Ride to a different neighborhood and bring a map along. Walk randomly for half an hour without checking the map. Then take out the map and find your way back to the car or transit stop.

12. **Robot Walk.** Walk like robots—stiffly, or only in a straight line, saying "bzzz" as you make turns to avoid obstacles.

13. **Simon Says Walk.** Take turns instructing each other: Simon says walk slowly, hop like a jackrabbit, walk backwards for three steps, and then walk on tiptoes.

14. **Log a Walk.** Suggest that your child keep a walk log or graph. Have her record how far she goes and how long she walks. When her walk is longer or shorter than usual, make note of what happened to lengthen the walk (avoiding a difficult homework assignment?) or shorten the walk (eager to get back for a phone call from a friend?).

15. **Changes Walk.** Look for everything that is undergoing even the tiniest change at the moment you pass, such as a twig bending under a bird's weight, a cat prowling after a squirrel, or evaporation of wetness on grass (though you can't see it).

Don't neglect things that are simply changed from a previous walk: Is there a hose uncoiled that wasn't out yesterday? Has someone begun replacing roof tiles? Is that a new car in the Smith's driveway? Was that flower in bloom last time you passed? Has the trash been collected?

16. **Geometry Walk.** Look for every possible shape along your way. Notice repeating patterns. Don't miss the ellipses and trapezoids, the diamond-shaped leaves, or the circular bases of street lamps.

17. **Rainbow Walk.** Seek out examples of each color of the spectrum (or each color found in your child's crayon box). Remember the colors of the rainbow by memorizing the name "ROY G. BIV," which is made up of the first letter of each of the colors (red, orange, yellow, green, blue, indigo, violet). Or choose one color for the entire walk and find as many examples of it, in all its shades, as you can.

18. **Twenty Questions Walk.** Variations of this familiar game will make the time fly. Judgment is required, too, as you choose items that are far enough ahead to still be visible for a while as you walk along. For example, "I see something red." "Is it bigger than a tricycle?" Or, "I see something smooth." "Is it on the other side of the street?"

19. **Get Crafty Walk.** Place some tape around your young child's wrist, sticky side out. Then she can easily pick up and attach fallen leaves and flower petals to make a bracelet. Cut the bracelet off carefully after the walk and keep it for a while as a memento. Make a point of collecting such nature bracelets from different environments.
    *Variation:* Simply hunt for stray leaves, feathers, dried seedpods, and other potential collage and craft materials. Bring them home to use later.

20. **Observation Walk.** Take a walk designed specifically to be written up later in your child's journal. (For more on keeping journals, see Chapter 2.) Help your child notice all sorts of sights that will make for an interesting entry: the moving van that indicates a new neighbor, the plumber's truck that could mean someone's having drainage problems, a pile of intriguing detritus on the sidewalk on trash day, road construction, or tree trimming.
    *Variation:* Instead of writing, have your child pretend to use a cell phone to relay reports on what he's seeing back to his "office." He should try to communicate clearly all the specifics of what's going on during this walk.

21. **How Mad I Am Walk.** Next time your child is angry, have her try the Inuit custom of getting rid of anger by walking as far as possible, noting where the emotion finally dissipates (you'll want to walk with your young child, but avoid conversation if she prefers). Thereafter, you can refer to episodes of fury as a "two-block mad" or a "mile-long mad."

22. **Silly Surprises Walk.** You be the leader. Every twenty steps or so, do something silly that your child has to imitate. Try jumping, hopping, or doing a dance step.

23. **Wonder Walk.** Spend your entire walk asking questions. Don't answer any, but take turns trying to make each question relate in some way to the one before it. For example: Why is the sky blue? What color is next to blue in the rainbow? What makes a double rainbow? Why does it sometimes rain while the sun is out? You may wish to pursue answers when you get home, but don't feel obligated to.

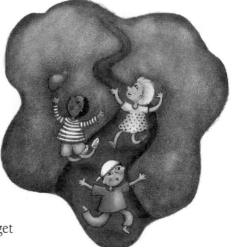

24. **Nature Walk.** Anywhere you walk, nature abounds. Many of the walks suggested here involve natural elements, but a true nature walk focuses on nature. For instance, how many different kinds of plants can your child locate? How many different kinds of grass? How many different shades of green or brown? How do the heights of growing things differ? How do the heights of hills differ? What colors do you see in a lake or river?

    *More examples*: Pick up a leaf and ask your child to find another tree with leaves of that same shape.

    Can you find any weeds growing through cracks?

    Can you find a spider web along a fence? Follow it. Is anything trapped in it? Observe the web closely and try to draw it when you get home (or bring a pad and pencil along on your walk).

    Notice birds. Do you see hawks or eagles circling? Can you find pigeons or sparrows on window ledges, on rooftops, on wires, peeking from behind store signs, or nesting on top of window air conditioners? Can you spot a roadrunner or a sandpiper?

    You may or may not see animals when you take your nature walk, but you can be detectives and seek out evidence of animals. Notice holes in the ground, chew marks on wood, paw prints, flattened grass, stray feathers, bits of nest material, and droppings.

25. **Our Tree Walk.** Choose and get familiar with one particular tree some distance from home. Consult a book to find out its scientific name. Take its picture in each season. Each time you visit it, notice how it's changed. You'll have to look hard if you visit often. Feel the bark, notice its patterns and colors, and see if it has any scars. If possible, have your child lie on

her back under the tree and examine the leaves and limbs. Are there birds or insects in or on the tree?

26. **Alphabet Walk.** Call out the first letter of everything you pass, such as "F" (fence), "H" (house), and "C" (cloud). Or get fancy and call out the second or last letter of each thing. You can either do this together or take turns. Explain less obvious choices, such as shadow, fleck, dust mote, or wing.

    *Variation:* Seek out words on signs that begin with each letter of the alphabet.

27. **Sounds of Silence Walk.** Walk as quietly as you can. Ask your child to listen very, very carefully. What can he hear? An insect buzzing, a lawnmower, a telephone, a dog barking, a car driving over a bump, running water, rustling leaves, construction equipment, or birdsong?

28. **Coordination Walk.** Can your child kick a small stone or a bottle cap for a whole block? Can she make it all the way around the block without stepping on a crack? Can you?

29. **Sense Walk.** Make a point of noticing everything sensory—from the whiteness of a cloud to the tinkling of a wind chime, from the smoky smell of a barbeque to the rough feel of a tree's bark. Sniff the flowers, notice the smell of the air after rain, feel the warmth of the sun and the cool of the shade. Appreciate the sense of taste when you get back and sip some cool water. Or taste the rain or snow. (For more sensory activities, see Chapter 3.)

30. **Bigger/Smaller Walk.** Take along a pair of binoculars or a magnifying glass. Experiment as you go along, noticing how different things look when you make them larger with a magnifier or binoculars, or smaller by viewing them through the wrong end of the binoculars.

31. **Flip a Coin Walk.** When you have enough time, let chance dictate where you walk. Flip a coin: heads means go right, tails means go left. Walk for five minutes or until you stop to examine something interesting. Then flip again.

32. **Texture Walk.** Take along crayons and plenty of thin paper or newsprint. Hunt for items you can make rubbings of. Hold the paper against the item and rub gently with the side of an unwrapped crayon until the shape of the item underneath appears on the paper.

33. **Bird Watching Walk.** Take along a bird identification book and a pair of binoculars. See how many different birds you can spot.

34. **Search for the Season Walk.** Search for and point out signs of the current season. In spring, hear the birds and see their nests; see flowers budding and grass sprouting. In fall, see leaves falling, cloudy skies, or whatever is typical of your region.

35. **This Earth Is My Earth Walk.** Seek out evidence of positive and negative environmental practices and talk about them. On the plus side, notice recycling bins, solar panels, gas-efficient vehicles, clear air, or ecologically suitable plants. On the minus side, notice oversized vehicles, wasted water, litter, dog waste, smog, or factory smoke.

    Make a point of strolling around the block on trash day so your child can observe how much garbage, recyclable and not, is accumulated by the families on only one block in only one week.

36. **Blind Walk.** Blindfold your child and act as his guide, leading him safely through a variety of experiences—stepping down and up, through a gate, onto grass—without too much explanation. Then ask him to talk about how he felt.

37. **Scavenger Walk.** Give your child a written list of items to locate during your walk, such as a yellow leaf, an ant, or a stone in the shape of an animal. If you usually see lots of people on your walks, include items such as a man with glasses, a woman with a briefcase, a person carrying a cup, or someone wearing sandals.

    *Variations:* Make up a list together and see who spots each item first. Or with an older child, make your scavenger hunt more challenging. Add the following types of items to your list: something friendly, something funny, something without scent, something scary, something wasteful, a sign that someone cares, something in disguise, a message, something you can't photograph, an item that won't be there the next day, or a boundary.

38. **Estimating Fun Walk.** When you begin your walk, choose an object— say, a mailbox or stop sign—and ask your child to estimate how many steps it will take to reach it. Then count and see how well she estimated. Now have her try again with another object. Challenge her to improve her step-estimating ability.

# Resources

*All the Backyard Birds* by Jack L. Griggs and Scott Edwards (New York: Harper Perennial, 1998). This American Bird Conservancy Compact Guide comes in regional editions. Color photos make it easy to identify the birds you see around you.

*Backyard Bird Identification Guide* by Jerry G. Walls (Neptune City, NJ: TFH Publications, 2000). Just as its title states, this handy guide will assist you in identifying common birds.

*Backyard Explorer Kit* by Rona Beame (New York: Workman, 1989). Ages 4–10. The kit includes a book on leaf and tree identification and a leaf-collecting album. See examples of all the major leaf and needle shapes and learn how to press the leaves you find.

*Birds Every Child Should Know* by Neltje Blanchan (Iowa City: University of Iowa Press, 2000). Ages 6–12. Nearly a century since its first publication, this clearly written guide is composed of story-like descriptions of more than a hundred commonly seen birds.

*Catch the Spirit: Teen Volunteers Tell How They Made a Difference* by Susan K. Perry (New York: Franklin Watts, 2000). Ages 10–18. Inspiring stories of teens who put countless hours into community service projects. You'll also find practical information on how to get started volunteering, including many suggestions about possible projects.

*Fun with Nature: Take-Along Guide* by Mel Boring, Diane L. Burns, and Leslie A. Dendy (Minocqua, WI: NorthWord Press, 1999). Ages 7–12. Descriptions of more than 150 animals and plants will help your child identify what turns up on a nature walk.

*House Styles in America: The Old-House Journal Guide to the Architecture of American Homes* by James C. Massey and Shirley Maxwell (New York: Penguin, 1999). This tour of homes is illustrated with two hundred color photos and includes tips on how to identify various styles, estimate a house's age, and more.

*The Kid's Guide to Service Projects: Over 500 Service Ideas for Young People Who Want to Make a Difference* by Barbara A. Lewis (Minneapolis: Free Spirit Publishing, 1995). Ages 10 and up. A clear and helpful guide for young people who want to help out, from simple projects to large-scale commitments.

*Minds in Motion: Using Museums to Expand Creative Thinking* by Alan Gartenhaus (San Francisco: Caddo Gap Press, 1997). An original collection of exciting ideas to help you help your kids get the most out of science, art, and history museums.

*Offbeat Museums: The Collections and Curators of America's Most Unusual Museums* by Saul Rubin (Santa Monica, CA: Santa Monica Press, 1997). This guide to offbeat museums includes photos, descriptions, and even directions for those with plans to visit.

*Trails, Tails, & Tidepools in Pails: Over 100 Fun and Easy Nature Activities for Families and Teachers to Share with Babies and Young Children* (Santa Monica, CA: Children's Nature Institute, 1999). For families to use with children ages 1–8. Search this book to find fun and simple activities, many adaptable for use in your own neighborhood.

# CHAPTER 6

# LEARNING COMES ALIVE AT THE CEMETERY

**A**n unusual way to bring history alive for your child is to take her on a cemetery visit. If she can read and understand what's written on gravestones, she's ready for a memorable learning experience as she digs for information, perceives connections, and discovers human stories.

You and your child probably won't be alone, since more and more families and students of all ages are making field trips to cemeteries, as people have done for generations. Whether their aim is to gain a healthier understanding of death or to mine the wealth of historical lore, folks are finding that cemeteries are not scary places but oases of tranquility. The gravemarkers and plaques found in memorial parks offer intriguing records of the changes each generation undergoes in its value systems.

When my own children were about six and eight, we made our first visit to a local graveyard. It turned into one of our most memorable outings. We explored in a leisurely fashion, made discoveries, hunted for who was oldest and youngest at death, compared names, and generally became more comfortable with this most integral facet of human life and culture.

# Preparing for Your Visit

To locate cemeteries in your area, first try your local telephone book under the heading, "Cemeteries and Memorial Parks." If you have a Visitors and Convention Bureau, the staff will have information about the facilities most frequented by tourists. Historical societies will know of others.

You may also notice graveyards as you walk or ride around town. Many are located in older neighborhoods or on the outskirts of metropolitan areas. You'll find some in churchyards, others in parks and grounds surrounding city, county, and state buildings. When you're traveling, don't miss the local cemeteries.

Before your first visit, discuss the "ground rules" with your child. Explain that since other people may be at the cemetery to pay their respects to deceased loved ones, it's imperative that everyone conduct themselves with dignity. As long as your child stays on the paths (walking, not running) and speaks in normal tones (he doesn't have to whisper), he won't offend anyone. The solemn atmosphere of cemeteries helps most kids refrain from inappropriate behavior.

Bring along a notepad and pencil in case your child wants to record oddities, make lists of names, or figure ages from birth and death dates. A calculator and magnifying glass may be helpful, too. And bring supplies for making rubbings, if your child is interested; see below for instructions.

Remember that most American children have very little firsthand exposure to death and its rituals. Your child's first impression is likely to be one of awe: So many people have died! Row upon row of gravestones, as far as the eye can see in all directions—like endless stars on a clear night—challenge one's vision of oneself as the center of the universe.

## Rubbing the Past the Right Way

A cemetery is the perfect place to begin the habit of collecting rubbings. (Get permission from the proper authorities first.) You'll need large, thin sheets of paper, masking tape, a fat wax crayon with the paper removed (or colored chalk), and a paintbrush or whisk broom (for cleaning off any dirt obscuring the words on a gravestone).

To make a rubbing, tape the paper tightly over the chosen gravestone and rub the surface with the edge of the crayon until the stone's details show up sharp and clear. Be sure no tape is left behind when your child removes the paper. Have your child note the date and the name of the cemetery where the rubbing was taken.

# What to Look for: Names and Dates

As you begin your tour, think of your explorations as an attempt to un-scramble puzzles. Be sure your child understands the common gravestone abbreviations, such as "b." for "born," "yrs." for "years," and "dau." for "daughter."

▶ Talk about how some people's names evolved from occupations, places of origin, and parents' names. (If she doesn't already know, tell your child where her first and family names come from or what they mean.)

  *Examples:* The family name of Miller refers to the occupation of milling flour. The family name of Paris suggests French origins. One of my sons is named Simon John. His father is John Simon, and *his* father was Simon John—following the tradition of some Lebanese families. My second son is named Kevin Michael, the "K" and "M" of which honor my own deceased grandfathers, Kalman and Meyer, a naming tradition in many Jewish families.

▶ Compare the last names on the older stones with those on more recent graves. Talk about whether the names suggest some changes over the years in residents' countries of origin. What sort of ethnic mix can you infer?

▶ Focus on first names. What used to be the most common ones for men? For women? Are those names still used much? Can your child find any particularly unusual names?

▶ Are there any famous people buried in the cemetery? The owners or managers may or may not agree to point out famous graves, but you and your child might come upon some well-known names on your own. In some communities, such as Hollywood, California, maps are available that direct tourists to the resting places of celebrities.

▶ Try to locate the stones at the opposite ends of time: the one with the oldest dates and the one with the most recent dates. Talk about some of the events and changes during the intervening years, decades, or centuries.

▶ Compare gravestones of males and females to determine who tends to live longer. Did more husbands outlive wives, or vice versa? Does it appear that adult life expectancy has changed over the years?

▶ How many deaths can be associated with childbirth? Child mortality? Mental figuring will enable your child to determine whether people died younger in past generations than they do now. Notice if any headstones record the cause of death. Such details were more often inscribed years ago than they are today. Take this opportunity to mention medical advances and improved health and sanitation practices.

▶ Is there a preponderance of headstones from one particular year? Work with your child to figure out why that might have happened. Could there have been an epidemic? A war? A natural disaster?

▶ Is there anything remarkable about the number of deaths by season?

# What to Look for: Relationships

▶ Looking at the gravestones of previous generations, what seems to have been the average number of children in a typical family? Do gravestones tell you anything about whether this number has increased or decreased?

▶ What can your child deduce about changing family relationships by observing the gravestones of individual families? How large did extended families used to be? What about today? Is it easy to find grandparents, great-grandparents, and grandchildren buried near one another?

▶ While colonial or early American gravestones usually represent only a single individual, the gravestones in modern cemeteries often name two or more people, nearly always husband and wife. See how true this is in the cemetery you're visiting. Notice stones already engraved with the names of still-living spouses.

# What to Look for: Beliefs

▶ What can you tell about people's beliefs and values by the inscriptions on their gravestones? Talk a bit about how different religions view the possibility of an afterlife. Some believe in reincarnation, although you aren't likely to find clues about this on the stones themselves.

▶ Talk about funeral customs of various societies and cultures throughout history.
   *Examples:* The Egyptians practiced mummification, the Romans generally preferred entombment, and the Vikings launched their dead in blazing boats. Hindus practice cremation, burning bodies on funeral pyres. Muslims bury their deceased lying on their right sides, facing Mecca, Islam's

holiest city. Also, many Muslims don't use coffins, since they believe dead bodies should be allowed to return to the earth. At some points in their history, Solomon Islanders have laid their dead on coral reefs as food for sharks. The Irish hold wakes; members of the Koryak tribe of northern Siberia play cards on the corpse. It's a Chinese custom to burn paper money at the graveside to ensure a happy afterlife for the deceased.

Anthropologist Peter A. Metcalf has studied the funeral customs of the Berawan, a small tribe in north central Borneo. The funeral rites are performed immediately after death for a period of two to ten days. Next, the bereaved family stores the corpse on a platform in the graveyard for at least eight months and up to several years. Then the family brings the corpse back to the longhouse (a communal hall) and entertains guests for six to ten days. During this stage, the family may take the bones of the deceased and clean them. Last, the remains are moved to a mausoleum.

This intimate interaction with the dead may seem strange to us. Metcalf reported that the Berawan found our customs equally strange, especially the practice of embalming (treating the corpse with preservative fluids). Consider visiting a funeral home with your child to learn more about the American way of dealing with death.

▶ Encourage your child to notice the variety of symbols engraved on headstones. These may range from angels and lambs (especially on children's graves) to hearts, flowers, heraldic designs, and specifically religious symbols.

Discuss the meanings of these symbols. Common themes include the passing of time, shortness of life, resurrection of the soul, and occupation of the deceased.

*Examples:* Simply put, birds stand for the soul, trees for paradise or eternal life, angels for heaven, willow trees for mourning, trumpets for victory, anchors for hope, and snakes for rebirth. Crossbones show life's brevity. Also look for hourglasses (life passing), candles (life snuffed by death), crowns (glory and righteousness), bells (tolling for the dead), and fruits (fertility and abundance). On Jewish stones, hands open with touching thumbs signify that the deceased was a member of the priestly line. A compass with a "V" indicates a member of the Society of Freemasons.

▶ If your visit coincides with a funeral, you may want to watch mourners arrive. Who arrives first? Notice people's clothing and talk about what's considered proper behavior at such an event. What is the significance of the religious rites performed? Be sure to observe from a polite distance.

# Digging Deeper: Related Investigations

▶ Budding geologists and casual rock hounds may enjoy finding the answers to questions like these: What kinds of rock are the markers made from? Why were these particular rocks chosen for this purpose? If the rocks aren't of local origin, where do they come from? Are different rock types used in different time periods? Do inscription styles vary by rock type?

▶ Notice how many old gravestones tilt. Sections of soil settle at different rates. What effects have wind, rain, pollution, and extreme temperatures had on the stones? An interesting fact: Many nineteenth-century granite sculptors died from lung disease caused by exposure to granite dust.

▶ Like everything else, monument designs go in and out of fashion. You may find examples of the massive floral designs that were popular at the turn of the twentieth century, or Egyptian motifs that were stylish in the 1920s. After the 1960s, a new freedom allowed quite a range of monument styles, while these days you're likely to discover very personal remembrances, from a surfboard to a color photo of the departed, encased in lucite and embedded in the granite. At some gravesites, you may even be greeted by the recorded voice of the deceased.

▶ Compare the styles of graves and headstones. Discuss how a headstone or marker can reflect a person's social status. What can you infer about a person or family from the kind of headstone chosen?

*Example:* More elaborate headstones—the ones with statues or ornate carving—might suggest wealth and high status. However, wealthy or prominent people sometimes choose simpler headstones because they have simple tastes or dislike ostentation.

▶ Your child may enjoy collecting unusual epitaphs. Emily Dickinson called them "marble stories." You'll find that these abbreviated biographies and autobiographies provide fascinating peeks into people's lives.

Perhaps you and your child will come upon an inscription like the one on the gravestone of Mary Buell in Litchfield, Connecticut, which aptly illustrates how the earth's population grows geometrically: "She died Nov 4th, 1768, at 90, Having had 13 Children, 101 Grandchildren, 274 Great G. Children, 22 Great G. G. Children, 410 Total, 336 survived her."

▶ An older child may enjoy making up her own "epitaph," perhaps including one or more versions of the inscription. Distinguish between the extreme brevity necessary on a headstone and the leeway permitted in a newspaper obituary. Keep this discussion on the light side by injecting humor into it.

*Examples:* Legend has it that a hypochondriac had these words inscribed on his grave marker: "Now they'll believe me!" The late comedienne Gilda Radner once wrote that when she died, she'd like to be buried with a working television. She wanted her tombstone to read: "Gilda Radner Program interrupted due to technical difficulties."

▶ Talk about which epitaphs were most likely chosen in advance by the deceased and which were probably chosen by surviving friends or relatives.

If both of you feel comfortable doing this, brainstorm all the different ways people can die, perhaps focusing on the most outlandish or far-fetched possibilities: tripping on a tombstone, walking under a falling piano, being buried in dandelion fluff. Point out the next time your newspaper carries a notice of someone dying in a freak accident. This activity doesn't have to be morbid. Use your best judgment of your child's propensity to worry.

▶ Many cemeteries have mausoleums, stone or marble buildings where the dead are kept above ground. Private family mausoleums are usually kept locked, but larger ones are often open to interested visitors.

▶ Some cemeteries contain buildings called columbaria, where the ashes of those who were cremated are kept. Explore these, too.

▶ Discuss all the people who may have been involved in the funeral and interment of those buried in the cemetery.

*Examples:* Did you mention the undertaker, member of the clergy, tombstone engraver, funeral director, embalmer, grave digger, cemetery maintenance crew, gardeners, security personnel, florist, caterer, casket maker, organist, coroner, cemetery architects and designers, newspaper obituary writer, personnel in City Hall's Vital Statistics department, and sympathy card publishers?

▶ Talk about euphemisms that people in our society (especially cemetery and mortuary employees) use when speaking of the dead.

*Examples:* Cemeteries are "memorial parks," and gravesites are called "interment spaces." People who've died are "the deceased" or the "dear departed"; they have "passed away" or "passed on," and they're "interred" instead of buried. Salespeople who approach the public about buying cemetery plots work in the "before need" department.

▶ Notice the flowers. What kinds are found in cemeteries? Are there particular occasions or times of the year when flowers are left on many of the graves? While you're at it, notice the flowery names for the avenues in some cemeteries: "Haven of Peace," "Slumberland," "Inspiration Slope."

# Resources

**The Cemetery Column,** *www.interment.net/column/.* This Web magazine features articles, photos, and special features all dedicated to the exploration of cemeteries and their inhabitants.

**Cemetery Do's and Don'ts,** *members.aol.com/ctgravenet/dosdonts.htm.* Get the lowdown on which general behaviors (including research practices) are suitable in cemeteries and which are not.

**Cemetery Junction,** *www.daddezio.com/cemetery/index.html.* This site is designed to help those interested in genealogy find information about their ancestors. Included are such features as directories and unique stories about cemeteries throughout the country.

***Country Churchyards*** by Eudora Welty (Jackson, MS: University Press of Mississippi, 2000). A collection of black-and-white photographs of cemeteries in rural Mississippi in the 1930s and 1940s, taken by author Eudora Welty.

***The Definitive Guide to Underground Humor: Quaint Quotes About Death, Funny Funeral Home Stories, and Hilarious Headstone Epitaphs,*** edited by Edward Bergin (Offbeat Publications, 1997). The author has put together an interesting collection of funny, funeral-related stories, headstone epitaphs, and quotes about death. Readers of all ages will see that even serious subjects can be approached with both respect and humor.

***Epitaphs to Remember: Remarkable Inscriptions from New England Gravestones*** by Janet Greene (Chambersburg, PA: Alan C. Hood & Co., 1993). A book of notable New England epitaphs from the mid-seventeenth century to the early twentieth.

**Find a Grave,** *www.findagrave.com/.* This searchable and browsable database provides photographs of and directions to the graves of noteworthy people. Includes dates of birth and death.

***Making Paper & Fabric Rubbings: Capturing Designs from Brasses, Gravestones, Carved Doors, Coins, and More*** by Cecily Barth Firestein (Asheville, NC: Lark Books, 1999). Learn the art of making quality rubbings.

***Soul in the Stone: Cemetery Art from America's Heartland*** by John Gary Brown (Lawrence, KS: University Press of Kansas, 1994). Over two hundred photos illustrate the cultural, historic, and aesthetic roles of gravestones. You'll also find insights into symbols and customs.

**Tombstone Traveler's Guide,** *home.flash.net/~leimer/.* An enthusiastic guide named Christina travels the world for inspiring tidbits from cemeteries, giving information on the meanings behind symbols, rituals, and tales.

# CHAPTER 7

# PLAYING AROUND WITH PHOTOGRAPHY

**A** child equipped with a camera has a distinct advantage: This relatively low-tech and inexpensive tool is almost as good as having an extra sense with which to investigate the world. Taking pictures is an excellent way for young people to become actively involved in looking at and thinking about places, people, issues, and things. When your child is no longer a passive observer but a participant in and recorder of life's pageant, he gains much more than technical skill.

Self-esteem is enhanced when a child operates a camera, since the photographer is in charge of selecting the photo site, composing the shot, and posing the subject. Science enters the picture, too, as the child learns about lenses, apertures, and what film to use in what light. Even with the simplest automatic camera, a child learns the advantages of thinking something through and of experimentation—great science lessons.

Photography also offers a uniquely personal means of communication, which can be of special benefit to the less verbal young person. As some writers feel most free to express themselves while "hidden" behind their written words, some photographers open up most comfortably behind their cameras. Even a highly verbal child learns a lot from focusing—literally—on the visual side of life.

> ### Pictures B.C. (Before Camera)
>
> A young child's first "photograph" doesn't have to be made with a camera. You can work with your child to create sungrams, or shadow images. Sungrams are made by placing objects on photosensitive paper and exposing the paper to sunlight.
>
> This technique introduces a child to the concept of negative images. It's a good first exercise in composition, because a child must create an original design for "photographic" reproduction. Inexpensive sungram kits are available in craft stores.

# Equipping the Young Shutterbug

Even the youngest child will enjoy a real camera. A simple one can give satisfactory results, but since film and processing will be your most costly outlay over time (unless you go digital—see "Should You Go Digital?" on page 89), it makes sense to invest in a camera that produces consistently good photos. A first camera needn't be expensive or complex. These days you can find fairly inexpensive—but relatively sophisticated—35mm cameras.

What about instant picture cameras, such as those made by Polaroid? Film is still relatively expensive for these and photo quality is variable, but they're useful for certain special occasions. Passing one around at a party and having every guest take a picture of something intriguing may result in an amusing collection. And kids, of course, love not having to wait for pictures to be developed.

If you own a good 35mm camera with manual settings, consider letting your child try it out. Some kids are fascinated by the challenge of fooling with settings; others are intimidated and return happily to an automatic camera. See how your child reacts.

Auto-focus cameras are great for the young and perhaps impatient beginner (the latter category fits many adults, too), because he can concentrate on the art of composing the shot instead of on the technicalities of lighting and distance. Still, if a child shows interest in moving beyond snapshot proficiency, he should have a camera with manual capability. When your child is ready, and if you're able to spend more, consider buying a single-lens reflex (SLR) camera, perhaps a used one. Not only do these cameras allow you to change lenses for greater flexibility, but what you see in the viewfinder is what you get when you develop the photo.

You can avoid flashbulbs and attachments for a while; there's plenty to photograph in sufficiently well-lighted places. In dimmer light, use fast film.

---

## Should You Go Digital?

Consider a digital camera for your child so her photos can go instantly onto your family's Web page or be emailed to pals and relatives. There are few things more gratifying for a budding photographer than immediately seeing on the computer screen how her photos turned out. Also, you can work with your child right away to figure out what went right with a picture and what she might try differently next time. She won't feel pressured (by you) to stop at twelve or twenty-four pictures, as there's no additional expense to "develop" extra shots.

Digital photos can be manipulated, improved, or enlarged quite easily with a number of popular software programs. Consider the joys of clutter-free storage, too. And with a high-quality color printer, any photo can be printed easily and clearly, so you can still try all the activities in this chapter that require photos in hand.

Like most high-tech items, digital cameras, though still expensive, are steadily coming down in price. If you and your child are already computer-savvy, digital could certainly be the way to go. You can manually choose the settings on the camera or opt for auto settings. Your main expense, after the camera itself and its batteries (rechargeables are a good investment), will be memory for the camera. Memory determines how many photos you can take and store in the camera (from only twenty to five hundred or more) before you must upload them to the computer. Less expensive digital cameras have less memory. They also have longer cycle times—the time you have to wait between shots—though it's still only seconds, usually. You'll also need to consider your camera's method of uploading, some of which are simpler than others. As with everything to do with computers, research thoroughly before buying.

---

# Getting Started

When you introduce photography to your child, don't try to turn him into an instant expert—and be especially slow to criticize his results. The point, at least in the beginning, is to encourage visual literacy and to turn your child on to images. Your child's vision will be different from yours. He may find something worthy in a weed patch, a pile of trash, or an old car. Or you may find

something aesthetic in these things, and he
may not. Art is personal and unpredictable.

I was thinking about the wide range of
subjects photographers choose as I looked
through a collection of prize-winning photos
from magazine contests. I came across the
following photo subjects: someone behind a
wet windshield; an old building; empty, wet deck chairs;
the sun setting over a lifeguard shack; a child drawing on the street with
chalk; rooftops; trees in autumn; an old barn; half a red car; an iron and iron-
ing board; bicycle spokes; the sole of a shoe; a kitchen chair; eggs on three
plates; brooms leaning on a wall; a fence; a cat; a man feeding pigeons; and
the reflection of clouds in a puddle.

When you first hand your child a camera, and before you load film into
it, have him open it and look through the back. Show him how, when you
manipulate the aperture ring in the front, he can see it open and close
through the back of the camera. Do this before even mentioning shutter
speed. Compare it to how we squint when we go out in the sun and open
our eyes wide in the dark. Let your child turn the aperture ring and look at
the numbers.

When discussing ISO (formerly ASA) numbers, keep the explanation simple. Use the analogy of a 100-watt bulb providing more light than a 50-watt
bulb. The darker the room, the more watts you need; the higher the ISO, the
more light the film attracts. That's why ISO 400 film is better for darker surroundings than ISO 200.

Allow lots of experimentation. It's not unusual for professionals to shoot
one or more complete rolls of film to end up with only one really satisfying
photo. Help your child figure out where the less successful shots went
wrong (encourage him to be interested, to see the fun in that, even if he
doesn't care, initially).

Most beginners simply "take" photos. They wait for a subject to present
itself, and then they shoot a picture of it. Once that becomes less interesting,
"creating" photos is next. This can mean staging a photo by telling the subject
what to do, or it might mean using props.

Children often need assistance framing a shot through the viewfinder—
especially with eliminating undesired elements from their photo composi-
tions. You might try this with one of your child's developed photos: If the
photo is mainly of a person, put your finger over the person and ask your
child what else there is to see. Is the "other stuff" in the picture important? Ask
your child to think about what was in his mind when he took the shot.

## Fourteen Tips for Young Photographers

1. Plan your photo before you press the shutter release. Keep it simple, with one center of interest (which doesn't always have to be in the center of the picture).

2. Look at what's in the background. Is it cluttered? Too busy or distracting? Is that what you really want to photograph? If not, move yourself or your camera. Remember that blank walls can make fine backgrounds.

3. Hold the camera as steady as you can, especially when gently squeezing the shutter release.

4. Make sure that fingers, straps, and the cap aren't blocking the lens.

5. Subjects who look stiff and posed aren't as interesting as relaxed subjects and people in action.

6. Close-ups are often more interesting than distance shots.

7. Practice using the viewfinder so no one's head is cut off in your photos.

8. Try shooting the same picture from different angles and distances. See which turns out best.

9. Don't angle your shot too much. When you get it printed, the picture will look as if everything is sliding off the paper.

10. Don't let lamps, trees, and poles appear to grow out of people's heads. Shoot from a different position.

11. Beware of glare from mirrors, windows, and picture frames. Move to the side and shoot your subject at an angle.

12. Take a tip from many professional photographers: Keep a simple log as you shoot rolls of film. For each picture, make a note of the date, the subject, and anything else you might want to remember later. Or, after your pictures are developed, write the month and year on the back of each print.

13. Many photos can be improved by cropping—using scissors—to cut away a boring or distracting background.

14. Handle and store your photos carefully. One easy way to store them is in three-ring albums with "magnetic" sheets—the sticky ones covered in clear acetate. These accept prints of all different sizes and allow for frequent rearranging. Photos can also be stored in various kinds of boxes, including small plastic or metal file boxes, or shoe boxes. (See "What to Do with All Those Photos," pages 97–98, for some creative ways to display your pictures.)

# Mastering the Medium

▶ Urge your child to use the camera to view things from unusual angles—close up, from above, from below, through branches. Start in and around your own home. Look for textures and patterns in the walls, fences, and pavement.

   *Examples:* "If I lay on my belly in the grass, I see a forest through the lens." "Your shoes would make a great picture. Pretend you're about to squish me—I'm a shutterbug!"

▶ Encourage your child to photograph the same subject from far away (long shots), from close up, and from a medium distance. The resulting photos will each emphasize a different aspect of the "story."

   *Example:* Try a long shot of baby brother playing, another photo showing only the baby's face and body, and a close-up of his hands on a toy.

▶ Experiment with light. Direct, midday sunlight has a bright, harsh quality, which often forces subjects to squint. Sometimes results are more pleasing on overcast days, late in the afternoon, or early in the morning. The angle of the light affects the photo's depth and definition.

▶ If your child knows how to set an f-stop and shutter speed, have her take several versions of the same photo (which is called bracketing), keeping a record of which settings she used. Later, analyze the results with her. Find out what she does and doesn't like about each photograph.

▶ Open your child's mind to the possibilities of "evolutionary" picture taking—that is, focusing on a single subject of personal interest over a period of time, seeking to capture subtle changes. This activity is best for somewhat more experienced photographers.

   *Example:* For a week or a month, your child takes photos of the outside of your home in all kinds of lighting and weather conditions. He doesn't have to shoot the whole house or building—maybe one brick, a section of siding, a step, part of the garden, or a window.

▶ Pair your child with a friend who has similar photography skills. Have them take photos of the same scenery and compare the results. This is a good way to help your child grasp how individual the photographic eye is.

# Picture This: Projects to Try

▶ Write a story or a nonfiction essay and take photos to illustrate it. Or take the pictures first, then write about them. Or use a photo to inspire a painting.

▶ Create a photo essay. Tell a story or illustrate a process using only pictures.
   *Examples:* Decorating a Christmas tree, baking a cake, refinishing a cabinet, cleaning out a garage, taking a walk.

▶ Create a family photo diary. Carry a camera around for a day or for several days, snapping pictures of family members. Try to catch everyone doing something characteristic and something out of the ordinary.
   *Examples:* The family eating a meal, little brother bathing, Dad brushing his teeth, Mom paying bills, the family pet frolicking, your child's bedroom as it usually looks. The diary might also include snapshots of the mail carrier, the gas station attendant, and others who are part of a day's events. Take a picture of your child to include in the finished diary.

▶ Suggest to your child that she try out unusual backdrops for her photos.
   *Example:* Create an interesting effect by laying a large mirror on the floor and placing an object on its surface. Include both the object and its reflection in the shot.

▶ Draw a large picture using sharp, contrasting colors. Then snap a photo of the artwork.

▶ Make photo books with themes. These can be as simple or as complex as your child chooses. Brainstorm creative book ideas together.
   *Examples:* One book could include only pictures of items beginning with the letter "B," such as book, baby, bottle, bird, and bread. Another could be portraits of stuffed animals. Another could show examples of nature in the city.

▶ Go to the zoo, camera in hand. Your child may find the visit especially interesting if she looks at the animals with photography in mind.
   *Variations:* Take a camera along on trips of all kinds. What used to be routine may become new when your child looks at her pictures—"Was that there last time? I never noticed it before."

▶ It may seem pointless to take photos of scenes already available on post-cards, but kids like to do it. So buy the postcards, too, and make comparisons. Where did the photographer stand to get that shot? What time of day was it? What season? What makes the postcard picture different from the photo?

▶ Visit the oldest neighborhoods and historic sites in your area to photograph interesting architectural features such as roofs, windows, porches, and cornices.

▶ Compile a large community map composed of photos of favorite stores and other neighborhood haunts.

▶ Put together a career album using photos of people in your community doing their jobs. You might include teachers, mail carriers, shopkeepers, police officers, fire fighters, farmers, and construction workers.

▶ Combine cooking and photography by taking photos of completed culinary successes. Then file the pictures with the recipes to create a kid's cookbook.

▶ When photographing the family pet, get down to its eye level. Attract the pet's attention and get it to look alert by crinkling paper or showing one of its favorite toys. (This is also a great way to photograph a very young brother or sister.)

▶ Your child may enjoy the double pleasure of combining gardening and photography. Suggest that he crouch down so his subjects (flowers, for example) are at eye level. Either fill the viewfinder with lots of flowers or zero in on a single stem or blossom.

   When the sun is low in the sky, sunlight from behind or to the side of a flower will emphasize its translucence. For a dewy, early-morning look any time of day, spray the flower with an atomizer before shooting it.

▶ Is your child a collector? Suggest that she start a photo collection focusing on one particular subject. The only constraints are the limits of her imagination.

   *Examples:* Sunsets, clowns, architectural oddities, dogs, fountains, fire hydrants, donut shops, doorknobs, playgrounds, cactuses, and cows.

▶ Draw or otherwise create backgrounds for stuffed animals or other toys. Then photograph the scenes.

▶ Teach your child the meaning of the words *symmetry* (similarity of form on either side of a dividing line; harmony; balance) and *symmetrical* (balanced or similar on both sides; well-proportioned; harmoniously arranged). Have him search out and photograph symmetrical images, such as a butterfly, two chairs facing a table, or windows on either side of a door.

▶ Compile an emotions album. Two or more children working together can pose to illustrate various emotions—anger, joy, sorrow, or puzzlement.

▶ "Mystery photos" are fun to take and share. The photographer chooses something familiar to photograph but tries to make it look mysterious—perhaps by showing only part of it or shooting it from an unusual angle.
  *Examples:* Try this with a common household object, an article of clothing, or something stored or boxed away. See if family and friends can guess what it is.

## Take a Photo Safari

Bring along a camera on an outdoor scientific expedition. Here are some ideas to try:

• Take photos that show gravity at work.

• Find and photograph animal homes—burrows, hives, nests, mounds, hollow logs, even doghouses.

• Document the impact of people on the natural scene. How about a collection of photos showing litter?

• Catch evidence of animal life—feathers, tracks, droppings, and footprints.

• Pretend you're a toad, a worm, or a bird. Take some photos that show how you see the world.

▶ Create photo comics. First, think of a story (it needn't be funny) and write a script. Then add a list of exactly what pictures you'll take to help tell your story. Get some friends or family members to act out your story while you take the photos. Vary your angles and distances. After the photos are developed, arrange them and glue them onto heavy paper or cardboard. (You can also crop them any way you want. Try pinking shears for an unusual effect.) Finally, design dialogue bubbles out of paper or self-stick labels, write your dialogue inside, and attach these to the photos.

▶ Your child can photograph a subject or scene that illustrates the mood of a favorite poem or song.

▶ If your child has photographed simple objects—balls, apples, cups, boxes, or flowers—suggest that he try drawing a picture of the object using the photograph as a model.

▶ Make a collage using parts of photographs and bits of magazine illustrations, with or without words cut from advertisements.

▶ From pictures taken at family get-togethers, create a "photo tree" that shows who's related to whom. This might be part of a family history book that also includes transcribed interviews with various family members.

▶ For a more advanced project, try composing trick shots. Even if the results are different from what your child anticipated, such photos will still provide practice in skills like choosing, planning, analyzing results, and comparing intentions with outcomes.

   *Examples:* Focus on a shoe poised menacingly above, a toy car made to look full-scale by its setting, or a toy animal posed with a mirror set up vertically between it and the camera to create a two-headed look.

▶ Try some "photo-fakery." Several years ago, a *Science Digest* contest challenged readers to create photos in two categories: UFOs and weird beasts. For UFOs, it was suggested that photographers throw a pie plate or a hubcap in the air. For weird beasts, possibilities included creatively decorated clay figures, double exposures of animals and people, and unusual shadows.

▶ Take a photograph of some object, such as a teddy bear, a toothpick, or a rock. Then take a picture of someone holding that photograph. Then photograph *that* photo, and so on, in an infinite regression.

## Make a Book of Changes

Work with your child to chronicle things that change over a period of time. Long after you think you're done with this, your child's sharpened awareness of her surroundings will keep resurfacing (as will your own, I promise you). Possible subjects for before-and-after photos include:

- empty lots with "_____ to Be Built Here" signs, followed by whatever is finally built
- old-building-to-new-building developments, including under-construction shots
- rivers at high water and low water
- oceans at high tide and low tide
- the same tree during the different seasons
- a carrot top, sunflower seed, or other seed before planting, during growth, in full bloom, and wilted
- babies, toddlers, or fast-growing pets at monthly or yearly intervals
- shopping areas or schools when they are crowded and when empty
- the price sign at a local gas station every few weeks
- an arrangement of favorite personal items that are periodically revised

# What to Do with All Those Photos: Seven Creative Possibilities

Your child's photographic masterpieces may delight you, but they'll soon overflow the magnets on the refrigerator and even the shoe boxes they're stuffed into. Deciding what to keep and display can be tough. First of all, you and your child do NOT need to hang onto every photo. If a picture is indecipherably fuzzy, lopsided, or uninteresting, encourage your child to toss it to make room for the better ones.

Try some ingenuity—and the following tips—as you look for ways to use and display favorite photos. You and your child (depending on his age) can do many of these projects together.

1.  **Art marks the spot.** Have your child choose a small photo or a portion of a larger one. Paste this to one end of a strip of cardboard that is 2 or 3 inches wide and about 8 inches long. Laminate (cover with clear adhesive paper) and use as a bookmark.

2.  **Pretty paper products.** Reduce the size of one of your child's photographic creations. Use a copy machine or scan it into a computer and reduce it. Paste this small reproduction onto a corner of a standard sheet of paper and photocopy (or duplicate on a computer). Enjoy this special stationery when you or your child writes letters. To turn a page into a greeting card, fold it into quarters.

3.  **Hold it.** Cover a wooden or cardboard box with a few selected examples of your child's photographic art—nature photos work well here—and coat with clear spray, like shellac. Use for storing stuff.

4.  **Colossal collage.** Ask your child to choose several photos. Crop and paste these onto a couple of large sheets of colored construction paper to form a single collage masterpiece.

5.  **Fancy frames.** Frame a photo by gluing it inside a box lid that your child has decorated. For unusual frames, use colored poster board or fabric glued to cardboard. Glue some twigs onto cardboard in the shape of a frame.

6.  **Good enough to eat.** Take a single photo, enlarged, or choose several. Arrange them to fit an inexpensive vinyl placemat. Laminate the photos with clear adhesive paper for a long-lasting, safe-to-eat-on mat.

7.  **Puzzle it out.** Choose a special photo to have enlarged to 8 x 10 inches. Paste it on a piece of cardboard and cut it up into puzzle pieces.
    *Variation:* Make photo puzzles out of wooden children's blocks. Choose six cubes, 1 inch on a side. Next, take several 4 x 6-inch photos and cut them into 1-inch squares. Glue these randomly onto the sides of the blocks until each block is covered. You'll never see the complete photo again, but you can mix and match the blocks to form creative, new images.

# Photographic Side-Trips

▶   You and your child can become a collector of props—items your child can use to enhance photographs. Once you're in the habit of seeking out such materials at garage sales and elsewhere, your child may get a great picture idea just by spotting some unusual prop.

    *Examples:* Costume jewelry, clothing, masks, stuffed animals, hats, eyeglasses, or toy cars.

▸ Photography has been around for 150 years, and older children may find its history fascinating. Some of the art's most famous twentieth-century practitioners include Alfred Stieglitz, Edward Steichen, Edward Weston, Walker Evans, Dorothea Lange, W. Eugene Smith, Henri Cartier-Bresson, Diane Arbus, and Imogen Cunningham. Check your local library for collections of their work.

▸ Read community calendar listings for photographic events such as gallery exhibits and photography exhibits at art museums. Take your child to a photography center. Outings like these motivate a child to experiment.

▸ Visit a photographer's studio or a friend's home darkroom. Encourage your child to ask questions, or you ask them.
    *Examples:* How is retouching done? What special techniques are used to produce unusual photographs?

▸ If possible, visit a photo lab where photographs are developed and printed (or just chat with staff members at your local discount developer when the store's not swamped with customers). Encourage your child to ask questions, or you ask them.
    *Examples:* How are slides developed? How are photos enlarged? What chemicals are used, and where do they come from?

▸ Study the editorial and advertising photographs used in various publications. Determine what idea or message the photographer was trying to get across.

# New Uses for Old Photos

▸ Pull out old family albums and study the photographs with your child. You can learn a lot about a person or an era from the things people chose to be photographed with and the ways they posed. I once bought a whole box of old photographs inexpensively at an antique shop. Though we didn't know the people involved, it was still fascinating to look for clues to their personalities in the unlabeled photos.

*Examples:* Are the people dressed up or casual? Are they involved in work or in leisure pursuits? Are they smiling? Are pets included? Are cars, farm equipment, or perhaps horses given a front-and-center position? Are small children held on parents' laps? For outdoor photos, notice the houses, other buildings, and natural settings. Or, if a photo was taken indoors, what rooms can you see? Can you tell what time of year the picture was taken?

▶   As you examine old photographs, remember that a single picture can raise many questions. Some can be answered by the photo itself, but others require additional research. Be wary of jumping to conclusions from insufficient information.

*Examples:* A man is shown holding a book. Does this mean he was an avid reader? Maybe and maybe not; perhaps the photographer merely posed him that way. A woman seems stiff and expressionless. Does this mean she had a rigid personality or never showed emotion? Not necessarily. In the past, before fast-action cameras and film, taking a photograph took a long time. People had to sit absolutely still, often in uncomfortable positions. Because photographs were expensive, being photographed was a special event, and people thought they should look serious and formal.

▶   Use a magnifying glass to study old photos closely, item by item. Pay attention to details like clothing decoration, jewelry, facial expressions, foliage, the lettering on signs and posters, the newness of a steam locomotive or automobile.

The interested child will likely ask questions about what she sees. Try to have resources on hand, like old mail-order catalogs (for dating the style of dress) and an atlas or travel guide (for learning more about where a photo was taken).

# Photos That Move: Video Camera Fun

If you own a video camera, your child has access to a method of photography that provides instant gratification, as well as numerous learning opportunities. Because feedback is fast and easy—just pop the cassette into the VCR—technical skills can improve quickly.

Many of the activities suggested in this chapter for use with a still camera work just as well with video. Here are more ideas to share with your budding videographer:

▶ Start simply. The best way to learn the basics of what your family's video camera can do is by taping a casual event, such as a picnic or a basketball game. Show your child how to operate all the controls and let him try everything. Encourage him to experiment with fade-outs. Remind him to move slowly and not to zoom and pan too much.

   Teach your child to limit individual scenes to fifteen seconds or so, instead of pointing the camera endlessly toward the same group of people doing the same thing. Remember: His questions and your instructions will both be recorded on the sound track.

▶ If you've ever thought of making a video inventory of your family's household belongings (very useful for insurance purposes), consider letting your child do the job.

▶ Do you have favorite relatives who live far away? Perhaps your child can tape a "video letter" for them. This might include scenes of everyone in the family doing something characteristic and of family members speaking directly to the distant relative.

▶ Have your child tape stories instead of just pointing and shooting. Doing so creates an awareness of plot, continuity, pacing, and the relative importance of events, all of which make for more interesting videos.

   *Examples:* The story of "How We All Got Ready for Jamie's Surprise Party," or "The Day of the Big Soccer Game," or "Painting the Bedroom."

   *Variation:* Carry this idea further by inviting your child to create a story. He can get together with friends, write a simple script, gather props, design titles, dress up, and either act or serve as the video camera operator. Then invite family members to the premiere.

▶ If your video camera doesn't have a character generator, a feature that allows you to make captions for your videos, your child can write her own captions with a wide felt-tip pen on cardboard. Film these at the start and at various points during a taping for a more polished look.

▶ Work together to make a documentary about baking cookies, planting a garden, repairing a fence, or even something as mundane as cleaning a room.

▶ Choose a family member as subject and tape his or her typical day. Include footage of such daily routines as teeth brushing, exercise, bed making, and eating. Consider staging some special events (subject receiving something exciting in the mail? an animated telephone conversation?). A pet can also be the subject of a day-in-the-life documentary.

# Resources

*Click: A Book about Cameras and Taking Pictures* by Gail Gibbons (Boston: Little, Brown & Co., 1997). Ages 4–8. This simple how-to book gives information on basic camera parts, how a camera works, what happens at the photo developer's shop, and taking pictures. The final pages offer a quick history of photography and "Fun Photo Facts."

*Click: Fun with Photography* by Susanna Price and Tim Stephens (New York: Sterling, 1997). Ages 7–12. An introduction to what can be done with a simple compact camera. Also comes packaged with a 35mm reusable camera and photo album in the *Click Book & Camera Kit* (Sterling, 1998).

**Eastman Kodak Online Library,** *www.kodak.com/global/en/service/library/tips.* This site offers an online library of materials to read or download, from "Close-Up Photography with 35mm Cameras" to "Picture-Taking in Five Minutes." Many of Kodak's publications are also available in print through their Information Center. Call 1-800-242-2424, ext. 10.

*A Female Focus: Great Women Photographers* by Margot F. Horwitz (Topeka, KS: Econo-Clad, 1999). Ages 4–10. Peruse this book for stories of famous female photographers alongside photos they're known for.

**Kodak's Guide to Better Pictures,** *www.kodak.com/global/en/consumer/pictureTaking/index.shtml.* Visit this site for picture-taking tips including the company's "Top 10 Techniques" for amateurs, ways to remedy problems, and an online tutorial in composition.

*Lights, Camera, Action: A Guide to Video Instruction and Production in the Classroom* by Bruce Limpus (Skylight, 1998). Ages 7 and up. For classroom use but suitable for families, too. Children learn new ways to use a video camera as they complete projects like creating a video documentary about a story they're reading or filming a commercial that demonstrates persuasive advertising.

*Magic: Stage Illusions, Special Effects, and Trick Photography,* edited by Albert A. Hopkins (New York: Dover, 1990). Ages 12 and up. Focuses mostly on stage magic but includes interesting information on photographic illusions as well.

*Make Fantastic Home Videos* by John Fuller (Buffalo, NY: Amherst Media, 1995). This illustrated guide is full of practical tips for making your home movies look more professional, including information on how to shoot birthday parties and other family events.

*My First Camera Book* by Anne Costick (New York: Workman, 1989). Ages 4–8. A teddy bear explains photo basics. Included with the book are a twelve-page photo album and a tiny, reusable camera.

*Shadow Play: Making Pictures with Light and Lenses* by Bernie Zubrowski (New York: Beech Tree Books, 1995). Ages 4–12. This activity book from the Boston Children's Museum offers lots of clearly explained activities, from the most basic (casting shadows on the sidewalk) to the more complex (making a shadow box and a box camera).

*Take a Look Around: Photography Activities for Young People* by Jim Varriale (Brookfield, CT: Millbrook Press, 1999). Ages 9–12. Black-and-white photos of the countryside taken by kids in a summer photography class led by the author illustrate a variety of photographic techniques. Beyond the great pictures, the book includes descriptions of the techniques, projects to try, and explanations of what makes each photograph shown so effective.

# CHAPTER 8

# USE YOUR HEAD: MIND-CHALLENGING PHYSICAL ACTIVITIES

**P**uppies, kittens, and children have at least one thing in common—they all love physical activity. For kids, whether they participate in sports, play games, dance, or move their bodies in less rule-bound ways, the benefits go far beyond the merely physical. Studies have shown that movement may enhance overall intellectual development. Yet for some bright children, the thrill of traditional sports, games, and exercises can quickly pall. To keep your child from becoming a sedentary specimen, it's smart to combine physical exertion with a healthy dose of mental stimulation. This chapter has dozens of ideas for your whole family to try.

## Cooperative Games, Winnerless Games

One way to put the fun back into tried-and-tired sports and games is by changing them into cooperative enterprises. Though the "New Games" movement has been around for decades now, many schools and youth athletic groups still teach physical education as though winning is all that matters. As you and your child will discover, game-changing can be a liberating experience.

The best games are those in which all players are fully engaged by the playing, not by the need to win. Players in a good cooperative game:

- laugh *with*, rather than *at*, each other

- are more interested in the playing than in the details of keeping score

- feel better about themselves both during and after the game (rather than feeling criticized or evaluated in front of the group)

- have a chance to be spontaneous, imaginative, and challenged

Some children initially resist the switchover from competitive to cooperative sports, thinking play is pointless without a clear winner. If this happens with your child, talk about it. You might mention that competitive sports still have a place, but that designing and playing "the other kind" can be both mind-expanding and helpful in preparing a person for a world that often rewards flexible thinking.

On a practical level, try these tips: Play with your child to show how it's done and how much fun cooperative games can be. Choose challenging games for an older child used to competition. Suggest that your child simply try a cooperative game to see if she likes it—and don't push.

Here's a sampling of games for you to try, suitable for a variety of ages.

▶ "Brussels Sprouts" is a tag game (invented by Pamela Kekich) in which "It" chases someone in slow motion, catches the other child, and links arms with him or her. Now they both become "It." The next person captured also links arms. "It" becomes larger and larger until everyone is included. Any time a player calls out "Lima beans!" the action changes to fast motion, or from fast motion back to slow motion.

▶ "Hug Tag" players have to hug another player to be safe. This game is great fun for parents and small children and has been known to get not-too-friendly siblings to hug and like it.

▶ "Double-Up Musical Chairs" can be played by any number of children. Start with one chair less than the number of children playing. When the music stops, someone has to double up on one chair. For the next round, remove another chair for more doubling up. By the last round, everyone piles on the same chair (and on top of each other, of course). No one is left out.

▶ "Human Knot" begins with ten or twenty people gathered closely together in a circle. Each person grabs the hand of two different people who aren't right next to her or him. The idea is to undo the "knot" without releasing handholds. (You twist and turn and put your arms over your shoulders.)

▶ "Reverse Score" can be played with various sports. Every time you score on the other team, *they* get a point. The player who scores switches immediately to the "winning" team, which is the team with more points—although that team won its points by being scored upon. (My family tried this with soccer at an eighth birthday party, with very amusing results.)

▶ "All on One Side" is a volleyball game with four or five players on one side, none on the other, and a balloon for a ball. The object is to get your team to the other side of the net and back as many times as possible. Each player volleys the balloon to another player and then scoots under the net. The last player to touch the balloon taps it over the net and scoots under. The receiving players try to keep the balloon in play and repeat the process.

*Variations:* Try putting two balloons into play at one time. Another version begins with players on both sides of the net. A player who hits the balloon over the net moves immediately to the other side. Everyone wins when the teams have switched sides completely without dropping the balloon.

▶ "Taking Coconuts" is a winnerless game from Papua, New Guinea, described in *Hands Around the World* by Susan Milord (see Resources, Chapter 12, page 179). Draw a large central circle on the ground, with four smaller ones around it. Place five coconuts (or balls) in the center circle. Each of four players stands behind the smaller circles. The goal of the game is to get three coconuts into your own circle, but the hard part is that you can't throw or roll them. You must take them one at a time from another circle, including the center one, and place them in your own. Play is very fast, and the game ends whenever you want it to.

# Creative Game-Changing

When two people of unequal ability—parent and child, older sibling and younger—play skill games, the one who always loses feels frustrated. The better player doesn't have much fun either, since there's no challenge when you expect to win all the time. And sometimes both winner and loser simply tire of the same old game.

Using flexibility and creativity, you can change the rules of the games you play. As long as both players agree, anything goes (except deliberately making mistakes or losing on purpose, since children see through those ploys).

Here are several suggestions for creative game-changing that will even the odds in many games and sports. They include handicapping, retaking moves, and other special privileges that make playing more enjoyable for everyone.

## Checkers and Chess

▶ Play one checkers game as a "test game." The winner counts how many checkers are left on the board and then starts the second game with that many fewer than the normal number.

   *Example:* If the winner ends up with five checkers on the board, next time he starts with only seven instead of the usual twelve. Continue this in subsequent games.

▶ Give the less experienced chess player several free moves at the start of the game. Or, in checkers, give this player more kings to begin with. Or declare her the winner if she gets a single king or three kings.

▶ If your child knows strategy, try this: If she can tell you a good move to make, you can't make that move.

▶ Once you reach the point where it's clear you're going to win (there's no way for your child to make a comeback), turn the board around and have your child play with your pieces until the end. (I owe this cooperative tip to novelist Jane Hamilton.)

▶ Eliminate competition altogether by having both players talk over each move, seeking and agreeing on the best ones.

## Other Board Games

▶ For games like Parcheesi, send the less adept player's piece back only ten spaces instead of all the way home. Or switch sides halfway through.

▶ In Monopoly, the less skilled player can receive $400 instead of $200 for passing "GO." If one player goes bankrupt, keep playing anyway for a predetermined length of time.

- In board games involving a race, like Candyland, set a timer for five minutes. After a card is drawn, either player can make the move, depending on whom it helps more (or hurts less). The game is won if both players get across the finish line before the timer goes off.

- When playing Scrabble or similar word games, look up words before placing them on the board. (This also enhances learning.)

- To make Chinese checkers a cooperative game, players coordinate their marbles' movements so they reach their destinations as close to simultaneously as possible.

## Bowling

- To even things up and make the game more fun for you and your child, try bowling each frame together. The less experienced player rolls the first ball, and the better bowler tries to "clean up."

- Use the official system of handicapping in bowling: Play the first game and then subtract the lesser score from the greater one. Give the player who scored less 75 percent of the difference with which to start the next game.

- Have each bowler compete against himself. The winner is the player who improves his own score the most from one game to the next.

## Card Games

- Play a game of solitaire together, alternating turns playing the cards. If the game "comes out," you're both winners.

- For five-card poker, let your child exchange four or all five cards, but limit yourself to one or two. Or let your child exchange one card at a time, up to five, in order to build the best possible hand.

## Ping-Pong and Tennis

- Set higher winning point totals for better players, lower for less experienced ones.

    *Example:* The better player has to make 21 points to win, but the less experienced player needs only 14.

▶ Play one game as a test game. Subtract the weaker player's score from the stronger player's score. For the next game, the stronger player must play the difference with her "wrong" hand (a lefty plays with the right hand and vice versa).

    *Example:* The stronger player gets 14 points, the weaker player gets 10 points. For the next game, the stronger player must play 4 points with her "wrong" hand.

▶ For Ping-Pong: Draw a box on the floor with chalk and confine the better player to it.

▶ For tennis: Require the stronger player to hit all balls into the white-outlined box used for serving. Or make it a rule that the better player has to let the ball bounce on his side before hitting it—no running up to the net.

▶ Forget about keeping score and just try to volley for as long as you can. Keep track or have someone time you with a stopwatch. Try to beat your own record.

## Team Sports

Many of the following tips come from the experience of physical education teacher Peggy Palumbo.

▶ Relax rules so no officials are needed and anyone can participate. Consider dispensing with scoring altogether. Or allow points for actions other than scoring, such as caring behavior and teamwork.

▶ Have players hold hands with a partner as they play.

▶ Every few minutes, have a certain number of players swap teams.

▶ When playing soccer, start with one ball and then add another, then another. With multiple balls on the field, everyone stays busy and involved. Celebrating after scoring is minimized because it happens so often. Or increase the number of goals. Place goals not only in the front and back of the field, but also on the sides.

▶ When playing volleyball, the two teams play until the agreed-upon time expires. Try unlimited hits on each side.

- Change the scoring in basketball so the stronger players get 2 points for a ball in, while the younger or less experienced players get 4 points for a ball in, 3 points if it hits the rim, and 2 points if it hits the backboard. Or have the object be for both teams to score a certain number of points in a given amount of time. For example, each team might need to score 10 points in 10 minutes. Often, when one team gets their 10 points, they'll cheer on the other team to do the same.

## Billiards

- For eight-ball, play a test game first. Count how many balls the less experienced player has left when the game is over. The stronger player starts the next game with that many extra balls.

- Another creative change is to require the more able player to bank every other ball.

- Other interesting possibilities: Have the better player switch hands (a right-hander plays with the left hand) or wear an eye patch to decrease depth perception.

- For cooperative billiards, one player shoots until she misses a shot. Then it's the next person's turn. Players try to set up the next person for a good shot.

## Frisbee

- Before play begins, players state which hand they will use for throwing and which for catching (or the same hand for both). They stand 15–20 yards apart and take turns tossing the Frisbee or similar throwing toy.

    If the catcher can't possibly reach the Frisbee at any time during its flight, she gets a point. If she might have caught it, the thrower gets a point (the catcher is the one who decides). Two points are awarded to the thrower if the catcher touches the Frisbee but drops it. Two points also go to the thrower if the catcher uses the wrong hand or catches it against the body.

    Play to 11 or 21 points, switching sides when one player reaches 6 or 11 points.

# Body-Brain Workouts

Here are more ways to enhance ordinary physical activities:

▶ Combine sports creatively. If unicycling isn't challenging enough, try juggling while doing it. Try shooting baskets from a unicycle. Experiment with combinations of volleyball and baseball.

▶ Play almost any ball game using water balloons.

▶ Find out how different animals get around. Then imitate their movements.
    *Example:* Your young child hops around the room like a cricket while you provide a staccato beat on a drum (or a cake pan) for him to follow.

▶ Try flying a kite by attaching a helium balloon to it. (Stay clear of power lines!)

▶ When playing basketball, the player who has just made a basket has to answer a question before the point is counted. Decide in advance what type of questions to use: trivia, personal, outlandish, or whatever.

▶ Look into folk dancing opportunities for families in your community. Not only is folk dancing good exercise, but it's also an excellent way to learn about other cultures.

▶ Play "Math Twister." Write some math problems on index cards or slips of paper. Write the answers in circles on a large piece (4 x 4 feet) of light-colored fabric. Have your child choose a card and answer the problem by putting his hand or foot on the correct circle and staying there. At the next turn, he puts another hand or foot in the circle with the correct answer. On the fifth turn, he takes his first limb and "reuses" it. Keep playing until your child loses his balance. (Problems can be 2 + 2, or 3 x 6, or the square root of 16, or whatever, depending on your child's homework.)

▶ Play a variation of the game "H-O-R-S-E," in which players take turns attempting various shots at a basketball hoop. When one player makes a shot, the next one must make the same shot or take a letter ("H," "O," and so on) as a penalty. A player is out of the game when she completes the whole word. Take turns choosing difficult or amusing words to use in competition.

▶ Your child may have played or watched a sport in which the umpire or coach communicated with players using hand signals. Challenge your child to make up a new set of signals for a homemade or an existing game.

Encourage your child to keep records of physical activities (such as pounds lifted, sit-ups completed, baskets made, and miles walked) by listing or graphing them on a computer or recording them in a journal.

An obvious adjunct to any recreational interest is a related magazine subscription. Specialty magazines exist for numerous physical activities. In fact, simply perusing the shelves at a well-stocked bookstore or library may suggest a whole new interest to your child.

# Weird Sports

Throughout recent history, unusual sports have been invented and enjoyed by hardy aficionados. See if your child can add to this list by collecting articles about other "weird" sports.

▶ "Skijaks" are 11-foot-long polyethylene pontoons that are a cross between skis and kayaks. You use them to propel yourself across the water's surface with an oversized, twin-bladed paddle.

▶ In "White-Water Ballooning," you take off into the sky and then descend into rapids along with your hot-air balloon.

▶ "Landsailing" boats, with wheels for "sailing" on dry land and a chassis that covers the pilot, were first made of scrap wood in 1931. Others were later converted from ice boats. Now their colorful sails are made of Dacron® and Mylar®.

▶ "Paraskiing" is the art of skiing uphill. Wearing a parachute, you're lifted by a gust of wind and carried toward the top of the mountain. Then you touch down on the snow with your skis and proceed down the mountain. Ski-chutes, designed for the unpredictable winds of Alpine slopes, are controlled by special vents that respond to a steering bar.

▶ "Wallyball," a cross between volleyball and racquetball, uses a slightly smaller, softer, rubber-textured volleyball. Players in teams of two, three, or four serve over an 8-foot-high net that's stretched across a racquetball court. They're allowed to hit the ball off one wall per hit. If the ball hits two walls or if it hits the opponent's back wall, a point goes to the other team.

Other weird sports are played only in people's imaginations. Here's one example; see if your child can make up some more.

▶   Under the heading "Silly Sports," a magazine once ran a short piece describing "Sky-Driving." Competitors drive cars out of a cargo plane at 10,000 feet and vie for a single empty parking space at a shopping mall. (Parachutes are packed in the trunks for safety, the article wryly adds.)

And let's not forget the strange and silly things people do to get into the record books. For example:

▶   Fifteen-year-old Michael Kettman of Florida once won a spot in the *Guinness Book of World Records* by spinning ten basketballs on his body for five seconds. He spent countless hours perfecting his technique. His equipment included some skateboard kneepads with attached metal rods on his legs and two wood contraptions for spinning balls on his head and stomach.
        Your child might also enjoy inventing outrageous physical stunts.

# Sports Science

Another way to enliven your child's interest in physical activity is to explore the scientific side of sports. Such an investigation offers other benefits as well. The child who analyzes a sport and understands something of its physics can incorporate this knowledge into his own movements for improved performance. And even a rudimentary knowledge of gravity, acceleration, kinetic and potential energy, and momentum will come in handy later in physics class.
        Increased awareness also adds a new dimension to spectator sports. You see the action differently once you know that a batter has less than 0.2 seconds to decide whether to swing at a 90 mph pitch, and that starting a swing 3 milliseconds too soon or too late will result in a miss.

▶   Peter J. Brancazio, a physics professor at Brooklyn College and an amateur basketball player, analyzed the trajectories of seventy-seven basketball shots to come up with this winning formula:

   • A high-arching shot is more likely to fall in the basket. (Brancazio found that all the best shooters favor the rainbow parabola over the line drive.)

- The slower the ball is delivered from the hand and the more feathery its flight, the better the odds that the shot will drop through the hoop. (Brancazio concluded that shooters should exert the least possible launching force.)

    Ask your child to try these basketball techniques for herself and evaluate the results.

▶ If standard kite flying has become old hat to your child, she may enjoy a stunt kite, which requires coordinating two strings and demands lots of active involvement. It's also fun to build a kite from a kit. Look for inexpensive kits in stores that specialize in kites or creative toys. Or your child can make a kite entirely from scratch using plastic sheeting and one-eighth-inch dowels. Talk about the kinds of material that seem to work best, and why. What is the relationship between the lightness of the kite or the length of its tail and its flightworthiness?

▶ Older children can design games requiring varying amounts of physical effort. To determine how much energy is expended, they can measure one another's heart rate, respiration, and perspiration.

    *Examples:* An easy way to measure heart rate is to locate, with the tips of your index and third fingers, your pulse—the pulsing artery between your wrist bone and the tendon on the thumb side of your wrist. Without pressing too hard, count your pulse for ten seconds (use a watch with a second hand). Multiply this count by six to obtain your pulse rate.

    How would you measure the amount you sweat during exertion? Brainstorm! Could you weigh a towel, wipe off your sweat with it, and then weigh the towel again? Could you measure how many cups of water it takes to replace lost fluids and take away your thirst, depending on the activity you've done?

▶ Ask your child to try adapting familiar games so physically challenged children could play them.

    *Examples:* How would you change a relay race or a tennis game if your partner was in a wheelchair? How could two people with limited arm power play volleyball?

▶ Because extended periods of weightlessness cause bone loss, scientists are researching new ways for astronauts to exercise during long space fights. Ask your child to work on solutions to this problem.

*Examples:* How could you compress a thorough workout into a short period of time so it wouldn't interfere with the demands of the space mission? How could astronauts run? (One possibility: Elastic cords could be used to keep a runner on the "ground" and provide resistance.) What about weight lifting in a weightless environment? (Scientists are considering artificial gravity.)

▶ How would you play earth games on the moon? Since the moon's gravity is one-sixth that of the earth, a football field would have to be six times as large, because players could throw the ball that much farther.

Can your child come up with ways to adapt other familiar games for play on the moon? What about for play on planets with stronger gravity than exists on the earth?

▶ Modern technology has revolutionized sports, and who knows what the future holds? Perhaps your child can venture some creative guesses. Just as an example of what advanced technology can do: Using wooden poles, track and field athletes improved their pole-vaulting performance over the years from a height of around 11 feet in 1900 to just under 15 feet in 1950. After the fiberglass pole was introduced, vaulters quickly achieved heights of more than 16 feet. Today's records are even higher.

Just as sports equipment evolves, so do new sports like inline skating, mountain biking, and snowboarding. What kinds of sports does your child think the future holds? Each time your family watches the Olympics, take note of what new sports have been added. On the Web, visit *www.espn.com,* which has an interesting section on "extreme sports."

With your child, investigate how world sports records have evolved over the last few decades. Make predictions of what these records may be five or ten years from now. Your child might write down these predictions and seal them in an envelope to be opened in the future.

## The Mind's-Eye View

Discuss with your child the impact of positive thinking on athletic performance. Some sports psychologists believe that the difference between two athletes who have neared the top of their sport is four-fifths mental. That is, athletes may be nearly identical in their physical conditioning, but their mental attitude will decide who wins.

Visualization is one technique many athletes use to foster positive thinking. They create mental images as a kind of rehearsal for what they're about to do; they picture something (a play, a strategy, a victory) with the intent to make it really happen later. Once they've visualized every step of the race or part of the sport, they feel more confident and more in control. Then they can loosen up and focus on the actual physical challenges.

Help your child learn to be a skillful imager, someone who can concoct and control his mental pictures. According to sports psychologists, visualization helps people learn and retain movements better. Can your child vividly imagine how a movement feels?

My son Kevin learned to ride a two-wheeled bike when he was only four years old by watching others do so. He went on to excel in a variety of sports by first closely watching experts, then imagining himself doing the same thing, then actually doing it. Similarly, some folks can watch a dance video and do it themselves right after. They're able to imagine themselves in the place of the experienced performers.

Effective visualization is all in the details. That means taking the time to think out every individual step of the sport or activity you're pursuing. As with any other skill, practice makes a person better at visualizing. Have your child try these exercises:

- Start small. Take a close look at someone's face, a flower, or a room. Try to see and memorize every single detail. Notice every eyelash, freckle, color, angle, and shape. Now look away and visualize what you've just studied. Speak into a tape recorder or write as much as you can describing that face, flower, or room. Repeat the process and see if you can create a more complete image in your mind.

- Take a mental trip through your favorite sporting goods store. Sit with your eyes closed. Imagine yourself walking into the store, walking up and down the aisles, picking up various pieces of sports equipment and trying them out (bounce the ball, swing the racket—carefully!). Now take an actual trip to the store, paying close attention to everything you see and do, following the order you previously imagined. When you come home, sit quietly and visualize it all again.

# Resources

*American Sports Poems,* selected by R. R. Knudson and May Swenson (New York: Orchard, 1996). All ages. An offbeat mix of poems on sports ranging from archery and auto racing to fencing, polo, and wrestling. Included are verses by such masters as Elizabeth Bishop, Anne Sexton, Randall Jarrell, Robinson Jeffers, and James Merrill.

*The Cooperative Sports & Games Book* and *The Second Cooperative Sports & Games Book* by Terry Orlick (New York: Random House, 1978 and 1982, respectively). All ages. Hundreds of games for children and adults that provide challenge without competition. Many are from other cultures.

*Everybody Wins: 393 Non-Competitive Games for Young Children* by Jeffrey Sobel (New York: Walker & Company, 1983). Ages 3–10. Use this book to find cooperative games that are easy to understand and implement. Games are arranged by type (such as partner games, old favorites, and ball games) and grade level. A helpful introduction explains non-competitive play and its benefits, and provides additional information for the leader of the games.

**Family Pastimes.** RR 4, Perth, Ontario, Canada K7H 3C6; (613) 267-4819; *www.familypastimes.com.* Request a catalog from this company, whose motto is "Play together, not against each other." You'll find board games, group games, and sports and game manuals.

*Keep Your Eye on the Ball: Curveballs, Knuckleballs, and Fallacies of Baseball* by Robert G. Watts and Terry Bahill (New York: W. H. Freeman & Co., 2000). Written for adults but can be shared with older children. Why are more home runs being hit than ever before? Does corking a bat really help a hitter? Find the answers to these questions and many more in this book on the physics of baseball.

*Looking Inside Sports Aerodynamics* by Ron Schultz (Santa Fe, NM: John Muir, 1992). Ages 8 and up. An introduction to the scientific principles of aerodynamics that explains various factors— gravity, friction, force—through visual studies of baseballs, footballs, Frisbees, and basketballs, and through other examples of sports physics.

**Neuroscience for Kids,** *faculty.washington.edu/chudler/outside.html.* This site includes directions for a variety of unusual games, such as "Synaptic Tag," "Neuron Chain," and "Brain Freeze Tag," all based on brain science and terminology.

*The Sporting Life: Discover the Unexpected Science Behind Your Favorite Sports and Games* by Susan Davis, Sally Stephens, and the Exploratorium (New York: Henry Holt, 1997). Ages 12 and up. This is an accessible book that parents and kids can share, featuring experiments and "physicist's party tricks" that illustrate scientific concepts.

*Sports Illustrated for Kids.* This monthly magazine, which also posts some features online, is available on newsstands or by subscription. It includes information on all aspects of sports, articles about kids and adults who excel in sports, ideas for games, and sports trivia. Write, call, or visit the Web site: *Sports Illustrated for Kids,* P.O. Box 60001, Tampa, FL 33660-0001; 1-800-835-6900; *www.sikids.com.*

*Sports Science for Young People* by George Barr (New York: Dover, 1991). Ages 12 and up. Explains how scientific principles affect the way athletes perform, particularly in football, basketball, and baseball.

# CHAPTER 9

# DIRT, WORMS, BUGS, AND MUD: KIDS IN THE GARDEN

**W**hen you introduce your child to an empty plot of earth and tell him it's his to garden, all he'll see at first is a large, dark-colored sandbox just waiting for him to dig and mess around in. There's nothing wrong with that. Once children start school, they rarely have the chance to work with messy substances. Gardening gives them ample opportunities to play in the dirt—digging holes and handling soil, peat moss, worms, water, even compost. Luckily, these are all vital to the process of coaxing nature to produce.

Children who garden grow in many ways. As they're taught to respect and cooperate with the natural world, they learn patience, how to plan, how to follow directions, and how to observe results. They develop an awareness of natural cycles. Their interest in nutrition and their feelings of self-reliance increase when the things they plant become foods they can eat and share with their family and friends.

Gardening is also an art. Combining various forms, sizes, and colors of plants into an attractive whole—creating living beauty—takes a good eye as well as a green thumb. The visually aware child will appreciate the aesthetics of planning a garden; the child who's less attuned to the visual can have her aesthetic sense developed by the parent who points out what to look for. Creativity blossoms as the child discovers that most of the "rules" of gardening are flexible and open to experimentation.

Gardening offers psychological benefits, too. Kids experience the joy of nurturing living things and seeing them develop, and they take responsibility for the care of something over a period of time. Gardening can be highly therapeutic for people of all ages, providing respite from more structured and competitive endeavors. And it makes an outstanding long-term family project.

"Gardens teach patience and gardens teach process," says Richard Stretz, a gardening writer, educator, and hybridizer of day lilies. "Those are not always lessons kids want to learn. But once you get them hooked, they'll be gardeners for life."

# Choosing a Place and Deciding What to Plant

Almost any home can support some kind of garden. You don't even need a plot of ground—many vegetables and flowers grow beautifully in pots, both inside and outside. Some neighborhoods supply a communal gardening area. Once you determine your own best place, you and your child can start researching and planning what to grow.

The Resources section for this chapter (pages 131–133) offers numerous starting points for investigation, including a few of the hundreds of Web sites devoted to growing things. Check the gardening sections of libraries and bookstores. Send for seed catalogs and study them.

What kinds of plants grow in your area, and how sturdy and disease-resistant are they? What time of year should you start them? Visit local nurseries for advice on what's appropriate for beginners in your part of the country. For speedier and more certain results, plant seedlings instead of seeds—though your child will miss out on the excitement of seeing that first sprout peeking through the soil.

Children like quick results, so keep in mind that fast-growing vegetables are good choices for turning young people on to the pleasures of gardening. Vegetables can be grown in a small area and are highly rewarding. Carrots and radishes grow fairly quickly and can be eaten raw—but since they grow underground, there's not much to see. Peas and beans grow into vines rapidly and are tasty to most kids. In fact, all vegetables taste especially good when eaten fresh from the garden. Children who grow their own tend to enjoy vegetables more than other kids do.

Container gardening offers distinct advantages: you can choose and control the soil and drainage, and you can avoid most garden pests. In larger containers (3- to 5-gallon pots), you can grow beans, carrots, peppers, tomatoes, corn, broccoli, cabbage, kale, leeks, even melons. Smaller containers (all the way down to 4- to 6-inch pots) are fine for growing peas (choose shorter peas, ones that grow to about a foot), lettuce, spinach, and Swiss chard. Choose in-between sizes for beets, eggplant, and cherry tomatoes.

*Tip:* Successful container gardening requires full sun and abundant water. The smaller the container, the less tolerant the plants are of drying out.

It's fun to grow fruit, although this usually requires space for trees or bushes. Also, most fruits grow best in warmer climates. Strawberries, however, are fairly easy to grow, can be grown in containers, don't require much space, and are perennials.

*Tip:* Take your child fruit-picking at a farm, orchard, or grove. Depending on your area, you might be able to pick your own apples, blueberries, raspberries, strawberries, oranges, grapes, or other fruits. Picking fruit is a great way to spend an afternoon, it's inexpensive, it gets you and your child out to areas you might not know, and you come home with great edibles!

Children often want to plant seeds left over from fruits (peach pits, apple seeds, watermelon seeds). If your local climate is conducive and you have the space, try planting some peach pits in a corner of the yard. Within about three years, some tasty fruit may appear.

Apples are another story. It can take up to twelve years for an apple tree to bear fruit, and, even then, odds are the apples won't taste good. Home-grown apple seedlings tend to be randomly cross-pollinated with crabapples. That's why fruit trees sold by nurseries are produced by grafting buds from known varieties onto root stock. Still, it never hurts to plant seeds and wait to see what happens.

Flowers come in an amazing array of forms and colors. The seeds themselves are available in a stunning variety. Some, like begonia seeds, are very small, while others, like tulip bulbs, are quite large. Although the most common flowers are generally the least expensive and easiest to grow, rarer types provide a special thrill to the diligent child. Annuals are fast and flower longer, but perennials return year after year. In your garden, try a few annuals and a few perennials.

Kids also like plants that appeal to various senses, such as fragrant mint or scented geraniums that smell like nutmeg, lemon, rose, or menthol. Ornamental popcorn is an especially delightful outdoor plant with a bonus— the kernels can be harvested and popped. Giant sunflowers add drama to any garden and are likely to grow taller than your child (and you).

Other easy and attractive plants to grow include flowering maple, hosta, daffodils, impatiens, piggyback plant, and strawberry begonia.

# Planning and Preparing

When starting out, think small. Garden chores can quickly become overwhelming for the child who plants too much.

If possible, get your child real garden tools and teach him to use and care for them responsibly. A watering can is easier for a small child to manage than a hose is (though hoses are more fun). If your child will be using a hose, it should have an adjustable nozzle with a fine spray.

Have your child draw a map of the proposed garden, showing where each plant will be placed. (*Tip:* If you're planting sunflowers or Indian corn, put them on the north side of the garden, so when they grow tall, they won't block sunshine from the other plants.) Let your child decide how to mark and identify what's planted, maybe by writing or drawing on wooden craft sticks or on the plastic markers sold at nurseries, or by attaching empty seed packets to sticks.

Depending on the size of your garden, help your child plan some walkways so he'll be able to reach all areas to care for the plants. Lay bricks or flagstone in the soil, or line the walkways with pebbles and cover them with wood chips.

Preparing the soil is critical. For a 5 x 5-foot garden, work a large sack of peat moss and a large sack of air-dried cow manure into the top 8 inches of soil. For potted plants, add some peat moss to a packaged soil mixture.

## Playing It Safe

Keep gardening fun by teaching your child these four basic safety rules:

1. Always wear gloves when working with tools or rough materials.

2. Always wear sunscreen when working outdoors.

3. Stay away from all garden poisons, including pesticides and chemical fertilizers. (If you as an adult choose to use these products, then you should be the one who handles and applies them.)

4. To avoid itchy discomfort later, always wash or shower after rummaging among plants or weeds.

## A Recipe for Homemade Compost

You may want to make your own compost to add to your soil. This takes about six weeks, so plan ahead. Follow these simple (if not smelly) steps:

1. Start with a garbage can's worth of grass clippings or leaves. Spread half on the ground and cover with an inch of soil.

2. Add a layer of bone meal or blood meal, available at garden supply stores.

3. Now add a layer of store-bought manure equal to the amount of clippings you've spread.

4. Follow with more layers of the same items (clippings, meal, manure). Then cover with a thin layer of soil.

5. Spread fruit and vegetable wastes from your kitchen—such as potato peelings, apple cores, and melon rinds—on top of this. (Never put meat or nonfood waste in a compost bin.)

6. Sprinkle the pile with water. Turn it all over with a rake or shovel once a week.

Eventually, microbial action will decay the whole organic mess so you can add it to the soil in your garden.

If you can tolerate the odor, you can concoct a smaller, simpler version of compost by letting a 5-gallon pail of leaves and soil molder away in a warm corner of a balcony or porch. Stir it up every week and keep it moist. Or put your ingredients into a large trash bag, tie it, and shake it every so often.

Other common (and odor-free) household wastes you can add directly to the soil in your garden or pots are coffee grounds, peanut or sunflower seed shells, loose tea, and crushed eggshells.

# Learning in the Garden

▶ Gardens can stand some neglect before things start dying. Still, the best results, as your child will soon discover, come from paying attention to each plant's individual needs. Your child will learn that plants generally like to be watered deeply only when they dry out (too much water kills more plants than not enough water does). Weeding is necessary not only for aesthetic reasons but also because weeds crowd the plants' roots and steal their nutrients. Rows of seedlings need to be thinned as soon as they begin to get crowded. Sometimes the tiny, thinned-out seedlings can be transplanted—worth a try if the thought of tossing them is traumatic.

▶ Answer your child's questions and ask some of your own. Have a couple of reference books on hand for the hard ones, like: Why do bees visit flowers? Why do you have to water, and how do you know when? Why do flowers bloom at different times? Why don't many plants bloom in the winter?

▶ How about planting an "Old Smoothie," the only modern thornless rose? It's available at nurseries or by mail order. If you do, talk with your child about why a thornless rose is so rare and about the ways various plants and flowers protect themselves against their enemies.

▶ It's fun to grow a flowering bulb indoors (though many are toxic, so supervise younger gardeners). First, cut a bulb in half to show your child the tiny embryo (plant) surrounded by fleshy layers of scales (food). Point out that the part of an onion we eat is really a bulb.

The process of making bulbs bloom indoors is called "forcing," and you'll need to buy bulbs especially prepared for this purpose. These are usually sold from late summer through late fall.

An easy bulb to force is the Tazetta narcissus, or paperwhite narcissus. Start by planting three or four bulbs in light potting soil, sand, or small pebbles. Use a pot without drainage holes. Cover the bulbs halfway, with their points sticking out (other types of bulbs should be fully covered by the planting medium; check the directions if you choose something besides paperwhites). Water and keep in a cool, dark place for ten days. Once the roots have anchored and the shoots are 3 inches high, move the pot to a cool, sunny window. Water regularly, keeping the roots wet. Expect flowers in about four weeks.

▶ Put landscaping in child-size language: describe it as "framing" some plants with others, as an artist frames a painting. As an example, place red flowers where they'll pick up the red of bricks or a redwood pot, blend with pink flowers nearby, or contrast with white flowers or walkways. This kind of activity helps your child develop a sense of color harmony and order.

▶ It's inevitable that pests will try to stake their claim to your child's garden. Together, research options for dealing with insects and seek alternatives to poisonous chemicals. Discuss the balance of nature, how each predator has prey, and how some insects—ladybugs, for instance—are good for the garden (they eat aphids that devour roses). Other invaders aren't a problem at all; worms, for example, aerate the soil and are great to have around. Some flying bugs pollinate other plants. (Perhaps a discussion of "the birds and the bees" is suitable here?)

## The Garden Journal

Suggest that your child keep a garden notebook or journal. As well as providing writing practice, a garden journal can become a useful record of gardening events, decisions, mistakes, and successes that your child can refer to from one year to the next.

- A loose-leaf binder works well for this purpose, since it allows for pages to be arranged and rearranged. Otherwise, any notebook or scrapbook will do.

- Things to keep track of include when specific seeds were planted, when they were fertilized, how long they took to sprout, and (for vegetables) when they were harvested.

- Have your child record sizes and colors of mature plants. Measure cabbages and sunflowers; count cherry tomatoes. Chart a particular plant's growth over the weeks.

- A garden journal is the perfect place to record needed information about specific plants. Near each plant's name or picture (perhaps cut from a seed catalog), your child can write down when to thin, when to transplant, and how long the plant takes to grow.

- Encourage your child to personalize his garden journal. He might draw the garden and individual plants and write his thoughts about gardening. He can include before-and-after photographs. If you order seeds from a catalog, suggest that your child cut out the catalog pictures, tape or paste them in the journal, and record important dates: planting, first sprout, first bud or flower. Over time, the journal becomes a kind of "baby book" for your child's growing plants.

- Here's a deceptively simple "assignment" for your child to include in a garden journal: Choose one flower and examine it very closely. Write down exactly what you see. (Help out with suggestions: "Notice the way the light and shadows connect." "Look deep inside the flower. What do you see?" "Examine the petals, the stem, and the leaves.")
  Most of us are accustomed to glancing at and commenting on nature—"That's such a lovely rose!"—but we rarely take the time to really see. For the older child, such a description can become quite lengthy.

▶ How about collecting and studying garden invaders, like insects? Even weeds lend themselves to collecting and arranging into weed bouquets.

▶ Make scarecrows to discourage pesky birds. An old shirt on a contraption of crossed sticks is a place to start. Add pants stuffed with newspaper or straw.

Another way to scare birds away from your garden is by tying aluminum pie plates or long, thin strips of foil to a nearby fence or tree.

▶ Discuss how different plants have been used throughout history to cure various ailments—and as murder weapons!

*Examples:* Two of the many plants with medicinal value are foxglove, from which we get the heart stimulant digitalis, and periwinkle, a variety of which is used in cancer chemotherapy. Toxic plants include hydrangea, oleander, philodendron, and the seeds or berries of plants such as holly.

# Pumpkins, Pussycats, and Pretty Little Birds

▶ Plant a pumpkin patch in the spring. Your child will enjoy Halloween more than ever this year if she's harvested her very own pumpkins. Pumpkins need some space, so try to set aside an 8 x 8-foot area of fertile soil for this project.

Soak some pumpkin seeds overnight in warm water before planting. To feed the seeds and keep them growing happily, plant them on a small hill composed of compost or manure, combined with some lime and some bone meal or fertilizer. Top this mixture with soil. Dig half a dozen holes an inch deep and plant a seed in each one. Then cover with soil. Water right away and frequently thereafter.

Once the seeds sprout in a week or so, begin weeding. Feed with more fertilizer every couple of weeks. Thin out the scragglier seedlings early on to give the rest a better chance. Once the rinds are orange and hard, your child can harvest her crop. Now she can:

• Carve a face in one or more of the pumpkins (a young child can use a marker to outline the face she wants you to carve for her). Try carving opposite expressions in each side of a single pumpkin, such as a happy and a sad face.

• Guess how much a pumpkin weighs and then weigh it. How close was your estimate?

• Estimate how many seeds are in a pumpkin and then count them. How close were you?

• Cook the seeds: For the amount of seeds you would get from a small pumpkin, toss with 1 to 2 tablespoons of your favorite cooking oil.

(Adjust the amount of oil to accommodate larger or smaller seed portions.) Salt to taste. Spread the seeds out on a baking sheet and roast them at 350 degrees for 15 to 20 minutes or until crisp and golden.

- Find a recipe for pumpkin pie that uses fresh pumpkin. See how it tastes compared to a pie made with canned pumpkin.

▶ Grow your own catnip, and your cat will thank you! Catnip is a member of the mint family. All you need is a small piece to begin—you can buy a small plant from a garden center or catalog. (Pet supply stores often carry ready-to-grow catnip plants.) Plant it in a well-drained sunny or partially shady area, in a mixture of soil, sand, peat moss, compost, and lime. Water, weed, and wait. After harvesting, you can dry some by hanging it upside down, out of the sun, in a dry, ventilated place. Then your child might want to design a little cat toy made of sewn- or glued-together felt (in a mouse shape or just a square to keep it simple) filled with dried catnip.

▶ Hummingbirds delight the senses, so plant some flowers that are likely to attract these tiny birds to your child's garden. Red is the main color that draws hummingbirds to a plant. They are particularly fond of red flowers with long, thin tubes that they can get their tiny beaks into. Here are some good choices, depending on your region of the country: fuchsia, trumpet vine, honeysuckle, cardinal flowers, scarlet larkspur, columbine, paintbrush, and monkey-flower. If all else fails, buy and hang up a red hummingbird feeder and keep it filled with sugary water. (Use four parts water to one part sugar. Mix, heat to boiling, and then cool.)

# Experiments for Budding Gardeners

When scientists do experiments, they start by proposing a problem to be investigated. A garden offers many opportunities for your child to experiment.

▶ Plant bean seeds in cups and devise various experiments with them. Some ideas to try:

- Measure the amount of water you use. Water the bean in one cup twice a day, the bean in a second cup once a day, and the bean in a third cup once a week. What's the best amount of water for optimum growth? What's the most successful watering schedule?

- Fertilize the soil in one cup and not in another. Which plant grows better?

- Add small drain holes to one cup and not to another. Which plant prospers more?

- Plant beans just below the surface, half an inch below, an inch below, and two inches below. Which works best?

- Point one bean up and one bean down. What difference does that make?

- Experiment with amounts and sources of light (such as a light bulb, direct sun, and indirect sun), a variety of moisture sources (such as milk and hot water), and fertilizing agents (such as liquid and animal fertilizers).

▸ It's fun to experiment with unusual growing mediums. Expect the following projects to get results, since they use seeds that will grow under almost any conditions:

- Moisten a small sponge and roll it in grass seed. Place it in a saucer of water on a windowsill. Watch what happens.

- Line the inside of an empty half-pint glass jar with blotting paper. Fill the jar with sawdust. Place corn kernels and bean seeds between the blotting paper and the glass. Water the sawdust regularly and watch the seeds send shoots up and roots down.

- Put some pebbles and water in a shallow pan. Add both a section of a potato that has an "eye" in it and the top of a carrot. The "eye" will sprout, and the carrot top will develop a fern.

- Use toothpicks to suspend a sweet potato in a tall glass so only the tip is in water. The potato will send out a leafy vine.

▸ Show your child how to start a plant in water from a cutting, so he can see the roots develop.
  *Examples:* A sturdy house plant like pothos is perfect for this experiment. Philodendron, coleus, and ivy are others (but be careful with philodendron, which is toxic). Cut a 6-inch section from an existing plant and place it in a glass of water. In a few days, roots will begin to grow.

▸ Rooting a cutting in a pot is easy, too.
  *Examples:* Using a sharp knife, cut a section from a side shoot of a coleus, chrysanthemum, or succulent; your cut should be a quarter-inch below a leaf. Dip the cut end in water, then in rooting hormone, and insert it in a damp rooting medium (a mixture of vermiculite and peat moss) in a shallow container. Or simply break off a piece of geranium, stick it in the pot, and wait for it to produce its own roots in a matter of weeks.

▸ Propagation and hybridizing are fascinating processes for the advanced gardener. Read enough about the subject to answer questions about how it's done, even if your child isn't quite ready to take these on independently.

▸ Not so easy to grow, but fascinating to kids, is the Venus flytrap. This carnivorous plant has "hinged" leaves that shut like a trap when the hairs on the leaves are touched (usually by a fly). A fly is digested in about ten days; each leaf digests three flies before withering and being replaced. Pot the Venus flytrap in sphagnum moss and place it in a dish of water in full sun to imitate the tropical jungle atmosphere this plant prefers.

▸ Research the particular growing conditions around your home or in a community garden area. Start by purchasing a soil-test kit. Plan experiments such as the following, and keep careful records:

- Plant seeds in two adjoining pots filled with soil. Does adding fertilizer to one make a difference?

- Compare germination rates of seeds you buy and seeds you save from other plants.

- Experiment with each of these variables: light, temperature, moisture, and proximity to other plants.

▸ Gardening questions designed to pique the curious child's interest include:

- Do compost additives (compost starters, worms) make better compost?

- Do plants thrive on music? (Studies have shown that some do, while others seem to prefer silence.)

- Which nutrients should be added to the soil, and where should they be added (to the top, or dug in below)?

- Can you grow plants not usually successful in your part of the country?

- Do old seeds sprout?

- How much money, if any, do you save by growing your own vegetables?

▸ Some greens and flowers are unexpectedly edible. You and your child may want to experiment by adding them to soups, salads, beverages, and desserts.
    *Examples:* The following are okay to eat, and some have nutritional value: peonies, pansies, nasturtiums, dandelions, day lilies, squash flowers, elder flowers, carnations, violets, marigolds, and sunflowers. Definitely *not* to be eaten are wisteria, holly, bird of paradise, hydrangea, oleander, poinsettia, and philodendron.

- Remember that the best science projects for kids are self-motivated.

    *Example:* My son Kevin once decided to plant some grass in a flower-pot on the front porch. He poured a handful of grass seed into a small pot filled with commercial leaf mold and fertilizer (which is not the standard procedure). He covered the seeds with about an inch of soil (quite a bit deeper than the instructions on the box suggested), watered them, and finally covered them with a piece of plastic wrap to keep the moisture in.

    Every morning he checked on their progress. Within only three days, tiny sprouts appeared. Within two weeks, he had a full container of grass—too full, since he noticed that the blades were crowding each other. He "mowed" them (with a pair of scissors). Altogether, this experiment lasted for about a month, until the blades turned yellow (the wrong growing medium? overcrowding? not enough sun on the covered porch?).

    At one point, Kevin took his personal "yard" to school, placed it in his locker, and enjoyed his friends' surprise.

# Gardening and Aesthetics

- Gardening literature can be interesting, even for the armchair gardener.

    *Examples:* For the youngest, don't forget the garden adventures of Beatrix Potter's *Peter Rabbit* or Ruth Krauss's *Carrot Seed*. Older children will be amazed at how articulate gardeners have described the beauty and poetry of the natural world in a wealth of literary (not just how-to) books and articles. See, for example, Christopher Lloyd's *The Adventurous Gardener*. (All these books are described in Resources, page 131).

- Flowers have a long and rich history. Your child may enjoy tracking down the little-known stories and backgrounds of some familiar flowers with the help of a book such as *100 Flowers and How They Got Their Names* by Diana Wells (New York: Algonquin Books, 1997). Add another dimension to gardening by exploring the traditional meanings of flowers.

    *Examples:* In many cultures, flowers have been assigned symbolic meanings since ancient times. Assigning such meanings became especially popular in Victorian England. A flower presented in an upright position implied a positive message; upside down meant the opposite. For example, a gift of an upright rosebud meant, "I fear, but I hope." If the gift was returned upside down, the message was, "Don't fear or hope."

    More flowers and their traditional meanings: carnation (fascination, woman's love); bluebell (constancy, kindness); passionflower (belief);

peony (shame); and rose (love, beauty). As with all symbols, multiple meanings and interpretations are possible. Ask your child to invent others.

▶ Melons, squashes, and gourds can be turned into garden sculptures.
   *Examples:* Suggest that your child carve his initials on a still-growing melon, squash, or gourd. Then have him watch the letters grow bigger over time. An inventor designed plastic forms to use for shaping eggplants, zucchini, and pumpkins into hearts, diamonds, even faces. Maybe your child can figure out a way to replicate this feat using homemade wooden forms.

▶ Carefully chosen containers can enhance the aesthetics of gardening. You and your child might enjoy constructing a window box together. Your child can easily paint or decorate inexpensive plastic or terra-cotta pots. Just about any kind of paint, except watercolor, will work. For decoration, glue on twigs, moss, glitter, buttons, or shells. When your child plants something in a pot she's decorated, she'll truly feel the project is hers.

▶ Once cut or plucked, your child's flowers need another pleasing home: a vase of some sort. You can buy these in splendid variety or make them out of common household containers like glass bottles. Encourage creativity.

▶ Take field trips to botanical gardens, greenhouses, and arboretums, all of which demonstrate the myriad varieties of plant life that can be grown with knowledgeable care. Many offer brochures that explain what you're seeing and can serve as starting points for conversation.
   *Examples:* Talk about native plants—types, characteristics, and needs. (In Southern California, where I live, native plants have to be drought-resistant, and many are succulents.) This could easily turn into a discussion of the broader implications of ecology: Should we use scarce water resources to keep our lawns green? What can happen when someone introduces a non-native plant into an area where it's likely to thrive?
   Some of the larger botanical gardens have "demonstration gardens," where your family may get ideas applicable to your own home garden. The gift shops in public gardens carry many unusual items related to plants and gardening, some of which may further ignite your child's interest.

▶ Visit a topiary garden. A topiary is a tree or shrub that has been clipped into a fancy, often whimsical, shape. If the idea appeals to your child, buy topiary forms from one of the mail-order horticultural supply companies. These are simply metal armatures on which vines can be trained and tied in the form of animals or whatever else you choose.

## The Art of the Japanese Garden

A visit to a Japanese garden will open your child's eyes to many artistic possibilities. The traditional Japanese strolling garden is laid out with a circular path around a pond stocked with koi (a type of fish). The Zen ideals of simplicity and understated beauty are worked into the landscape.

All the elements, from the plants to the rocks to the water, are arranged symbolically. Rocks are usually grouped in threes, fives, or sevens. Three rocks placed on top of one another may, for example, suggest a crane. Two flat rocks on either side of a tall one represent Buddha flanked by two disciples. Water suggests purity. In some gardens, you'll see rocks, pebbles, and sand arranged in a meandering pattern to suggest the effect of water. Black pines symbolize eternity.

Different interpretations are possible, so consult brochures or ask staff members for information about symbolism.

- Try creating a sand garden in the Japanese tradition, which may have started with Soseki Musoo, a fourteenth-century Kyoto philosopher. Sand gardens contain only sand, rocks, and moss, which symbolize water, mountains, and forests, respectively. The sand is raked into lines resembling lake ripples. Rocks of unusual shapes are arranged artistically, usually asymmetrically. There's a famous Japanese temple garden in which fifteen stones are placed in such a way that no matter where you stand, you can count only fourteen at a time.

  For your garden, use white sandbox sand. Before adding the sand, remove all weeds and pack the earth tightly, or put a sheet of plastic over the bed. Use stones, a path, or some kind of ground cover as a border for the sand garden.

  As your child plans and creates her own sand garden, encourage her to develop a story or interpretation to go along with it.

  You might also consider buying a copy of *The Zen Gardening Kit* by Daniel Abdal-Hayy Moore (Philadelphia: Running Press, 1992), which includes a book and a small Zen rock garden in a wooden frame. We had fun with one of these in our family, keeping it on the living room coffee table where anyone could use the tiny rake to rearrange the sand and stones. Someone once added a tiny bunny to the mix. Also available by Moore is the *Mini Zen Gardening Kit* (Philadelphia: Running Press, 2000).

- You can add a touch of Asian design to almost any garden by including Japanese lanterns, driftwood, statuary, pottery, or a small basin used as a pool.

- Ikebana, or flower arranging, is another Japanese gardening art, considered a form of sculpture. It relates to Eastern philosophy and centers around the beauty and peacefulness of nature. Ikebana is said to enhance one's ability to see everything with more sensitivity.

  Practitioners of ikebana are concerned with the lines and shape of each leaf, blossom, and branch. Their arrangements tend to be asymmetrical. To more accurately replicate nature, they typically use more green than do flower arrangers in the West.

  The artistically inclined child might enjoy learning how to do ikebana, but all children stand to benefit from some exposure to it—especially since most kids think that flower arranging means simply sticking cut flowers in a vase.

# Resources

*The Adventurous Gardener* by Christopher Lloyd (New York: Lyons Press, 1998). For older children to adults. The writer, a horticulturist, believes "the best gardening is experimental." He makes even familiar gardening chores exciting.

**Armstrong Garden Center,** *www.armstronggarden.com/hortguide.html.* Armstrong Garden Center offers a multitude of free, online horticultural guides with details about growing flowers, fruits, vegetables, and more.

*Carrot Seed* by Ruth Krauss (New York: Harper Trophy, 1989). Ages 4–8. Everyone warns a young boy that the carrot seed he's planted won't grow. The boy continues to care for his plant, however, and surprises everybody with the results.

*The Complete Adventures of Peter Rabbit* by Beatrix Potter (New York: Viking, 1984). Ages 4–8. A collection of the four stories featuring Peter Rabbit and his mischievous cousin, Benjamin Bunny.

*Earth Child 2000: Earth Science for Young Children—Games, Stories, Activities, and Experiments* by Kathryn Sheehan and Mary Waidner (San Francisco: Council Oak, 1998). Ages 4–8. Lots of fun activities to increase a child's respect for the earth, including an extensive chapter titled "Wonders in a Garden."

*A Field of Sunflowers* by Neil Johnson (New York: Cartwheel Books, 1997). Ages 4–8. A nice introduction to these bright, showy flowers.

*Garden Crafts for Kids: 50 Great Reasons to Get Your Hands Dirty* by Diane Rhoades (New York: Sterling, 1998). Ages 6–12. Learn how to grow potatoes in tires, build a gardening tool station, create a composting station, and more. Clear, simple explanations of plant physiology and discussion of other garden-relevant wildlife such as birds and bugs make this a great teaching resource as well as a how-to book.

*The Garden Explored* by Mia Amato and the Exploratorium (New York: Henry Holt, 1997). Ages 12 and up. This brief but clever book addresses the whys of gardening, as well as the hows and whens. Simple experiments and facts provide a wealth of useful information, such as why plants respond better to watering at certain times of the day, how to improve the quality of the soil, and what makes some "weeds" desirable additions to the garden.

*Grow Your Own Pizza: Gardening Plans and Recipes for Kids* by Constance Hardesty (Golden, CO: Fulcrum Publishing, 2000). Ages 7 and up. This unusual activity guide includes garden plans for creating many kinds of pizza, as well as how-tos for "planting" cake and ice cream, carrots stuffed with spinach soufflé, chocolate zucchini cake, and dozens more recipes. Even though additional ingredients must be gathered from the store, the fun of growing a pizza garden should outweigh any energy (and small amount of money) spent.

*Growing Vegetable Soup* by Lois Ehlert (Orlando, FL: Harcourt Brace, 1990). Ages 4–8. This brightly illustrated book is the story of a father and child sharing the simple joys of planting, watering, and watching seeds grow in their garden. They cook up their rewards into a delicious vegetable soup, the recipe for which is included.

*Jack's Garden* by Henry Cole (New York: Mulberry, 1997). Ages 4–9. Using the traditional "This is the house that Jack built" format, *Jack's Garden* begins, "This is the garden that Jack planted." Cumulative words and pictures show how the parts of nature connect and grow together. Around each framed picture, small, realistic, labeled illustrations show the links in increasing detail: the names and types of seeds, tools, clouds, and insects. A page of gardening suggestions is included.

*The Kids Can Press Jumbo Book of Gardening* by Karyn Morris (Buffalo, NY: Kids Can Press, 2000). Ages 4–8. Tips, checklists, and information on how to attract butterflies, what vegetables to grow, which flowers smell the sweetest, and more.

**KidsGardening,** *www.kidsgardening.com.* This is the National Gardening Association's youth site. It features email pals, activities, discussions, a catalog of products, and much more.

*Linnea's Windowsill Garden* by Christina Bjork (New York: Farrar, Straus and Giroux, 1988). Ages 4–9. In this exploration of a child's indoor garden, fictional Linnea tells readers about her orange tree, shows how to take a cutting, and trims an avocado plant.

*My Backyard Garden* by Carol Lerner (New York: Morrow Junior Books, 1998). Ages 6–12. Kids will find advice on getting a garden started, a month-by-month care calendar, and sample garden plans in helpful detail. Also by the same author and publisher is *My Indoor Garden*, which provides helpful guidance for kids who want to grow potted plants.

**National Gardening Association,** *www.wowpages.com/nga.* Search the site's library, find gardening links, connect to the kids' site, and lots more.

**Nor'East Miniature Roses, Inc.,** *www.noreast-miniroses.com/culture.html.* This site features an extensive article on "Miniature Rose Culture." Miniatures are extremely appealing to kids; most need only sun and water to thrive. Micro-minis grow well indoors.

*Ready, Set, Grow! A Kid's Guide to Gardening* by Rebecca Hershey (Pacific Palisades, CA: Goodyear Publishing Co, 1995). Ages 4–8. Includes plant tips, garden riddles, puzzles, crafts, activities, and a garden journal.

**Smith & Hawken.** P.O. Box 6907, Florence, KY 41022-6900; 1-800-940-1170; *www.smith-hawken. com.* Request a catalog from this respected mail-order firm, which, among other gardening supplies, sells good quality, scaled-down versions of garden implements for children.

*The Terrace Times, www.windowbox.com/beagle/archives.html. The Terrace Times* is a monthly e-newsletter published by Windowbox.com. Check out the helpful archive of articles about container gardening and growing plants in small spaces.

*Tiger Lilies and Other Beastly Plants* by Elizabeth Ring (New York: Walker & Co., 1996). Ages 6–12. Describes and illustrates twelve plants that have some animal characteristics, from the way they look to the way they act. Includes a glossary.

**Veggies Unite! Gardening Page,** *www.vegweb.com/gardening.* This page of a vegetarian Web site offers a variety of tips on container gardening, growing specific vegetables, and more.

*The Victory Garden Kids' Book: A Beginner's Guide to Growing Vegetables, Fruits, and Flowers* by Marjorie Waters (Old Saybrook, CT: Globe Pequot Press, 1994). Ages 3–13. Step-by-step instructions for growing a garden, including specifics for thirty crops.

**The Virtual Gardener,** *www.gardenmag.com.* This online magazine contains informative articles, tips, and a message board. Get helpful information about vegetables, flowers, animal control, and more.

# CHAPTER 10

# MIND SNACKS: RECIPES FOR KITCHEN LEARNING

**I**f you enjoy cooking, both you and your child are lucky—it will be easy for you to share your enthusiasm for the culinary arts. Even if cooking isn't a favorite activity for you, try thinking about food preparation as a valuable way to help your child learn.

Kids are automatically attracted to the fun it looks like you're having when you cook. After all, you get to mess around with different ingredients, you get to smash some of them and scrunch or pound others, you get to choose flavors and textures, *and* you get to experiment.

A willingness to experiment is the key to both fun and learning in the kitchen. Personally, I'm a strict recipe-follower. That, too, has its pleasures for a surprising number of children, but most often the fun comes from fooling around with a variety of substances and seeing what comes out of the oven or the pot.

It helps to develop the mindset (useful in almost *all* activities) that there's no such thing as a failure, whether the end result is edible or not. Between the pleasure of creating and the hoped-for delight of eating comes more learning than you can shake a steak at. For instance, if a recipe calls for an ingredient you don't have, and you substitute something else that doesn't work at all, your child will learn the value of thinking ahead and of using suitable substitutes. Cooking also sharpens math and science skills, provides lessons in nutrition, and encourages artistic and aesthetic interests.

If you're game to try (almost) anything your child prepares—including fried peanut-butter sandwiches—she'll be more willing to sample new foods you suggest at home and in restaurants. Encouraging your child's more inventive creations also builds her self-esteem.

Even preschoolers can be involved in food preparation. When they say, "Let me do it!" let them. By school age, most kids can handle many kitchen activities, from menu planning to measuring, mixing, timing, and actual cooking. Include cleanup chores as part of the agenda and lend a hand if your child is still young or easily overwhelmed.

At age eleven, my son Kevin, already an expert at baking several kinds of chocolate-chip cookies, tackled a triple-layer checkerboard cake made with three pans and two flavors of cake mix. The results were less than aesthetically pleasing, but he figured out a better way to bake it the next time around.

# Getting Started

Enticing cookbooks for children abound (see Resources, pages 145–146, for suggestions). When considering which ones to try, make sure the recipes are clear enough for your child to understand. For example, if a recipe asks you to "sift," is that term explained? If you're a pretty basic cook yourself, like I am, your child's cookbooks will have to spell everything out. It helps to have access to a grandparent, neighbor, or friend who knows his or her way around the kitchen.

It also helps to have on hand at least one comprehensive (adult) cookbook that doesn't take anything for granted. I have referred countless times to my 1949 edition of *The Good Housekeeping Cookbook,* which my mother gave me years ago. That's where I once looked up how to make macaroni when another recipe I was using assumed I already knew that much. (One of the basic tenets of being both a good learner and a good facilitator of learning is a willingness to be ruthlessly honest about what you *don't* know.)

Well before an actual cooking session, choose one or more recipes with your child, list the ingredients you'll need to buy, and shop for them together. If possible, add a little extra to your food budget for experimenting. (Think of cooking as an art or craft worth the expense, like finger painting or photography.)

Make certain you have on hand all the kitchen equipment you'll need, including the right knives, mixing implements, bowls, and pans. Halfway through a recipe is no time to discover an item is missing. A nice touch for a child is a heat-resistant, clear glass pot or pan that allows you to see the food as it cooks. I have a large sauté pan with a glass cover, which is almost as much fun (though it's heavy and a bit fragile).

### Kitchen Safety

Keep cooking a safe family activity by following these six simple guidelines.

1. Make it a rule always to turn pot handles inward, away from the edge of the stove.

2. Teach your child how to use knives safely (and never when in a hurry).

3. Emphasize the power (and the power to harm) of blenders, mixers, waste disposers, food processors, stoves, and ovens, including microwaves. Compare these appliances to power tools such as drills and chain saws and teach your child to treat them with respect.

4. Point out that a pot or pan stays hot long after it leaves the stove. So do the burners on an electric range, long after you've turned them off. So do many foods (and some dishes) heated in a microwave oven. Teach caution.

5. Make sure that your child always wears a large apron when cooking as protection from hot splatters.

6. Have plenty of oven mitts and thick potholders available. Your child can practice using these on cold dishes before handling hot ones.

# Over-the-Counter Learning

Cooking can be an artistic form of self-expression. Your child will enjoy putting his personality into his culinary concoctions. Once he knows the basics, allow him as much freedom as possible, and see what happens.

▶ Point out how foods can be made to appeal to all the senses. Talk about colors and combinations, aromas, and textures, as well as flavors.

▶ Encourage creativity in the forms food can take.
   *Examples:* Pancakes can be made in any animal shape by pouring the body first, then adding legs and a head. (A friend of ours, when his children were small, made this a Sunday morning ritual. His children took turns calling out types of animals, while he designed pancakes to order.) Use cookie cutters to cut out sandwiches. Add cucumber slices to the bottom of a hot

dog bun, and you have a car. Create a monster by using small, round dinner rolls for sandwiches and adding grapes on pretzel sticks for eyes.

- Allow your child to combine foods in unaccustomed ways, or to use unexpected colors. When my son Simon was small, he wondered why food never seems to be blue. So we made cupcakes using blue food coloring. His curiosity was satisfied, and the cupcakes tasted fine.

- Show your child how to substitute healthier ingredients for the ones called for (such as using lowfat milk instead of whole milk), or to change some aspect of a recipe (such as reducing the amount of sugar). Realize that sometimes the results will be delicious and sometimes they won't.

    I once read that the goal of cooking classes is to liberate students from cookbooks. A worthy goal for your at-home cooking school might be to free your child from the fear of failure. Learning how to rescue a dish that has gone wrong can be more educational than learning how to prepare it in the first place.

- Make up recipes from scratch and then name them appropriately or amusingly. Or your child can invent a name and then prepare something that tastes the way the name sounds. (Yellow Boomerangs? Slippery Slides?) Or adapt literary allusions to fit foods. (A muffin of one's own? The tabouli not taken? My kingdom for a quesadilla?)

- List all the basic dishes your family commonly eats. Then brainstorm ways to change them by altering their form or by combining their ingredients in new recipes. Since you don't have to actually prepare everything mentioned, encourage your child's uninhibited flow of ideas. A strawberry and ham shake might work; peanut pancakes could be delicious.

- Explore with your child the vocabulary of cooking. *Dice* means to cut into tiny squares shaped like dice. *Mince* means to chop into very tiny pieces. *Purée* means to make food into a smooth, thick liquid, usually using a blender or food processor. *Simmer* means to cook just below the boiling point so small bubbles rise to the surface. *Sauté* means to cook food in an open pan in a small amount of oil.

▶ Kids enjoy making their own items, such as individual meat loaves, cup-cakes, or single-sized pizzas. Little loaf pans and baking dishes are useful at times like these.

▶ Math skills are often called on during cooking. Have a conversion chart available for when your child wants to make more or less than a recipe calls for. Math is also needed when a package of something doesn't come in the amount required in a particular recipe. Supply a variety of measuring utensils, such as a kitchen scale and multiple sets of measuring cups and spoons.

▶ Since snack foods are often favorites (for some children, these provide a large part of their daily nutrition), make healthful snack-designing a priority.
*Examples:* For homemade ice pops, shakes, or blender creations, stay well stocked with frozen fruit juice concentrates, cans and jars of juices, frozen fruits, fresh fruits, yogurt, milk, oats, nuts, nut butters, raisins, honey, and cinnamon.

▶ Take your child shopping to choose fresh ingredients and dressings for a home salad bar. Try to include at least one vegetable that neither of you has ever tasted. Turn a salad into a meal with homemade biscuits.

▶ Introduce your child to the world of herbs and spices (since salt is generally far overused anyway). Has your child tasted parsley, sage, rosemary, or thyme? How about basil, tarragon, dill, or curry?

▶ Once your child figures out that one cup of uncooked rice equals three cups of cooked rice, or that one large onion makes a cup of chopped onions, or that a stick of margarine equals half a cup, have him note these details in his recipes to save time on subsequent occasions.

▶ If your child thinks bread comes in three varieties only (the soft, white kind; the wheat kind; and hot dog buns), expand this limited repertoire.
*Examples:* Try Middle Eastern pita, Mexican tortillas, Scottish scones, and the breads of other lands: chapati from India, limpa from Sweden, and men pau from China. Point out that in many cultures, bread is extremely important as a ceremonial food. For example, in Latin America on All Souls' Day, the dead are remembered by taking bread offerings to cemeteries.

# food Trips: Going Beyond the Kitchen

▶ If you have a computer, let your child enter recipes on it. He might want to computerize some ingredient lists for your favorite recipes.

▶ Enthusiastic young cooks enjoy playing restaurant. First, request a tour behind the scenes of a local fast-food eatery or, if you know someone in the restaurant business, ask for a peek at the kitchen. At home, suggest that your child make (or pretend to make) two or three kinds of cookies or other simple, popular foods. Then challenge her to design a menu for her restaurant, complete with a decorative cover. She can list selections for each meal she'll be serving, with side dishes, drinks, or desserts. Help with spelling as necessary. Your child and her friends can take turns being the restaurant manager, cook, server, and customer. You might help out by supplying pads for taking orders, play money, and plastic dishes—though most kids can improvise with whatever's at hand.

*Variations:* Suggest that your child design a menu of imaginary foods, space-travel foods, or monster foods.

▶ Teach about foreign cultures while your child learns to prepare various international dishes.

*Example:* Choose a country and look it up in an atlas. Write to its embassy in Washington, D.C., and request recipes for popular national dishes. (Your librarian can help you find the address, or find it yourself on the Internet.) While you're waiting for a reply, explore the ethnic groceries in your area. You might find Asian food stores; Italian, Middle Eastern, African, or Caribbean groceries; and Jewish delicatessens. Often such shops carry regional cookbooks with notes that can tell you a lot about a culture and an area's climate, economy, and history.

If there aren't any ethnic groceries nearby, wander the foreign-foods aisle at your supermarket. Ask someone who works at the store to explain the uses for unusual ingredients.

▶ Seek out specialty food outlets such as creameries, poultry farms, perhaps even a sausage factory, any of which might make an interesting field trip.

▶ Visit your local farmers' market. Go in the early morning and watch the stands being set up. Browse among the large variety of produce, plants and flowers, and handicrafts. The farmers' market I know in downtown Los Angeles is like a series of small, ethnic neighborhood markets laid end-to-end.

*Tip:* Stalls may charge for shopping bags, European-style, so bring your own and save money (and be environmentally responsible). Do this at supermarkets, too. Some will deduct a bit from your bill for each bag you supply yourself. If your store doesn't have this policy, your child might help you compose a letter to the manager suggesting it.

▶ Learn to eat with chopsticks. Many commercially packaged chopsticks come with printed instructions. Or visit an Asian restaurant and request a lesson. Once you and your child master this feat, celebrate with a Japanese-style family dinner. Everyone removes their shoes and sits on large, flat pillows or mats at a low table (perhaps your coffee table). Get takeout food or try a few recipes.

▶ Enroll your child in a cooking class. Some supermarkets and many kitchenware stores offer classes for kids, as do some community centers and schools.

▶ Discuss what it means for a food to be "in season." Foods in season tend to be at their least expensive and often their tastiest. Different foods are in season at different times in various parts of the country. Talk about how important climate and weather are to what you find in your local supermarket.

*Example:* Sometimes the prices of certain vegetables and fruits are much higher than usual at your local market, due to—perhaps—an unexpected chill having destroyed much of the crop in faraway states or countries.

▶ Model smart shopping for your child.

*Examples:* Make price and quality comparisons for different food items. For example, buy a generic muffin mix and a well-known brand. Does the taste difference justify the price difference to you? How about to your child? Compare price to quantity—is it always more economical to buy the larger size, or to buy two of something if the second is half-price? Figure out what it would cost to buy the ingredients to make a particular fast food at home. Is the time saved by having a restaurant prepare the food worth the expense? Which seems better: to know the nutritional content of what you're eating, or to take your chances with fast food? Collect and use coupons for a month; calculate how much money you've saved.

▶ Encourage your child to compile his own cookbook of tried-and-true recipes, perhaps illustrated with drawings or photos. Or he may prefer collecting recipes he'd like to try someday. Help him find a cookbook format that works. He might want to ask friends and relatives for their favorite recipes.

*Examples:* All-in-a-jumble-in-a-box is what some people prefer. Others paste favorite recipes in a medium-sized loose-leaf binder (my own method) or write them on 4 x 6-inch or 5 x 7-inch cards and file them away. Others create a computerized personal cookbook.

▶ Buy a copy of a magazine devoted to cooking. A subscription might motivate your child to experiment with new recipes.

▶ With your child, watch cooking shows on TV. Try to duplicate some of the preparations.

## Pasta Pointers

- There are 600 shapes and varieties of pasta, all of them easy to prepare.
- Pasta is properly cooked when it's *al dente,* which means firm "to the tooth."
- Sometimes carrots are used to color pasta orange, or spinach to make it green.
- Tubes and twists are best for chunky sauces to cling to; spaghetti, linguine, and other straight noodles are preferred for smoother sauces.

Your child might enjoy learning about and trying different types of pastas. Here are nine of the most popular:

- **spaghetti**—long, round strands; from *spago,* which means "length of string" in Italian
- **lasagna**—flat, wide noodles usually layered with sauce and cheese
- **conchiglie**—shell-shaped macaroni; from the word meaning "seashell"
- **manicotti**—large cylinders, usually stuffed with a filling; from the word meaning "small sleeves"
- **farfalle**—bowtie-shaped pasta; the word means "butterfly"
- **elbow macaroni**—curved tubes; from *macarone,* meaning "dumpling"
- **rotelle**—wheel-shaped, meaning "wagon wheel"
- **ravioli**—meat- or cheese-filled squares of pasta dough
- **fusilli**—curly spaghetti or macaroni, meaning "twists"

# food Science

▶ Help your child make the connection between calories consumed in food and calories burned through exercise. As part of your conversation, talk with your child about the uselessness of fad diets and the outright harm some of them can do to a person's health. Make sure your child understands that it's great to be active so long as the desire to burn calories isn't taken to extremes or used to make up for eating a nutrition-poor diet. Use this chart as a starting point for discussion. The number of calories burned is based on a person who weighs 130 pounds. Fewer calories would be burned by a person who weighed less than this.

| One hour of exercise | Calories burned |
|---|---|
| Swimming (crawl) | 686 |
| Basketball | 499 |
| Cycling at 12–14 mph | 499 |
| Roller skating/inline skating | 437 |
| Walking at 4.5 mph | 312 |
| Sitting and reading | 70 |
| Sitting and watching TV | 47 |

To enter weights and times for various activities, visit The Fitness Partner's Activity Calculator Web site at *www.primus web.com/fitnesspartner /jumpsite/calculat.htm.*

▶ Talk about junk foods. What's in them? Are baked snacks better for you than fried snacks? What can you tell from the food label? How about reduced-salt, reduced-sugar, and reduced-fat snack foods? Make a point of showing your child that reduced-fat cookies, for example, may have much more sugar and even more calories than the regular kind. Point out that sugar-free ice cream, for another example, may have more fat—and no fewer calories—than the kind with sugar.

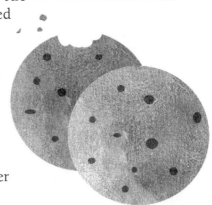

Fast foods are not normally labeled with their nutritional content, but nearly all the big chains now offer a sheet or pamphlet of information on request. Ask or send for these so you can make comparisons. *The Completely Revised and Updated Fast-Food Guide* (see Resources, page 145) provides a detailed rundown on every aspect of this American staple.

▶ An older child may be interested in investigating her school lunch program. Get her started with some thought-provoking questions.

*Examples:* Are the meals nutritionally balanced? Are they attractive? What proportion of a typical meal could be labeled junk food? Are additives used? Is there much waste? Do the teachers have the same menus as the students?

▶ Before your next grocery-shopping trip, take a few minutes to explore food labels with your child. Check out a U.S. Food and Drug Administration Web site that offers a nine-page, printable article called "Guidance on How to Understand and Use the Nutrition Facts Panel on Food Labels" at *vm.cfsan.fda.gov/~dms/foodlab.html.* (Or call 1-888-SAFEFOOD, 1-888-723-3366.) One fact to note is that what a label calls a "serving" is often a lot less than what you or your child might consider a *real* serving. Talk about the benefits of limiting the percentage of fat and sugar and increasing the percentage of dietary fiber eaten each day. Discuss how ingredient lists are ordered (from largest quantity to smallest). Talk about what "low cholesterol" and "low fat" (versus "fat free" and "reduced fat") really mean.

Packaged foods often include company Web sites on their labels. Suggest to your child that he visit the sites of a couple of his favorite foods to see what the companies choose to highlight.

Next time you're food shopping, ask your child to find a product label that shows no saturated fat, or more grams of fiber than of sugar, or a "% Daily Value" for sodium (salt) of more than 20 percent for a single serving. ("Percent Daily Values," as most labels will tell you, "are based on a 2,000 calorie diet. Your daily values may be higher or lower depending on your calorie needs." Twenty percent of a day's daily value of salt in one serving is quite high, but not hard to find.)

▶ This simple experiment shows how chemicals from our body (the enzymes in saliva) break down starch molecules. Have your child spit into a small jar of baby-food bananas or sweet potatoes. Leave the jar unrefrigerated overnight. By morning, the enzymes in the saliva will have turned most of the starchy food into a liquid.

▶ It's easy to observe the chemistry of foods when sugar dissolves in hot water, gelatin changes from a liquid to a solid in the refrigerator, yeast causes dough to rise, water boils into steam, and a soft-boiled egg blackens a silver teaspoon (the sulfur in the egg white does it). Stop your child before she tries to stir something hot with a metal spoon, explaining that metal conducts heat. Steer her towards a plastic or wooden spoon.

▶ Make carrot curls and ponder why they do what they do. Using a vegetable peeler, shave off long strips of carrot and pop them into a bowl of ice water. The strips will curl because the fibers on the outer edges of the carrot are longer and more stretched out from growing. Ice water tightens the stretched fibers and makes them curl.

▶ Other scientific conversation starters: Each adult consumes about half a ton of food and drink every year. The small intestine, which separates what your body can use from what it can't, is about twenty feet long in adults. The human stomach contains hydrochloric acid, which is powerful enough to dissolve cement and would burn your finger if you touched it.

## Table Manners

- Everyone enjoys food more when it's served in a pleasing environment. Your child can help brighten family meals by making place cards or napkin rings, folding paper or cloth napkins in pretty shapes, or designing a centerpiece for the table (a stuffed-animal tableau?). Encourage him to help you arrange food attractively on the plate. Try eating by candlelight for a special treat.

- Talk about table manners. Discuss differences between what's acceptable at home, at a friend's house, and at a restaurant.

- Point out how food customs and etiquette change from one era to another, and from country to country.
  *Examples:* In some traditional Middle Eastern cultures, people eat with their hands from a communal dish. Right-handed European diners don't switch their fork from their left hand to their right when cutting and eating food, as do many people in the United States. Instead, they use their left hand both for cutting and for eating (lefties use their right hand). Try it.

# Resources

*Alphabake! A Cookbook and Cookie Cutter Set* by Debora Pearson (New York: Dutton Books, 1995). Ages 3–8. Why not learn the letters of the alphabet while becoming familiar with kitchen skills? This book comes with a tin cookie sheet and a set of plastic, oven-safe cookie cutters in the form of letters.

**CFSAN for Kids & Teens (Center for Food Safety and Applied Nutrition)**, *vm.cfsan.fda.gov /~dms/educate.html*. This site about nutrition and food safety includes a coloring book, word match, crossword puzzle, quiz, and more.

*The Completely Revised and Updated Fast-Food Guide: What's Good, What's Bad, and How to Tell the Difference* by Michael Jacobson, Ph.D., and Sarah Fritschner (New York: Workman Publishing, 1992). Be well informed before you choose your next fast-food meal.

*Creepy Cuisine* by Lucy Monroe (New York: Random House, 1993). Ages 9–12. Recipes that sound repulsive (Wild Lice, Vomit Vinaigrette, Gangrene Scrambled Eggs) but are quite edible.

**Epicurious**, *www.epicurious.com*. This site contains kid-friendly recipes, as well as a food dictionary, cooking tips, and information on cooking basics and food etiquette.

*Gobble Up Science: Fun Activities to Complete and Eat* by Carol A. Johmann (Huntington Beach, CA: Learning Works, 1996). Ages 6–12. What in nature is safely edible? This book gives information on how to make a dandelion salad, a cake using violet paste, and more.

*The Healthy Body Cookbook: Over 50 Fun Activities and Delicious Recipes for Kids* by Joan D'Amico and Karen Eich Drummond (New York: John Wiley & Sons, 1999). Ages 8–12. The activities and recipes in this book teach biology and use simple household ingredients.

*The Hole in the Wall Gang Cookbook: Kid-Friendly Recipes for Families to Make Together* by Paul Newman and A. E. Hotchner (New York: Fireside, 1998). More than seventy celebrity recipes, plus photographs and letters from the campers at the Hole in the Wall Gang Camp for seriously ill children.

*Kids Can Cook: Vegetarian Recipes* by Dorothy R. Bates and Suzanne Havala (Summertown, TN: The Book Publishing Co., 2000). Ages 9–12. This spiral-bound cookbook contains vegetarian recipes that have been kitchen-tested by kids.

*Kids Cook! Fabulous Foods for the Whole Family* by Sarah Williamson and Zachary Williamson (Charlotte, VT: Williamson Publishing, 1992). Ages 4–12. Creative recipes for every meal, written by two kids.

*Kids Cooking: Scrumptious Recipes for Cooks Ages 9 to 13,* edited by Chuck Williams (Alexandria, VA: Time-Life, 1998). Ages 9–13. This cookbook features a color photo of each finished recipe, pictures of each piece of equipment needed, and illustrated, step-by-step instructions.

*Loaves of Fun: A History of Bread with Activities and Recipes from Around the World* by Elizabeth M. Harbison (Chicago: Chicago Review Press, 1997). Ages 8–12. Harbison not only provides a history of bread from ancient times to the present day, but also includes two dozen recipes and five activities related to bread making or bread ingredients. The text is lively, and directions for recipes and activities are clearly written.

*The Mash and Smash Cookbook: Fun and Yummy Recipes Every Kid Can Make!* by Marian Buck-Murray (New York: John Wiley & Sons, 1998). Ages 6–12. More than fifty recipes with names and ingredients that appeal to kids (like Spaghetti Soup and Green Monster Mash). Most of the recipes don't require the use of a stove; instead, kids get to use their hands to mash, bash, pound, and smash up the wacky dishes.

*Pretend Soup and Other Real Recipes: A Cookbook for Preschoolers & Up* by Mollie Katzen (Berkeley, CA: Tricycle Press, 1994). Ages 4–8. Nineteen easy, tasty recipes using healthful ingredients.

*Science Experiments You Can Eat* by Vicki Cobb (New York: HarperCollins, 1994). Ages 8–14. This is a science book, not a cookbook. The results, however, are all edible, and you can learn a lot about kitchen chemistry.

**The Searchable Online Archive of Recipes (SOAR),** *soar.berkeley.edu/recipes.* Search this site for more than 70,000 recipes, all searchable by type (main dish, snack, holiday foods, special diets, cooking for/with kids), region, and ethnicity.

**USDA for Kids,** *www.usda.gov/news/usdakids/index.html.* The USDA (U.S. Department of Agriculture) has useful information on food safety, nutrition, the food pyramid, food-related science, backyard conservation, and more.

**Veggies Unite!,** *www.vegweb.com.* A good online resource for vegetarians or any lover of vegetables (both adult and child). Filled with vegetarian recipes, related pages (gardening, veggie poetry, veggie testimonials, and a recipe exchange where you can post and respond to questions), and reference tools (such as a culinary dictionary and measurement conversions).

# CHAPTER 11

# THE JUNIOR GEOGRAPHER

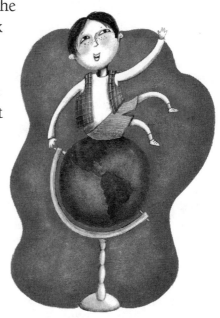

**W**hen my colleague's son Max was five, he knew that Madeline, the children's book character, lived in "an old house in Paris." His parents had shown him Paris on a map and told him that he'd have to take an airplane and fly over the ocean to get there. They'd discussed the Olympics with him, explaining that the games take place in different cities around the world and that athletes come from many countries to compete. He knew he lived in Rockville, Maryland—whenever they would visit a friend, he'd ask his mother, "Do they live in Maryland, too?" He could even point to the United States on a globe.

Even young children like Max are able to grasp that a map or globe represents places in the real world. According to psychologists who have researched children's sense of place, most kids as young as three can use a simple map to find something hidden. For instance, if you were to show your preschooler that you'd "hidden" a toy behind a chair in the living room, and then were to show him a simple map of the living room and ask where the toy is hidden, he'd probably be able to point to the correct spot on the map. By five, almost all kids can manage this.

If you showed a young child—once she'd gotten the idea that a map represents a larger space—a piece of paper (a simple hand-drawn map) indicating with an "X" where a toy was hidden in her sandbox, she could probably go and dig up that toy with surprising accuracy.

# It's 10 A.M.—Do Your Kids Know Where They Are?

Despite the potential kids have to learn map skills, most Americans have only a foggy notion of geography. Tests have repeatedly shown that American students don't perform as well on geography as do their peers in other countries. And even though many states have implemented new geography courses and standards at the high school level, schools haven't substantially changed the curriculum in the lower grades. As a parent, though, you have the opportunity to help make geography an intriguing and even creative activity for your child.

According to Matt Rosenberg, professional geographer and geography guide for the Web site *About.com*, kids need to learn geography because they need to understand that there are places besides just home and school. They also need to understand the connections between those places.

"Geography helps kids build their mental maps," explains Rosenberg, "which helps them put the whole rest of the world into perspective as they get older. So when they hear something on the news, they have a sense of where it's happening. Home is your first mental map—how to get from the bed to the bathroom—and then you need to build on that so that you can fit the whole world into your mental map and grasp how it all relates to home."

Keep in mind that geography involves more than maps. Geography is actually a form of basic literacy. It's a way of thinking about the world, a way of asking questions about how people, land, and other resources relate to each other. As your child grows, sharing geography-related activities and games will help increase her understanding and appreciation of her place in the world. Your child gains so much by knowing that the city or town she lives in is part of a larger region, state or province, country, continent, and world. (Chapter 12, on cultural diversity, suggests additional ways to deepen this global awareness.)

An added reason to introduce your daughter, in particular, to geography is that girls typically don't do as well as boys on geographic tasks and tests. Thus, by working with your daughter—and making geography fun—you'll be giving her the skills and confidence she needs.

Another plus is that, even if a sense of direction is largely inborn and hard-wired, it can be helpful to spend time practicing the skills of locating oneself in space. By playing at geography now, your child may spend less time lost and confused later.

# Maps and More

How to begin? Help your child get a good grounding in geography by making it part of your lives. Begin with the concrete—maps and globes—and work your way toward more abstract concepts.

▸ Beginning when your child is a preschooler, talk about maps. Tell your child that a map is simply a handy way to show the world in a small space. What direction is at the top of every map? (Make it clear that north is not always "up," however.) Explain the tiny symbols in the corner of the map. Make a point of using directional language. Say, "We're going north today, to visit the zoo," and "When we turn left here, we'll be going east, toward the ocean."

▸ Put signs indicating direction (north, south, east, west) on the walls of your child's room or any other room of your home. Give your child instructions that make use of these, such as, "Please go sit in the chair near the west wall of the living room."

▸ To make the purpose of maps more obvious, ask your child to dictate or write a "word map" for someone who wants to know how to reach his school or some other location from your home. For example, "Turn left at the stop sign, turn right at the oak tree, go three miles. . . ." Then draw a simple map to the location, including street names, and compare the two ways of giving directions. (Your child may find, as I sometimes do, that word maps do the trick quite well. However, finding where you are, mid-journey, on a word map can be confusing at times.)

▸ Hang up a map of the world where everyone in your family can see it. As you read the newspaper or watch the TV news with your child, point out locations of stories. Ask your child to find these places on the map and place stickers on them. Introduce the idea of scale and explain that an inch can represent a block, a mile, or fifty miles.

▸ Buy a globe, if you don't already have one. Compare the globe to a standard flat map and notice how the shapes of the countries are different on each. (A globe shows countries in more accurate relationships geographically than a map does.)

▸ Turn a map or globe upside down and see how that affects your perceptions of the world. Does it make a difference when South America is above North America, or Africa is above Europe? Tell your child about a map published by an Australian company called "McArthur's Universal

Corrective Map of the World," which shows Australia in the center. You might sketch such a map for your child (put the United States or some other country in the center) so he can grasp how this might change a person's perception of where his country is in the world.

▶ When your child is five, get her a compass. Show her how to find north and mark it on the maps she makes herself. Then, when she's a little older, point out the midway points: northeast, southeast, northwest, southwest.

▶ Make a compass. You'll need a bowl full of water, a steel sewing needle, a cork or piece of foam, a magnet, and a piece of tape. Magnetize the needle by rubbing the magnet across it ten times in the same direction. If your needle will stick to a piece of metal (such as your refrigerator door), then it's sufficiently magnetized. Attach the side of the needle to the cork with tape and put it in the bowl of water. Your child will discover that the needle always points the same way (north), no matter how the compass is turned.

▶ Laminate maps, or parts of one map, to use as breakfast place mats. Put your child's daily vitamin in a new location—a different neighborhood, city, state, or country—each morning. Ask, "Where's your vitamin?" and have your child name the location. You might also have your child figure how far the vitamin "traveled" since yesterday.

## Open-Map Quiz

Make up some questions that can be answered by looking at a map of the United States, such as:

• How many states begin with "A"?

• How many states have only one syllable in their names?

• Which states have north, south, east, or west in their names?

• Where does the Mississippi River meet the Missouri River? (Introduce the idea of how big cities evolved from trading centers that were located near rivers or river junctions.)

On a world map or globe, have your child find all the countries that border particular bodies of water. For example, Norway, the United Kingdom, Denmark, Germany, and the Netherlands all border the North Sea.

▶ Hang a city or town map in a central location and place stickers on (or circle with a brightly colored marker) all your family's "hangouts": school, place of worship, grocery store, electronics superstore, hardware store, park, post office, bank, movie theaters, video store, or favorite pizza place.

▶ Map the familiar. On a large sheet of paper, have your child draw a detailed map of his room. You can help draw the outline, and he can draw the furniture in the correct spots. Add windows and doors. How about a map of your home, inside and outside?

   Now map the entire neighborhood. First, take a walk. Point out street names on corner signs, house and business addresses, apartments, schools, fire stations, and childcare centers. Suggest that your child decide on a set of symbols to represent trees, hydrants, water, power lines, farms, fields, businesses, or parks. Show these in the map's key.

   Your child might like to make some of the landmarks out of cardboard or blocks of wood.

▶ Take a walk in your neighborhood, making a point of turning several times (try one of the many walks described in Chapter 5, pages 71–77). After you return home, draw your young child a simple map of where you went, noting the main points of interest, such as a bus stop, willow tree, or broken gate—whatever you both noticed. Have your child move a finger along the path you took, showing which way you went at each turn. Ask, "Which direction did we turn after we stopped to look at the willow tree?"

▶ Give your child a local map and ask him to choose a spot some distance from your home or street. Then have him direct you to that spot with clear instructions: face north, go two blocks, turn west, go one block. See if you can find the location by using his verbal directions.

# Everyday Geography

Here are more ways to help you make geography a familiar, enjoyable part of your child's life:

▶ Help your child find out, by reading labels, where her clothes and toys were made. Then locate those countries or cities on a map or globe.

▶ Ask friends and relatives to send your child postcards from their hometowns, vacation spots, and travels.

▶ Introduce your child to hobbies and collections that stimulate the study of geography, such as coins, stamps, dolls, flags, or maps.

▶ Draw a family tree indicating the country of birth of each family member. You might also place pins or stickers on a world map showing where family members (or friends) were born, live, or have lived.

▶ Increase awareness of places by singing songs with your child that refer to geographic locations. For starters, try "This Land Is Your Land," "Home on the Range," "Red River Valley," and "London Bridge."

▶ Focus on the natural wonders of your own area. Go on a nature walk, making notes so you can then map the locations of the tallest tree, the largest cactus, the highest hill, a large crack or fissure in the ground, a flower bed, or a spot where leaves collect on the ground. Follow this "trail map" and add to it another time.

▶ Talk about how people shape and modify their environments, and how environments shape the way people live. If people stopped mowing and trimming the vegetation in your area, what would it look like after a year or two? After ten years? Discuss how people can adapt to very harsh terrains, such as living in extremely cold or hot places. Ask your child to consider how people's lives would change if the sun didn't set each night, or if it didn't come up each morning.

▶ After dark, shine a flashlight on a globe from several feet away. Show your child how one half of the world experiences night when the other half has daylight. By slowly rotating the globe, your child can turn night into day for country after country. Find the windows in your home where the sun first appears in the morning and where it sets.

▶ Introduce time zones. If you know people who live in other time zones, discuss what they might be doing at "your" 8 A.M. and "your" dinnertime.

▶ Discuss the place names in your area. What language did they come from? What might they tell you about the history of your location?

▶ Help your child find out the weather in other regions and countries by looking in the newspaper or on the Internet. Online, try *www.intellicast.com* (don't miss the site's Education Pages) or *cirrus.sprl.umich.edu/wxnet* (which features hundreds of links to other weather sites).

   Your child might like to choose a "sister city" and check out its weather frequently. What's it like in Bombay today?

# Geography Games

Show your child how much fun geography can be by sharing the following games and activities:

▶ **Mother, May I Travel?** Take turns being the leader ("Mother"). A player asks the leader, "Mother, may I take two giant steps to the east?" The leader may either okay the move or suggest another: "No, but you may take four baby steps to the west." If two children are playing, the first player to reach the leader becomes the new "Mother." If you're playing with one child, switch places when your child reaches you.

▶ **Zoo-ography.** As you plan a trip to the zoo, cut out small pictures of the animals you expect to see. You might also buy a set of animal pictures when you get to the zoo. At the exhibits, read the placards describing the native habitats of each animal. (Take notes.) When you get home, have your child tape the animal pictures on a large world map to show each animal's origin.

▶ **Treasure Hunt.** Hide a small toy in the park, in the backyard, or somewhere around your home. Give directions to your child to find it, either orally or written down in the correct sequence. For example, "Go two steps north, one step south, three steps east." For the child who needs it, provide a small map with the directions marked. Orient your child so north on the map is in line with north in the place where the treasure is hidden. Once your child is familiar with more advanced directional terms, such as northwest and southeast, you can include them in treasure hunts.

   *Variation:* Plant clues in various locations for your child to follow. For example, "To find the next clue, go two steps north and one step east."

▶ **Dinner in Madrid.** Once a month, plan to "spend an evening" in a different foreign city. Choose by spinning a globe and having your blindfolded child touch a spot. (If a city isn't touched, choose the nearest one or spin again.) Let's say your first stop is Madrid. Start by getting one or more books about the city from the library or by searching the Internet for information. Send for travel brochures from the visitors' bureau of Spain (or visit the library, the Internet, or a travel agency). Search out some authentic Spanish recipes.

On the night of your "visit," your child can make place mats (use clear vinyl adhesive to laminate) out of maps of Spain or of Madrid (get these from the auto club, a map store, an airline magazine, or by copying from a library book or printing from the Net). She can also make a centerpiece that in some way relates to Madrid. Have your child help you prepare at least one food typically eaten there.

*Variation:* Plan a trip around the world, stopping at a different location each night. The older the child, the more realistic you can make your travels (for example, it might take only one day to drive across Ireland, but if you stopped at museums or archaeological sites, it could take two or three).

▶ **Design-a-Town.** Begin with a large, blank piece of paper. Ask your child to invent a "perfect" town or community and to draw as realistic a map of it as possible. Show structures in the town and the geography surrounding the town. Thus, the map might include a nearby lake, mountains, farmland, factories, neighborhoods, schools, or government buildings. How will the people get needed materials and power? What ten community services are most important to a community? Where will each be located? Invite your child to give imaginative names to each feature on the map. Talk about how this invented town differs from the place you live.

This game helps kids understand the challenges pioneers faced when inhabiting a new area, how names of places may have been chosen, and the impact of the natural environment on human communities.

*Variation:* Forget about realism and make a totally mythical map. Choose a theme (monsters? bubble gum? the Internet?) and lay out and name features of this place (Monster Mountain? Gumball Falls? Cyber Province?). Don't forget the usual mapping elements: an indicator of north, a key with symbols, a mileage scale, and an explanation of the various colors.

▶ **Geography Twister.** Tape the edges of large sheets of paper (or newspapers) together, forming a giant playing surface that covers a 6 x 6-foot area of the kitchen floor (or other uncarpeted room). Using markers, and masking tape to form the outline, copy the main features of a map of your area onto the large sheet of paper. Then have one or more children stand in the center of the map. Give them directions such as these: Put your right hand on the Santa Monica Mountains. Put your left foot east of the San Diego freeway. Put your right hand north of the Los Angeles River.

*Variation:* Older children can play this on a map covering a larger area or representing several countries. You could then call out directions such as, "Put your right foot on a country where people speak German."

## Ride, Drive, Fly, Eat

Homemade games can be as much fun as those that are store bought. Consider making and playing this one. It will help children increase their recollection and understanding of directions, and since they've helped make it themselves, they may enjoy it more than many other games.

1. Make a game board by cutting a 10 x 10-inch piece of cardboard or tagboard. Divide the board into one hundred 1-inch squares, or "blocks" (ten across and ten down).

2. Print START at the top right corner and END at the lower left corner of the game board. Label the top, sides, and bottom of the board NORTH, WEST, EAST, SOUTH.

3. In one block of each row of squares, place a small picture of an item of food, drawn or cut from a magazine. Scatter the pictures so no food items are right next to each other.

4. Make forty direction cards (playing-card size, or use 3 x 5-inch index cards). Label ten each with N, S, W, and E, and place them facedown in a pile.

5. Make markers that represent vehicles by drawing or pasting small pictures onto cardboard and cutting them out, or use vehicle pieces from another game.

6. Find a single die.

Place your vehicle markers at START. Take turns choosing a direction card, rolling the die, and then moving your marker that many blocks in the direction indicated. If you land on a picture of food, you get to collect it. The game ends as soon as any one player lands on the END block. The winner is the one who has collected the most food items.

# Resources

*Atlas in the Round: Our Planet as You've Never Seen It Before* by Keith Lye and Alastair Campbell (Philadelphia: Running Press, 1999). Ages 9–12. This atlas shows countries from an overhead perspective and is more accurate than an atlas of flat maps. Includes more than 120 full-color photos.

**Carmen Sandiego Junior Detective Edition** (The Learning Company). Ages 5–8. This software program allows children to solve fictional crimes in sixty locations around the world as they learn map skills and see actual photos of countries. For children nine and older, check out "Where in the World Is Carmen Sandiego?" Find these games at your favorite store or order from the Web site, *www.learningco.com*. Another option is to visit *www.carmensandiego.com* to play the free Internet version of this popular game.

*Discover the United States of America: Puzzle Book* by Lara Bergen (Norwalk, CT: Innovative Kids, 1999). Ages 7–12. A foam puzzle of the U.S. is part of this colorful book, which features facts about each state and amusing illustrations. Write, call, or visit the Web site: Innovative Kids, 18 Ann Street, Norwalk, CT 06854; (203) 838-6400; *www.innovativekids.com.*

**Distance Calculator,** *www.indo.com/distance.* This uncomplicated site calculates the distance between any two cities in the world (as the crow flies). It also provides a map showing the two places.

**Eartha Global Explorer** (DeLorme). Ages 10 and up. This CD-ROM lets families explore detailed relief maps made from satellite imagery and plan real or imaginary trips around the world. Create plane, rail, or road-ferry routes and let Floyd, your animated travel agent, point out interesting places along the way. Find it at a local store, or visit *www.delorme.com.*

*Earthsearch: A Kids' Geography Museum in a Book* by John Cassidy (Palo Alto, CA: Klutz, 1994). Ages 9–12. A multifaceted introduction to geography that covers everything from rocks to recycling. Bound into the book are eighteen different "exhibits" (such as foreign coins and rice) that inspire questions answered by the text and photos.

**Family Expeditions,** *www.nationalgeographic.com/familyxpeditions.* This National Geographic site features an interactive atlas and numerous activities for families to share.

**GeoSafari** (Rand McNally). Ages 8 and up. This CD-ROM has questions about geography, history, and science. Available from Rand McNally stores, 1-800-234-0679, or *www.randmcnally.com/rmc/home.jsp.*

**GeoSafari Game of the States** (Educational Insights). Ages 8 and up. With this board game, players learn map skills and gain cultural information as they play their way across the U.S. Search your favorite store or order online at *www.educationalinsights.com.*

**GeoSafari Globe** (Educational Insights). Ages 3 and up. An easy-to-read, 12-inch world globe mounted on a rotating stand, just right for seeking out where world events are taking place. Also find GeoSafari Talking Globe and GeoSafari Talking Globe Traveler for ages eight to twelve. Search your favorite store or order online at *www.educationalinsights.com.*

*Helping Your Child Learn Geography* (U.S. Department of Education, 1996). A booklet of maps, activities, and lists of resources. Write: Consumer Information Center, Pueblo, CO 81009, or read the booklet online at *www.ed.gov/pubs/parents/Geography/intro.html.*

**Houghton Mifflin Social Studies Center,** *www.eduplace.com/ss/index.html.* Features the GeoNet game for children ages nine and up, in which players answer geography questions based on national geography standards.

**Inflatable Animal Globe** (Action Products International). Ages 3–7. An inflatable, 16-inch globe that shows animals in their native lands. Check your local store or order online at *www.apii.com.*

**Kids Web Geography,** *www.kidsvista.com/SocialStudies/geography.html.* Check out this site, which focuses on virtual tours of places around the world and on maps and cartography.

*The Kingfisher Young People's Atlas of the World* (New York: Kingfisher Books, 1997). Ages 6–12. This atlas has photos, illustrations, maps, and charts of facts and figures.

**K12online.com,** *www.k12online.com.* A Rand McNally site that's a great geography resource. It includes activities and products for kids, as well as products for parents and teachers.

**My First Amazing World Explorer** (DK Multimedia). Ages 5–10. The activities on this CD-ROM begin with the creation of a passport that allows children to sign in and track their progress throughout the game. Players can then visit faraway places, send postcards, and collect stamps in their passports. Order online at *www.dkonline.com/dkcom/dk/1cat.html.*

*National Geographic World.* Ages 8–14. This magazine published by the National Geographic Society has colorful features and activities about the planet, animals, nature, sports, and more. Call 1-800-638-4077 to subscribe, or check out the online edition at *www.nationalgeographic.com/world.*

*National Geographic World Atlas for Young Explorers* (Washington, DC: National Geographic Society, 1998). Ages 6–12. Colorful photos, clear maps, and brief cultural tidbits.

**National Weather Service,** *www.nws.noaa.gov.* Everything you want to know about the weather.

**Parks Canada.** 25 Eddy Street, Hull, Quebec Canada K1A 0M5; 1-888-773-8888; *www.parkscanada. gc.ca.* This government organization can provide maps, brochures, and information regarding Canada's many national parks.

*The Reader's Digest Children's Atlas of the World,* edited by Colin Sale (Pleasantville, NY: Reader's Digest, 2000). Ages 6–12. Maps and facts, plus hands-on projects and activities.

**Travel the World with Timmy!** (IBM). Ages 4–7. This computer game offers kids an interactive passport to the sights, sounds, and customs of three countries—Argentina, Japan, and Kenya. Besides the games, puzzles, and other activities, children can create stories from given elements and hear them read aloud in English, Swahili, Spanish, or Japanese. Find it at your favorite local or online store.

**Uncle Happy's Train Game** (Mayfair Games). Ages 6 and up. As players deliver products by drawing tracks on a wipe-off board of the U.S., they learn the location of the states. Search your favorite store or contact Mayfair Games at (708) 458-3900; *www.coolgames.com.*

**The U.S. Department of the Interior.** P.O. Box 37127, Washington, D.C. 20013-7127. This government office offers maps of more than three hundred parks, scenic trails, battlefields, and historic sites that are under the care of the National Park Service. Also search the kid-centered Web site, *www.doi.gov/kids/,* which offers geography links for children.

**The U.S. Geological Survey.** This government office produces all kinds of maps covering the entire world. For more information, call 1-888-ASK-USGS (1-888-275-8747) or visit *library.usgs.gov/faq.html.* Also check out the USGS Learning Web, *www.usgs.gov/education/,* for maps, resources, and links.

**Where in the World?** (Aristoplay). Ages 8 and up. This world awareness/geography game for 2–6 players includes 195 country cards and may be played in a variety of ways. Available from Aristoplay, 8122 Main St., Dexter, MI 48130; 1-800-634-7738; *www.aristoplay.com/where.htm.*

**World Wall Map, Laminated** (Rand McNally) Ages 3 and up. An inexpensive, 32 x 21-inch world map with a write on/wipe-off laminated surface. Available from Rand McNally stores, 1-800-234-0679, or *www.randmcnally.com/rmc/home.jsp.*

# CHAPTER 12

# CULTURAL DIVERSITY: IT'S ALL RELATIVE

**N**ot too long ago, *culture,* for many of us, meant looking at celebrations, rituals, foods, and dress from faraway lands. While learning about such traditions is always worthwhile— and fun—our understanding of culture has expanded. To explore culture with your child, you can also investigate your own neighborhood, community, and country—even explore your family.

Culture, on a very basic level, refers to commonalities that run through a group of people with a shared heritage. Religion, ethnicity, and race reflect culture; so do shared history, attitudes, and beliefs. Your child, like most people of any age, is likely to believe that her culture—her way of doing things—is the "right" one and that others are a bit "funny." Most of us take for granted the givens of our own community or society until something makes us aware that people of other backgrounds don't always experience life the same way we do.

As you undertake a casual study of other cultures with your child, aim for an appreciation of differences. Avoid accepting or fostering stereotypes. As Amy Klauke of the multicultural children's magazine *Skipping Stones* phrased it, "We walk a tightrope when we explore cultural diversity, because we don't want to create more generalizations to replace the old ones." Help your child appreciate both Western and non-Western cultures. Ideally, an awareness of cultural diversity leads to an awareness of individual differences, increased appreciation of the incredible variety of human attributes, and flexible thinking. These habits of mind should naturally lead to less prejudice and stereotyping.

The activities and topics in this chapter, ranging from the earthbound to the "cosmic," can be starting points for discussions. Whenever possible, turn your conversations to hands-on experiences. Before you delve in, here are some ideas to keep in mind.

- **Traditional foods, celebrations, and songs are part—but not all—of a culture.** The complexities of culture are difficult for younger children to understand, so it makes sense to begin with what's more tangible and concrete, such as traditional foods, dances, and songs. As your child gets older, discuss the more abstract concepts related to culture: How do people of a given culture regard aging and death? Raising children? Time? Personal space?

- **Studying culture isn't only about looking at differences.** While this may be what stands out, it's also interesting to look at commonalties. All people, for instance, have the same basic needs for nurture, food, shelter, communication, and companionship.

- **All members of a cultural group are not the same.** Individuals are just that—individual.

- **Like many things, cultural practices change over time.** It's not unusual for some children (especially younger ones) to believe, for example, that all Native Americans live in tepees or that people in Scotland always wear kilts. These misconceptions will continue (often without your knowledge) until someone dispels them.

- **We all form and use stereotypes, often without realizing it.** This is universally true. Your child will be more comfortable talking about cultural differences and stereotypes with you if you begin by admitting that there's much you yourself need to learn and many attitudes you need to examine.

- **Everyone is part of a culture.** A child who sees the beautiful traditional dress of one group may be saddened if he doesn't believe he has something similar in his family. Reminding a child that culture is so much more than what the eye sees can help. Does your family have a special greeting whenever you see each other after a long time? Do you have particular rituals around dinnertime? What kind of routines do you follow at bedtime? All of these questions relate to culture.

# Learning About Basic Needs

Finding out how people of other cultures meet their basic needs for food, clothing, and shelter provides some of the most obvious contrasts to your own culture. Such an investigation also offers chances for a range of sensory experiences, and thus is a good starting point for younger children.

▶ To broaden your child's awareness of how foods can differ, venture together into restaurants that offer authentic ethnic foods.

*Examples:* Many kids have tasted egg rolls, tacos, and spaghetti. Why not try something from Ethiopia, Thailand, India, Israel, or Germany? My son Simon quickly took to the unusual flavor of Thai iced tea, a sweet drink he encountered at a Thai restaurant when he was ten.

*Variation:* Search newspapers, cookbooks, and the Internet for recipes that represent foods from other cultures. Decide on some to try. If possible, shop for ingredients at a store that specializes in foods of a particular country or region. Take your time and explore the shop. Ask questions.

▶ People in other countries have their own styles of dress. In the library or on the Internet, look for pictures of clothing from various cultures. Or look through magazines and compare how people dress in different parts of your country. Browse in specialty doll stores to see the clothing, often detailed and authentic, on the many international dolls. (Point out to your child that the clothing on these dolls is often ceremonial—dress that people once wore routinely but now wear for cultural celebrations.) For great pictures of children from various countries, seek out the book *Children Just Like Me* (see Resources, page 178).

*Examples:* Talk about what it would be like to wear Bavarian lederhosen, a Korean hanbok, a Ghanaian dashiki, a Muslim hijab, or many layers of cloth, as is the custom in the Arabian desert. Wrap a sheet, sari- or kimono-style, around your child.

▶ People also live in a variety of structures. Maybe you live in an apartment building in a large city. How would your life be different if you lived in a rambling farmhouse miles from town? If you lived in a house built on stilts as protection from animals? In an igloo (which Inuit people built of sod, wood, or stone when permanent, of blocks of snow or ice in a dome shape when temporary)? In a mud hut?

▶ Talk about different climates and how they influence people's lives. Climate affects cultural development much more than most children realize.

*Examples:* How might the life of a child in one of Canada's Northwest Territories differ from that of a child in Los Angeles, California, or on the island of Fiji? What if you lived where the night or the daylight lasts for six months at a time? Where it rains nearly every day of the year? Where it hardly ever rains? How would this affect your moods? Your activities?

# Exploring Cultural Attitudes

Attitudes toward important parts of life—childhood, growing up, aging, illness—differ widely from society to society. Here are some examples and questions to use as conversation starters with your child.

▸ Each state in the United States has a legal age at which young people are considered adults, usually eighteen or twenty-one. In many societies, certain behavior is required before a child is given the privileges of adulthood. What does your child think it means to be an adult?

In some societies and cultures, the crossing of the line from childhood to adulthood is clearly marked by ceremonies and rites of passage. Think about and discuss any rites of passage your family observes.

*Examples:* In many Jewish families, boys and girls mark their religious adulthood at age thirteen with the ceremony of Bar Mitzvah for boys and Bas (or Bat) Mitzvah for girls. Some cultures celebrate graduation from particular levels of school as a rite of passage into adulthood. And still others mark adulthood after a child has performed a predetermined act, such as spending time alone in the wilderness or plowing a field independently.

▸ Youth is highly valued in some cultures, while other cultures honor and value age. Birthdays are big occasions for many elderly people of Latin American or Asian descent, since advancing years often bring additional power and prestige; being called "the old one" is an honor. In many families in the United States, birthday celebrations often get less and less elaborate the older a person gets.

Ask your child to consider these questions: Do you think it's a good thing or a bad thing to be old in the country you live in? What about being young? What is something you can do to honor both an elderly and a young person you know? (Make a "You're Appreciated" certificate? Write a poem about the person? Sing him or her a song?)

▸ Talk with your child about various cultures' funeral customs and attitudes toward death. (See Chapter 6, pages 82–83, for more on this subject.)

▶ Different cultures have different norms when it comes to privacy or "personal space." Talk with your child about your family's views on privacy. Do you read each other's mail or email? What is your policy about opening closed doors?

   *Example:* People from some cultures share one bedroom or even one large bed with the entire family. In other cultures, children sleep in rooms separate from their parents. And in others, there isn't a "bedroom" at all, but rather one room that serves all purposes. What kind of sleeping arrangement is comfortable for you?

▶ The expanding discipline of transcultural medicine or cross-cultural health care teaches health-care workers to be sensitive to cultural differences that may lead to conflicts or misunderstandings. The ways people react to pain and sickness, as well as their beliefs about medical treatment and death, are deeply ingrained in their culture. Certain Native Americans, for example, won't take red pills for religious reasons. People from some cultures prefer doctors to start an exam with some casual conversation, while others expect formal politeness.

   Discuss how your family deals with illness. Do you rest when you're not feeling well, or do you carry on normal activities? Do you drink a special beverage when you're ill—a particular tea or warm milk, perhaps? Does a person who's sick get to play and watch TV, or is he expected to stay in bed?

# Nodding, Nose-Tapping, and Other Body Language

Depending on where you are in the world, body language and common gestures mean entirely different things. What's funny or friendly in one culture may be rude or even obscene in another. A gesture meant to comfort may instead provoke anxiety or antagonism.

Many people who travel widely educate themselves about these cultural differences, but anyone—traveler or not—can learn about and appreciate how much is conveyed by the unspoken.

▶ Nodding the head to signify yes is not a universal gesture. To some people from Greece, Turkey, and various Middle Eastern regions, nodding means no. The way many Westerners wave good-bye is the same way some Middle Eastern cultures indicate "come here."

Suggest that your child make up some entirely new gestures. How about touching the tip of her nose to mean "I'm curious—please tell me what you're talking about"? Or puffing her cheeks to indicate impatience; "*When* can I go outside and play?"

▶ In Great Britain, people tap the side of their nose to show that something is confidential. The sign many Westerners use to indicate "OK" (touching the tip of the forefinger to the tip of the thumb), means "you're worth zero" in France and Belgium, and something vulgar in Brazil, parts of southern Italy, Greece, and Turkey. Placing your index finger to the temple, with the other fingers curled, can mean "that person is smart" in the United States, but "that person is stupid" in Europe. It can also mean the opposite in both places, depending on the context.

Suggest that your child make a collection of gestures or body language she notices people using. Can she think of other gestures with multiple meanings?

▶ Different cultures have different ideas of how close people should be when speaking with one another. Many men in the United States subconsciously stand 18 to 20 inches from another man while talking—and a few inches farther from a woman. In France and Latin America, people are generally comfortable standing closer, about 13 inches from a conversational partner.

Have your child experiment with moving closer or farther away than usual when talking with a friend. How does the friend react?

▶ In some cultures, people tend to look directly at their conversational partners. In others, it's considered respectful to keep eyes cast downward while in conversation. Discuss these differences with your child, noting your own style.

▶ In Japan, a listener uses short answers, called *aizuchi*, to show he's paying attention to a speaker. Aizuchi includes words like *ee* (which means yes), *soo-desu-ka* ("Is that so?"), and *soo-deshoo-ne* ("It must be so."). If the listener doesn't use these words frequently, the speaker feels uneasy.

Can your child think of any equivalents in English? (How about "Hmmm" or "Uh-huh"?)

▸ In some cultures, when one person is speaking, the other person isn't supposed to interrupt. A pause is the cue for the second person to speak. But in other cultures, interrupting the speaker is considered a normal part of conversation. And still in others, circumstances, such as mealtime, change the dynamics of conversation, and everyone can talk at once. What are the standards for interrupting during conversations in your family?

*Variation:* Some studies of men and women in conversation have found that men interrupt more often to change the direction of the conversation, whereas women more typically interrupt to express agreement or understanding. Notice if these generalizations apply in your home and talk about this with your older children.

# Time Traveling

Your child may be surprised to learn that the Western concept of linear time isn't shared by everyone. The Hopi Indians, for example, have no verb tenses in their language for past, present, and future. Some Eastern religions speak of transcending time to enter eternity. And our individual perception of time can differ depending on our age or stage of life; often the older we are, the faster time seems to go.

Many North Americans are very conscious of the need to be "on time." In other cultures, especially those in southern Europe and Latin America, it's permissible to be late, even for business appointments. When a host in South or Central America wants dinner guests to arrive at 7:30, he has the option of telling them to come at 7:30 "American time." Otherwise, guests are likely to arrive closer to 10.

▸ When California psychologist Robert Levine, author of *A Geography of Time* (see Resources, page 179), worked as a visiting professor in Brazil, he noticed that clocks everywhere were set to vastly different times and that no one seemed to mind. He also reported that while many students were relaxed about arriving quite late to his classes, many also stayed long after class was over, something his American students seldom did.

A study Levine later carried out showed that Brazilian students defined being late for lunch as arriving thirty-three-and-a-half minutes after the scheduled time, compared to only nineteen minutes for California students. When he translated a time survey into Spanish for a Mexican sample, he found that even the language of the questionnaire presented a problem, since the verbs "to wait for," "to hope for," and "to expect" are all translated in Spanish as *esperar.*

When you call your child for supper or to do some chore, how many minutes do you wait before you feel she's "late"? Is her perception the same as yours?

▶ We often talk about life in different countries as being "fast-paced" or "slow-paced." In another study he carried out, Robert Levine tried to determine a country's "pace of life." He and his researchers measured the accuracy of a country's bank clocks, the speed at which pedestrians walked, and the average time it took a postal clerk to sell a customer a single stamp. Then they ranked different countries around the world.

Japan ranked first, for fastest pace of life. The United States came in second and England third. Italy, Taiwan, and Indonesia were among the countries with the slowest pace.

Travelers from fast-paced countries who are visiting slower-paced ones sometimes get frustrated and annoyed when they don't get what they want "right away." But there are different paces of life within any given country, too. City life is often considered faster-paced than suburban, small town, or rural life. There are also different paces of life in different regions of any given country. Talk about this with your child. What pace is your family used to? What does your pace of life have to do with where you live?

▶ If your family lives by the clock, it may be enlightening to spend a weekend day without any reference to time. Put your watches in a drawer, cover all the clocks, and don't check the time on the computer, radio, or TV. See what happens.

# Learning About the Arts

You can learn a lot about a culture by studying its arts. For example, the aesthetics of music vary widely among cultures. The instruments differ, as do the rhythmic and harmonic patterns. Yet there are similarities as well.

While a banjo is a traditional instrument in Japanese and Zambian cultures, the instruments are only vaguely like the American bluegrass banjo. And some American folk musicians play fiddles, which aren't at all like those that Chinese or Iranian musicians use.

In Western music, rhythm is usually a regular pulse, divided into regular groups. In the music of sub-Saharan Africa, the rhythms are extremely complex. Tuning and musical scales are  different, too. In the Far East, the stress is on pitch and on tiny, intricate intervals. Most Indian classical music has a solo melody line, a rhythmic accompaniment, and a drone. And much African music is primarily percussive, played on drums, rattles, bells, and gongs. What are some similarities? Composer and conductor Leonard Bernstein studied music from around the world. Believing there might be a worldwide "musical grammar"—a language all cultures speak— he gave a fascinating example: Children all over the world, on every continent and in every culture, tease each other with the exact same two or three notes, the ones used to sing or yell, "Allee, allee, in free!"

▶ See if your library has selections of music from various cultures and regions to share with your child. If not, well-stocked music stores always carry a variety of foreign offerings. (Also check Resources, page 178.)

▶ Encourage your child to create and play homemade instruments that resemble instruments from other cultures.
    *Examples:* Make a xylophone styled after those found in Ghana: Set pieces of wood across a shoe box and play it with a pencil. Pot and pan lids can easily double as gongs like those used in Southeast Asia. Panpipes used by Peruvian Indians can be approximated by joining together a series of different-sized tubes. Stretch a string across a board, raised slightly at the ends by bridges; this resembles the Appalachian dulcimer or the ancient Egyptian monochord. Drums can easily be made from coffee tins and other cylindrical containers. Fashion a flute or a whistle by blowing across the top of a soda bottle.

▶ When your child is a competent enough reader to feel comfortable with subtitles, rent a foreign video (or seek out one of the few foreign films that have been dubbed into English). She'll begin to observe differences between films made abroad and those she's used to seeing. A few good ones to try are *Red Balloon, My Life as a Dog,* and *Le Grand Chemin.* The same Japanese director who made the critically acclaimed *Princess Mononoke* (which, although animated, is itself too adult-themed and violent for children) also made two excellent, animated films for young kids: *My Neighbor Totoro* and *Kiki's Delivery Service.* They're available both dubbed into English and with English subtitles.
    Discuss movies as cultural clues: How are personal relationships shown? How does the movie portray violence? What does the movie show you about the country and time period in which it was made?

Notice the slower pacing of some foreign films. To a youthful audience used to instant foods, speedy Internet connections, and the fast pace of American commercials, action films, and music videos, foreign films might seem slow. Talk about what effect the directors are aiming for with this more placid pacing.

▶ There's a rich choice of multicultural children's literature available in bookstores, schools, and libraries. Seek out books representing the views of people from other cultures, or search for books such as Arabic or Japanese fables or different versions of familiar stories like "Cinderella."

▶ Explore other arts with your child. Learn about mask making as practiced by some Native Americans, Brazilians, Zimbabweans, and others. Find out about the martial arts, which hold a special position in some cultures. (Young children especially will wonder how something that looks like fighting can be called an "art.") Your child might like to take a class in one of the martial arts. (See *Dr. Webster-Doyle's Martial Arts Guide for Parents* in Resources, page 178.) Look into dance, puppetry, and Japanese gardening and screen painting.

▶ In the Islamic religion, it's forbidden to use images of living creatures in art. That's why much of Muslim graphic art consists of floral themes, geometric figures, and Arabic script.

See if your child can draw a picture using geometric figures and the shapes of letters in artistic ways.

▶ If possible, take your child to see a Chinese, Japanese, or Hmong dance troupe. Many Asian dancers use facial expressions and hand gestures to communicate the message of the dance.

Suggest that your child make up and perform a dance in which facial expressions and hand gestures tell a story, with a minimum of foot movement.

# Learning About Language

▶ *Aloha,* which means love, is used for both hello and good-bye in Hawaiian. *Shalom,* which means peace, is used for both hello and good-bye in Hebrew.

With your child, learn how to say hello or some other common word in several languages. Observe the similarities and differences.

▶ Introduce your child to the concept of an international language. Estimates vary widely, but it's likely that more than two million people around the world speak Esperanto, which was invented by Dr. Ludwig L. Zamenhoff of Poland and first presented to the public in 1887. Esperanto uses mostly Latin roots and has a consistent, logical, simplified grammar. Spelling is phonetic.

*Examples:* Nouns in Esperanto always end with the letter "o," adjectives with "a." Plurals of nouns are formed by adding "j," pronounced like the "y" in *toy.* Root words are combined to form words like *horsehouse,* which quite sensibly means the place where a horse lives (used instead of "stable"). Hello is *saluton.* "The pen is blue" becomes "La pumo estas blua."

Find out more from an international Web site, *www.esperanto.net,* or a U.S. site, *www.esperanto-usa.org.* Request a free information packet online or by calling 1-800-ESPERANTO (1-800-377-3726).

▶ Some languages have more than one word for what English speakers think of as a single entity. Since ice is so important in their lives, the Inuit people reportedly differentiate among the various kinds, from slush ice to black ice. (This isn't completely clear-cut, however. In *They Have a Word for It,* Howard Rheingold speaks of the Inuits' nearly 170 words for ice. Geoffrey K. Pullum, however, in *The Great Eskimo Vocabulary Hoax,* insists there are only two Inuit words for ice. See Resources, pages 181 and 179.)

Have your child choose something important to her—stickers, ice cream, or telephones, for example—and make up words for different kinds.

▶ Dr. Vitaly Shevoroshkin, a Russian linguist at the University of Michigan, studied 140 European and Asian languages to determine if there ever existed a common ancestral language from which all others descended. After locating the fifteen oldest, most stable words in all the languages, he theorized that these words were in the vocabulary of a common language spoken 12,000 years ago.

See if your child can guess which fifteen words or concepts he identified as oldest.

(Answer: The fifteen words stand for the following concepts: I/me, two/pair, thou/thee/you, who/what, tongue, name, eye, heart, tooth, no/not, fingernail/toenail, louse, tear—as in crying, water, and dead.)

▶ Every society has evolved words to soothe its infants, with most lullabies depending on monotonous sounds and rhythms for their calming effect. *Lull* comes from Roman times, when the word *lalla* was used to quiet babies.

Here are some examples of the lull-words used in lullabies around the world: *ai lu lu* (Poland), *arroro ro ro* (Spanish-speaking countries), *a-ya ya* (Trinidad), *baloo, baloo* (Scotland), *bayu bayu* (Russia), *bom pe, bom pe* (Cambodia), *ma ma ma* (Yuma Indian, United States), *nen nen* (France, Japan), *shoheen-shal-eo* (Ireland), *su su su su* (Estonia, Poland, Ukraine, Sweden), *yo yo yo yo* (the Bantu tribe of Africa).

Make up a new lullaby with your child, using some of these lull-words.

# Gods and Gardens: Comparative Mythology

Comparative mythology in its simplest form—learning how diverse cultures have developed similar myths to explain how the world works—is worth introducing to school-age children. Though this is a complex subject, it's important to understand that the myths we're raised with aren't the only ones, and that all cultures have their own myths, equally meaningful to them.

▶ The works of Joseph Campbell are recommended reading for the parent who wants to converse knowledgeably on the topic. Or watch the six-videotape set of the PBS series *Joseph Campbell and The Power of Myth, with Bill Moyers* for a fascinating tour of comparative mythology (see Resources, page 179).

▶ Timeless symbols appear in myths and in our dreams. These symbols also appear frequently in works of art from around the world. For example, a garden appears in the mythologies of many cultures, as do floods. The snake of Judeo-Christian legend is a bringer of life in the myths of other cultures; a cobra protects the Buddha while he meditates.

Look for common symbols the next time you look through a book of art or visit an art museum with your child. For example, an egg often stands for creation or rebirth; a sun rising can also mean rebirth; a sunset may mean death; a lighted candle represents the brevity of life; milk and water represent life; children symbolize innocence; sheep stand for gentleness; clowns symbolize the imagination or the childish side of the personality.

## Family Folklore

Don't forget that your own family has a history and its own folklore. By discussing what you know of these, you'll be teaching your child how your family is both similar to and different from others around the world.

Suggest that your child interview you or other relatives, using a tape recorder, video camera, or paper and pencil. She can make up her own questions or begin with these:

- What region(s) or country (countries) did our family come from?

- Do we celebrate special occasions like birthdays, weddings, and holidays the same way our ancestors used to celebrate them?

- How did you celebrate holidays when you were young? What special games or food can you remember?

- Do you know any dances, songs, or language from "the old days"?

- Do you have any old costumes, toys, crafts, or recipes from our family's past?

Your child can also find out about family folklore by asking, for example, "Do you know of any special family 'rules'?" (For instance, in some families, you never go outside without wearing sunscreen. A friend of ours and his sister made up this rule when they were growing up: You can only eat one piece of popcorn at a time out of the bowl.)

Some books that may help your child get started:

*How to Tape Instant Oral Biographies* by William Zimmerman (Cincinnati: Betterway, 1999).

*The Family Tree Detective: Cracking the Case of Your Family's Story* by Ann Douglas (New York: Firefly, 1999).

*Do People Grow on Family Trees? Genealogy for Kids & Other Beginners* by Ira Wolfman (New York: Workman, 1991).

▶ While readers of the Old Testament learn that "in the beginning" the world was dark until God said, "Let there be light," people in the Banks Islands of Melanesia learn another description for the beginning of the world: "In the beginning, there was light. It never dimmed, this light over everything." This and other creation tales may be found in Virginia Hamilton's *In the Beginning: Creation Stories from Around the World* (see Resources, page 179).

Before or after doing some research on creation stories, suggest that your child brainstorm all the ways he thinks the world might have started. Encourage him to develop the most imaginative creation story he can.

# Fourteen More Ways to Appreciate Cultural Diversity

1. After your child has met someone new, talk about what makes this person different from your child or from another friend. Hairstyle? Height? Skin shade? Food preferences? Family make-up? Frequency of smiling? Shyness or assertiveness? Clothing? Wittiness? Friendliness? Life goals? Religion or beliefs? The point is that superficial markers of traits such as gender, race, age, and appearance are often much less outstanding than other forms of difference, and that these more genuine differences are what make us interesting. Now talk about the ways your child and this person are alike.

2. Ask your child to close her eyes, spin a globe, and see which country her pointing finger stops on (or near). Research that country and choose one of its customs to observe for an hour or a day. If the finger lands on your own country, learn about the customs of people from another region.

3. Finding yourself in an alien environment can be very disconcerting. Almost everyone who emigrates from one country to another has this experience. If your family hasn't encountered this personally, use role play to help your child understand what it means to switch from one cultural environment to another. One or both of you can pretend you've just arrived in your country. Walk around your home or neighborhood paying special attention to what might be different, unique, or strange.

4. Attend local craft shows or fairs. You're bound to see folk art and crafts that represent different regions or even countries, and you may find something that relates to your own heritage. If they're not too busy, ask the artisans about the cultural significance or tradition behind their crafts—some will even have free brochures that you can take.

5. Discuss with your child how you experience your culture differently now than your ancestors did one, two, or five generations ago. This home-based historical perspective adds insight to the study of worldwide cultural differences.

6. Get copies of foreign newspapers or magazines from several English-speaking countries, such as the United States, Canada, Australia, or England. Notice the subtle differences in the way the language is used. (For a source of copies, see "Multinewspapers" in Resources, page 180.)

7. Ask to be placed on the mailing lists of local colleges and universities. When they hold ethnic or other cultural events or exhibits, you'll know about them and can attend with your child.

8. Visit art, anthropology, and specialized ethnic museums with your family.

9. Consider attending the services or special activities of various religions. You and your child will be introduced to some of the differences in religious rituals and beliefs—plus you'll be exposed to other cultural elements, such as architecture, music, and language. Call ahead of time to the places of worship (temples, mosques, churches, or synagogues, for example) to find out whether and how visitors are invited to take part.

10. Choose a country and plan an imaginary trip. Check the Internet, the library, or a travel agency for information and maps. Take into consideration what kinds of clothing you'll need for that country's climate. What regions will you visit? What sights will you see? How will you prepare?

11. Using travel brochures as a model, have your child design a brochure about your own community. What will he highlight? What makes your area special and worthy of visiting? Do many people that live there or work there? Are there many shops? Parks? Animals? What about your community is a source of pride for its residents? Talk about what these facets tell you about your community's culture.

12. Encourage your child to call you on sweeping generalizations or stereotyping you might make. You may surprise yourself—as I did when I asked my son, "How's your new math teacher? What did he say about your first paper?" Kevin responded in a quiet voice. "*He?*"

13. With your children, compile a scrapbook of articles from newspapers and magazines relating to "structural inequality"—that is, ways in which discrimination against one group or another is upheld by the government or other institutions. This is much easier than it sounds. Articles appear frequently on issues such as discrimination against gay people in the military, against members of minority groups who apply for home mortgages,

against women in hiring and promotion, against older adults through mandatory retirement, and against people with limited English proficiency in government agencies. A related issue is lack of access for disabled people in public places.

14. Share elements of your culture (family or broader) with your friends and invite them to share their cultures with you, perhaps by way of a friendly get-together with "culture sharing" as the theme. You and your child might be surprised to find out that your friends have traditions, customs, and beliefs that you never knew about before.

## Pen Pals: The Write Stuff

Exchanging letters with someone in a foreign land offers many benefits to children. It's a great way to learn about different customs, broaden one's perspective, improve letter-writing skills, have fun exchanging postcards, photos, and souvenirs, and maybe even make a lifelong friend.

Suggest to your child that when she writes to someone whose native language isn't English, she shouldn't use abbreviations, slang, or colloquial expressions. Give her some ideas of what to write about to get her started, such as extracurricular activities, where your family lives, what you typically eat, occupations of the adults in the family, what holidays you celebrate, or what you like about school.

Here are some places where your child can find a pen pal in another country:

- GeoMail, the National Geographic Pen Pal Network. Ages 6–16. Write to National Geographic Society, Dept. GeoMail-OL, P.O. Box 96088, Washington, D.C. 20090-6088. Or print the order form you'll find online at *www.nationalgeographic.com/kids/ngo/penpal/*.

- Keypals (a feature of the Young Writers Club), *www.cs.bilkent.edu.tr/~david/derya/keypals.htm*.

- Penpals for Kids, *kidspenpals.about.com/kids/kidspenpals*. This Internet treasure trove for young pen pal seekers includes topics to write about, many places to seek a pen pal, and numerous related resources.

- Student Letter Exchange. Ages 9–19. For an application, send a self-addressed, stamped envelope to Student Letter Exchange, 211 Broadway, Suite 201, Lynbrook, NY 11563, or find an order form online (you have to print it and mail it in with a small payment) at *www.pen-pal.com*.

# Holidays Around the World

Every culture has its own unique holidays and celebrations. Even those that are widely celebrated, like May Day, are observed differently in different places. For example, on a Saturday in May, children in the Netherlands celebrate Luilak, which means "lazybones." Early in the morning, children all over the country gather in groups and walk through towns, making as much noise as possible to wake up the "lazybones" and to trick the "winter demon" into going away.

In the paragraphs that follow, I've listed a few of the many cultural celebrations and holidays that are celebrated around the world and in our own communities. Some of these are based in history, while others are rooted in religion, ethnicity, or myth. This short list is just a small sample that illustrates the many types of holidays and celebrations people observe. Begin by learning more about some of the days and events listed here, then consider looking for one of the many books that describe additional cultural celebrations.

▶ The Hindu Festival of Lights, called Divali (also spelled Dipawali), is an autumn celebration culminating in a holiday that lasts nearly two weeks. Although the practices of Hinduism vary by region, most Hindus consider Lakshmi, the goddess of prosperity, to be the reason for the festival. Believers build a temporary altar inside their homes, where they place coins and other symbols of wealth. Sweets are exchanged, and lamps are lit both inside and outside homes.

▶ December 26 marks the start of Kwanzaa, a seven-day holiday for black families to celebrate their African heritage. Kwanzaa means "first" in Swahili. The holiday, introduced in the United States in 1966, gets its rituals from African harvest festivals. On each of the seven days, a family member explains one of the principles on which the celebration is based (unity, self-determination, collective work and responsibility, cooperative economics, purpose, creativity, and faith) and how he or she practices it. Children receive gifts relating to black culture, and on December 31 an African feast is held.

▶ The Chinese New Year is a traditional spring festival celebrated by many people of Chinese descent. Find out what "year" it was when your child was born; 2001 ushered in the "Year of the Snake." To determine Chinese years, talk with a local Chinese restaurant owner or merchant or visit these Web sites: *www.man darintools.com/calconv.html* and *www.new-year.co.uk/ chinese/* (the second site also lets you send Chinese New Year's cards, read your fortune, and more).

▶ Another cultural New Year is Tet, the seven-day celebration of the Vietnamese New Year. The word is an abbreviation of *Tet Nguyen-Dan,* which means "the first morning of the first day of the new year." During Tet, many Vietnamese families plant a New Year's tree called *Cay Neu* in front of their homes (a bamboo pole is often used as a Cay Neu). Leaves are removed from the tree so that it can be wrapped or decorated with red paper, which symbolizes good luck. The last ritual of the New Year celebration is the taking down of the Cay Neu.

▶ Native Americans' Day is observed in the state of South Dakota and is dedicated to the remembrance of the great Native American leaders who contributed so much to the history of the state. This legal holiday is recognized on the second Monday in October. Festivities are organized throughout the state including events with Native American speakers, singers, and storytellers, and hands-on activities for children.

▶ The Kite Festival, an annual ritual in the town of Santiago Sacatepéquez, Guatemala, is held at the village cemetery as a celebration of a cultural myth. It's told that long ago, when evil spirits were believed to disturb the good spirits in the town's local cemetery, a magician suggested a way to get rid of the evil spirits—fly kites. Believing that the evil spirits were frightened by the noise of wind against paper, the villagers followed the magician's instructions. Kites have supposedly been flown in the cemetery as an annual event ever since, and today, the youth of the village work for weeks making detailed and intricate kites.

▶ Many holidays are solemn, sacred occasions. Ramadan, for example, is the sacred ninth month of the Islamic year, which is based on the lunar calendar. During the entire month, Muslims fast during the day and eat small meals and visit with friends and family in the evening. Ramadan is a time of worship and a time to strengthen family and community ties. The sighting of the new moon at the end of Ramadan marks the celebration of Eid ul-Fitr, which means "feast of the fast breaking."

▶ Other ethnic celebrations you can commemorate: Japanese Girls' Doll Festival (March 3), Greek Independence Day (March 25), Asian-Pacific American Heritage Week (the first week in May), Cinco de Mayo (May 5), American Indian Day (usually the fourth Friday in September), Oktoberfest (starts September 21), Ch'usok (a Korean harvest moon festival of thanksgiving, celebrated in late September or early October, in which the graves of ancestors are visited and feasts are enjoyed).

# Global Game-Playing

Learning about the variety of sports and games played around the world can be a fascinating topic to share with your child. For instance, what we know as soccer is called football in many other countries. Kickball is played as a spiritual ceremony among the Hopi Indians of the southwestern United States. And in a game called Indian kickball, played by the Tarahumara Indians of northern Mexico, an oak-root ball or stone ball is kicked by teams of three to six players along a course of twenty to forty miles.

Here are some games your family may enjoy learning about and even trying.

▶   A Chinese game called "Helping Harvest the Land" is symbolic of the communal living in the People's Republic of China. Two teams of four members each line up at the same side of the play area, usually dirt, with the equipment—a toy hoe, plastic flowers, watering can, and tricycle—at the opposite side. The first team member runs across the play area, picks up a hoe and hoes the ground five times, then returns to his or her team. The second team member plants the flowers and runs back. The third waters the flowers. The fourth picks the flowers, places them in the tricycle's basket, and then rides the trike back. The first team to complete the cycle wins.

▶   "London Bridge" has variations in other countries. In Italy it's called "Open the Gates." In Latin America it's played with a fruit theme: Each player is given the name of a fruit, which must be kept secret. The arch (made by players' hands) is dropped on the person suspected of having the name of the fruit being sung about ("Here's a woman selling apples, selling apples, selling apples . . ."). If the guess is wrong, the player is released.

▶   Some of the games we play today have long histories and are played using homemade equipment in other cultures. Tic-tac-toe and tug-of-war are seen everywhere. The game of Dominoes was invented by the Chinese at least three centuries ago. Modern European dominoes consist of twenty-eight pieces, including blanks. Chinese dominoes have thirty-two pieces and no blanks. Inuit people play with dominoes made of walrus ivory, marked with higher values but played like European dominoes.

Consider modifying a set of dominoes to imitate the way these other cultures play the game.

▶   "Cat's Cradle" is played in almost every country of the world, with people in widely separated regions making some of the same string figures. The Japanese and the Chugach Eskimos call it a girls' game, but Navaho Indian men are experts at weaving string figures. If neither you nor your child knows how to play Cat's Cradle, find someone who can teach you.

▶  "Maq," the name of an Inuit game from the Canadian Arctic, means "silence." Players sit in a circle. One player enters the middle of the circle and points to another player. That player must say "Maq" (pronounced "Muk") and then remain silent and straight-faced while the person in the middle uses gestures and expressions in an effort to make the other person laugh. If the person in the middle succeeds, the one who laughed replaces him or her in the middle. Consider playing this game at your child's next birthday party.

▶  Playing "Know Your Potato" is a good way for children to learn to appreciate individual differences. Each person selects a potato and looks at it closely. Then everyone dumps their potatoes in a pile, mixes them up, and tries to find their particular potato. The point is, although all potatoes may look alike, you'll discover differences that make each one unique.

# Resources

*All Families Are Different* by Sol Gordon (Amherst, NY: Prometheus, 2000). Ages 7–13. Various kinds of family units are described and illustrated. At the end of the book, the reader can draw his or her own home, school, self, and family.

**American Library Association: Coretta Scott King Award Books,** *www.ala.org/srrt/csking/cskaw in.html*. The Coretta Scott King Award Books are listed annually by the American Library Association on its Web site. The award recognizes African-American authors and illustrators of children's books whose works carry on the legacy of Dr. Martin Luther King Jr. and his wife Coretta Scott King.

*An Amish Year* by Richard Ammon (New York: Atheneum, 2000). Ages 5–7. Spend time with Anna, an Amish fourth-grader, as she goes about her chores and daily life through the seasons.

**Anti-Defamation League.** 823 United Nations Plaza, New York, NY 10017; *www.adl.org*. The B'nai B'rith's Anti-Defamation League publishes a catalog of materials that can be used to teach communication and respect among diverse groups. The League's Web site includes news and information about combating hate, anti-Semitism, terrorism, and more. The organization also provides tools for teachers and parents, such as a seven-page article entitled "Talking to Your Child About Hatred and Prejudice."

*Best-Loved Folktales of the World,* edited by Joanna Cole (Landover Hills, MD: Anchor, 1983). All ages. This anthology of more than two hundred folk and fairy tales from around the world provides ample proof of the universality of certain themes across cultural and historical lines.

*Chang's Paper Pony* by Eleanor Coerr (New York: Harper Trophy, 1993). Ages 4–8. This "I Can Read Book" takes place in San Francisco during the gold rush of the 1850s. The story focuses on Chang, the son of Chinese immigrants, who longs for a pony that his family can't afford.

*Children Just Like Me* by Susan Elizabeth Copsey, Barnabas Kindersley, and Anabel Kindersley (New York: DK Publishing, 1995). All ages. Published to coincide with UNICEF's fiftieth anniversary, this book records the efforts of a photographer and teacher who traveled the world for two years, meeting and talking to children.

*Cornhusk, Silk, and Wishbones: A Book of Dolls from Around the World* by Michelle Markel (Boston, MA: Houghton Mifflin, 2000). Ages 6 and up. Colorfully illustrated narratives, one paragraph per doll and one doll per page. Included are histories of the Akuaba Doll from Africa, Dairi-Sama Dolls from Japan, and the Nina, which was used in the mid-nineteenth century to smuggle medicine for sick Confederate soldiers.

*Culture Quest World Tour*, *www.ipl.org/youth/cquest/*. This site is part of the Internet Public Library. Simply click on a region and explore that area's games, recipes, national parks, and more.

*Dancing Wheels* by Patricia McMahon (Boston, MA: Houghton Mifflin, 2000). Ages 6–14. Experience a unique form of diversity by going backstage with a dance company called Dancing Wheels, comprised of a sit-down dancer in a wheelchair and her partner, a stand-up dancer. Illustrated with colorful photographs.

*Dr. Webster-Doyle's Martial Arts Guide for Parents: Helping Your Children Resolve Conflict Peacefully* by Terrence Webster-Doyle (New York: Weatherhill, 1999). A martial arts instructor explains that this discipline involves much more than physical skills. Martial arts also teach confidence, positive social values, treating others with respect, and how to avoid and resolve conflict peacefully. There's an extensive chapter on what parents can do at home to teach these skills.

*Dreaming in Color, Dreaming in Black and White: Our Own Stories of Growing Up Black in America,* edited by Laurel Holiday (New York: Archway, 2000). Ages 12 and up. An abridged version of an adult anthology of childhood remembrances. African-American adults tell their personal experiences with racism while they were growing up. Powerful and harrowing.

*EarthBeat!* P.O. Box 1460, Redway, CA 95560; 1-800-409-2457; *www.musicforlittlepeople.com*. This company explores and celebrates diversity while focusing on music. Recordings include American folk songs, African songs of liberation, Persian soul music, Polynesian dances, Latin American lullabies, and more. The catalog also features crafts and musical instruments.

*Exploring World Art* by Andrea Belloli (Los Angeles: J. Paul Getty Museum Publications, 1999). Ages 8–12. Open this book to find forty art images and objects, along with information about the cultures that produced them.

*Faces.* Ages 9–14. This periodical about world cultures publishes nine issues per year built around themes and including stories, articles, crafts, recipes, and games. Call or order online: 1-800-821-0115; *cobblestonepub.com*. The same company also publishes *Footsteps,* a magazine celebrating African-American history and achievement. See *www.footstepsmagazine.com* for more information.

*Families* by Meredith Tax (New York: Feminist Press, 1996). Ages 9–12. A book about all kinds of families (animal and human), with a strong focus on love.

*Families: A Celebration of Diversity, Commitment, and Love* by Aylette Jenness (Boston: Houghton Mifflin, 1993). All ages. Seventeen young people describe their families in their own words, illustrated by the author's photographs. Represented are families with adopted children, stepfamilies, and ethnically and religiously mixed families, among others.

*A Geography of Time: The Temporal Misadventures of a Social Psychologist* by Robert V. Levine (New York: Basic Books, 1998). A fascinating, anecdote-rich account of how each culture defines and experiences time. Levine explains, for example, how some people don't understand the concept of "wasting time," while others follow "event time" rather than "clock time." This adult book has concepts that can be understood by children ages eight and up with a little help from parents.

*The Great Eskimo Vocabulary Hoax and Other Irreverent Essays on the Study of Language* by Geoffrey K. Pullum (Chicago: University of Chicago Press, 1991). In this book for adults, the lead essay traces the idea of multiple Inuit words for ice.

*Hands Around the World: 365 Creative Ways to Build Cultural Awareness and Global Respect* by Susan Milord (Marco, FL: Garreth Stevens, 1999). Ages 4–10. Activities to share with children, from simple crafts to celebrations of unusual holidays.

*The Hero with a Thousand Faces* by Joseph Campbell (Princeton, NJ: Princeton University Press, 1989). This introduction to comparative mythology is a must for parents who want to explore the topic in depth with their older children.

*I'm Like You, You're Like Me: A Child's Book About Understanding and Celebrating Each Other* by Cindy Gainer (Minneapolis: Free Spirit Publishing, 1998). Ages 3–8. Simple words and colorful illustrations invite young children to discover, accept, and affirm individual differences.

*In the Beginning: Creation Stories from Around the World,* told by Virginia Hamilton (Orlando, FL: Harcourt Brace, 1991). Ages 8 and up. This illustrated volume contains twenty-five stories from many cultures, showing the different ways each has explained the genesis of the world or of humankind.

*Joseph Campbell and the Power of Myth, with Bill Moyers.* This six-videotape set of the PBS series will take you (and your older children) on a fascinating tour of comparative mythology. If your video store or library doesn't carry these tapes, write, call, or visit the Web site: Parabola, 656 Broadway, New York, NY 10012; 1-800-560-MYTH (1-800-560-6984); *www.parabola.org/videos/vid library2.html.* An audiocassette version (HighBridge, 1993) is also available.

*Journey Between Two Worlds* series (Minneapolis: Lerner Books, 1996–98). Ages 10–12. Each book in this series describes the difficult, often dangerous life of a refugee family in their native country and their subsequent journey to the United States. Readers will learn how the family has adjusted to a new culture while still preserving the traditions of their homeland. Titles include *A Bosnian Family, A Kurdish Family, A Hmong Family,* and many more. Request a catalog from Lerner Publishing Group, 1251 Washington Avenue North, Minneapolis, MN 55401; 1-800-328-4929; *www.lerner books.com.*

*Kids Explore America's Jewish Heritage* by Westridge Young Writers Workshop (Santa Fe, NM: Avalon Travel/John Muir Publications, 1996). Ages 9–12. This book, one of a series, presents a look at Jewish history, food, holidays, arts, famous firsts, heroes, and stories. There are also suggestions for hands-on fun. Other titles include *Kids Explore America's African American Heritage, Hispanic Heritage, Japanese American Heritage,* and *Heritage of Western Native Americans.* Call 1-800-788-3123.

*The Land I Lost: Adventures of a Boy in Vietnam* by Huynh Quang Nhuong (New York: Harper Trophy, 1986). Ages 9–12. A book of true stories about a Vietnamese boyhood, including vignettes about various relatives, crocodiles, pythons, and a pet water buffalo.

*Little Daniel and the Jewish Delicacies* by Semadar Shir (New York: Adama Books, 1988). Ages 3–10. A little boy eats his way through a year's worth of Jewish holidays in hopes of growing taller. In the process, he learns the meanings of the various foods and religious customs.

*Material World: A Global Family Portrait* by Peter Menzel (New York: Random House, 1995). All ages. Some of the world's leading photographers spent one week living with a statistically average family in various countries, learning about their work, their attitudes toward their possessions, and their hopes for the future. Then a "big picture" shot of the family was taken outside the dwelling, surrounded by all their material goods. The book provides sidebars offering statistics and a brief history for each country, as well as personal notes from the photographers about their experiences. *Material World* is a lesson in economics and geography, reminding us of the world's inequities but also of humanity's common threads.

*The Multicultural Game Book: More than 70 Traditional Games from 30 Countries* by Louise Orlando (New York: Scholastic Trade, 1995). Aimed at teachers of grades 1–6 but also useful to parents.

*Multicultural Games: 75 Games from 43 Cultures* by Lorraine Barbarash (Champaign, IL: Human Kinetics, 1999). While intended for elementary and middle-school educators, this book is also useful to parents. Activities are presented in a standard, easy-to-use format that includes information about where the game originated, the appropriate age group, the competition level, instructions for playing, and more. Each game has two special elements that help kids discover other cultures and learn more about their own. "Did You Know?" provides a brief fact about some aspect of the culture and is designed to stimulate questions and discussion. "Culture Quest" suggests additional activities that encourage deeper investigation.

**Multinewspapers.** Box 866, Dana Point, CA 92629; (949) 499-6207; *www.worldwidenewsletter.com/catalog.jhtml*. This company offers single copies of and subscriptions for English-language newspapers published around the world, from Iceland to Fiji.

*People* by Peter Spier (New York: Doubleday, 1988). Ages 4–8. This richly illustrated, oversized picture book demonstrates the diversity among people by comparing eye shape, children's games, forms of shelter, occupations, religious beliefs, and more.

**Planet Earth Music.** P.O. Box 789, Ukiah, CA 95482; 1-888-216-4029; *www.planet-earth-music.com*. This company offers a wide selection of music from around the world.

*Skipping Stones: A Multicultural Children's Magazine.* Ages 8–15. This nonprofit publication provides an avenue for children of various backgrounds to share experiences through their stories, poems, and artwork. Games and activities help kids compare and contrast various cultures. Published bimonthly during the school year. Write, call, or visit the Web site: *Skipping Stones*, P.O. Box 3939, Eugene, OR 97403; (541) 342-4956; *www.efn.org/~skipping*.

*Small World Celebrations* by Jean Warren and Elizabeth McKinnon (Torrance, CA: Warren Publishing House, 1988). For parents of children ages three to five, this book explains how to celebrate sixteen international holidays through art activities, games, songs, and snacks.

*Somehow Tenderness Survives: Stories of Southern Africa,* edited by Hazel Rochman (New York: Harper Trophy, 1990). Ages 12 and up. A collection of ten short stories by well-known writers (Doris Lessing and Nadine Gordimer, among others) who tell what it was like to grow up under apartheid. Grim, enlightening, and, unfortunately, still necessary.

*Talking Walls* and *Talking Walls: The Stories Continue* by Margy Burns Knight (Beltsville, MD: Tilbury House, 1995, 1996 respectively). All ages. A unique approach to cultural studies that asks, "What are the stories behind the great walls of the world?" Includes the Western Wall in Jerusalem, the Lascaux caves, the Great Wall of China, and some unexpected ones, such as the wall of messages outside the home of Chile's famous poet, Pablo Neruda. Also by the same publisher and author: *Who Belongs Here? An American Story.* There are also excellent, extensive activity guides for the *Talking Walls* and *Who Belongs Here?* books. Call or visit the Web site: 1-800-582-1899; *www.tilburyhouse.com.*

*They Have a Word for It: A Lighthearted Lexicon of Untranslatable Words and Phrases* by Howard Rheingold (Louisville, KY: Sarabande Books, 2000). All ages. This book is full of useful words for which there are no equivalents in English.

*Tortillas Para Mama and Other Nursery Rhymes in Spanish and English,* selected and translated by Margot C. Griego, Betsy L. Bucks, Sharon S. Gilbert, and Laurel H. Kimball (New York: Henry Holt, 1987). Ages 2–8. A collection of traditional Latin American nursery rhymes, many accompanied by instructions for finger play.

*The Travelers' Guide to Asian Customs and Manners* by Elizabeth Devine and Nancy L. Braganti (New York: St. Martin's, 1998). Written for adults, this is a handy manual detailing do's and don'ts for seventeen Asian countries. For example, you'll find out in what country it's impolite for a man to wink at a woman and that it's rude to say "thank you" when complimented in South Korea (you should deny the compliment). The same authors also have books on European, Middle Eastern, African, and Latin American customs.

**U.S. Fund for UNICEF.** 333 East 38th Street, New York, NY 10016; 1-800-FOR-KIDS (1-800-367-5437); *www.unicefusa.org.* This nonprofit organization offers videos about children from around the world. Ask for the UNICEF catalog, which includes international greeting cards, other paper products, children's toys and games, and seasonal items.

*Video Letter from Japan.* Ages 9 and up. Individual tapes in this series of six videos cover a day in the life of a Tokyo sixth-grader, a look at two families in northern Japan, school life in Japan, and other subjects. Each twenty-five-minute video comes with a teacher's manual and poster. Other videos about Japan and Korea are available. Call the Asia Society at 1-800-ASK-ASIA (1-800-275-2742). The society's AskAsia Web site, *www.askasia.org,* includes features for educators and for children, including activities and e-pals.

*We Can All Get Along: 50 Steps You Can Take to Help End Racism* by Clyde W. Ford (New York: Dell, 1994). For adults, with some ideas to share with children. The fifty steps in this thought-provoking guidebook help readers develop a personal program for eliminating racism, from noticing unintentionally racist language to identifying—and voting against—institutionalized racism.

*Wisdom Tales from Around the World: Fifty Gems of Story and Wisdom from Such Diverse Traditions as Sufi, Zen, Taoist, Christian, Jewish, Buddhist, African, and Native American* by Heather Forest (Little Rock, AR: August House, 1996). Ages 9–12. Fables, parables, and folktales, some new, some familiar.

# CHAPTER 13

# BEHAVIOR FOR BEGINNERS: A BIT OF PSYCHOLOGY

The science of psychology has many branches. From sleep researchers who study dreams, to experimental psychologists who work with human subjects in the field and lab, to social psychologists who study how people act in relationships, all psychologists work at understanding some aspect of human complexity. While courses in psychology are rarely available to children before their mid-teens, much about this fascinating field lends itself perfectly to parent-child discussion and exploration. After all, what could be more interesting to children than themselves?

## Dreamwork

*For several months around the time of his parents' divorce, Simon spent his nights flying. During the day, the fifth-grader was caught up in conflicts between his mother and father, but once asleep, he simply waved his arms and took off.*

*Simon enjoyed the incredible feeling of freedom and control in these dreams. In some dreams, however, arm-flapping didn't work, and he had to stay on the ground and face whatever came along.*

◆ ◆ ◆

*Kevin always loved the idleness of summer. A few days before he was to begin junior high, he dreamed he came to school unprepared. He had to take tests he knew nothing about. He didn't know anyone, and he couldn't find his locker.*

*When he woke up, relieved it had only been a dream, he immediately asked his mother to take him shopping for some new notebooks and school clothes.*

My children really had those dreams, but both scenarios—dreaming you can fly and dreaming you're thrown into a situation for which you're utterly unprepared—are very common. Talking about dreams is a good way to begin introducing your child to the workings of the human mind. Dreams are a universal human experience that begin in infancy, and they have a way of bringing out feelings that might not otherwise find expression. By helping your child tune into his dreams and find ways to share them, you're giving him a safe means for communicating feelings. Our waking minds can use dreams to better understand our lives.

Share these facts: The younger the child, the more time he or she spends dreaming. While newborns dream 45 to 65 percent of their sleep time, or nine hours a day, children two to five years old dream for about two hours. From five to thirteen, children spend 15 to 20 percent of their sleep time dreaming. The average adult who sleeps eight hours spends only one of them dreaming.

It seems that at least two-thirds of the dreams children recall are negative ones, so don't panic if all your child can tell you about are bad dreams. The incidence of nightmares tends to peak between ages five and seven, when children go to school for the first time and are subject to many new demands. Bad dreams also appear to be more memorable. The happy, adventurous dreams, as well as the mundane ones, are more easily lost upon awakening.

According to experts, it's important that parents not try to interpret children's dreams for them. When kids are ready, they'll make the connections themselves.

Dreams have their own logic. Just as with adults, a child's dream of food may relate to attitudes about parents (one of many possible interpretations)— or it may just mean the dreamer is hungry. Recently, before elective surgery, I dreamed I ate some toast, but because I knew I wasn't supposed to eat before the procedure, I became anxious in the dream. I'm pretty sure this merely reflected my anxiety about the upcoming surgery in general.

The dreaming mind changes things around, which is one reason so many creative ideas come out of the dreaming state. We each develop our own dream symbols, the significance of which we may not be able to grasp easily. Beware of simplistic, one-symbol-fits-all interpretations. The best way to interpret a dream is to determine what it means to *you*.

If your child tells you about a dream, you have an opportunity to help her explore its possible meanings in her life. This is a superb emotional and practical skill to help your child learn at an early age. Joan Mazza, a psychotherapist with a special interest in dreams, suggests you ask your child to talk about the feelings in the dream. Your child may need prompting. Try saying something like, "That sounds scary (funny, exciting). Were you feeling scared (happy, delighted, surprised) during that dream?"

To help your child discover connections between emotions in dreams and circumstances of daily life, ask, "What does that dream make you think of? Did something happen yesterday that reminds you of that dream?" You can ask more sophisticated questions as your child matures, such as, "I wonder if something happened recently that relates to that dream in some way." Kids sometimes talk more readily about a dream than about "real life." For example, if a child is being bullied at school, she may be ashamed or afraid to admit it. The distress she's reluctant to express to a teacher or family member may be revealed in a dream. Mazza suggests caution, however, about taking a child's dream too literally, since the characters and events portrayed there may represent someone or something else.

---

### Plants and Pajamas

The McDermotts were getting ready to move to a nearby neighborhood. Four-year-old Rory asked, "Are we going to be taking our plants?" Her father reassured her that they would. Two days later, Rory had this dream: "I was at school and I was in pajamas. I felt nervous, but then I felt pretty good. But not as good as when I'm home in my pajamas."

When people dream of being naked or inappropriately dressed in public (a very common dream), this usually has to do with feeling overexposed. According to Patricia Garfield, a clinical psychologist and dream researcher, Rory's dream suggests that she was feeling somewhat vulnerable at the moment. "In this situation, she's feeling like things are out of place a little bit, that things may not feel right or that she may be in an awkward situation after the move." Her question about bringing the plants suggests that she's anxious about having her favorite things around her in her new home.

If your child dreams that she's undressed or inappropriately dressed in public, you might say, "A lot of people have that dream. I have it myself sometimes. It sure is uncomfortable not being in the right clothes. Have you ever felt uncomfortable or out of place like that when you're awake?"

If you're going through some transition or change and your child reports an uncomfortable dream like this, it's a clue that she's feeling anxious. Give her extra attention and reassurance.

---

You can help your child feel in control of his dreams by teaching him the concept of "lucid dreaming" or "creative dreaming." A lucid dreamer who dreams something scary can learn to take action or get assistance within the dream, thereby changing the dream's direction.

Some kids pick up lucid dreaming on their own. Patricia Garfield interviewed children who said that if they didn't like a dream, they just "changed the channel." Other children can be taught these simple techniques:

1. As you fall asleep, say to yourself over and over, "I'm dreaming." Soon you will be, and you'll begin with some sort of awareness that you are, indeed, dreaming.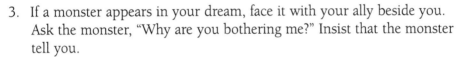

2. While you're awake, choose someone or something to be your dream ally—maybe a parent, a friend, or a stuffed animal. (Some children choose religious figures or superheroes, depending on what they've been exposed to and feel comfortable with.)

3. If a monster appears in your dream, face it with your ally beside you. Ask the monster, "Why are you bothering me?" Insist that the monster tell you.

4. If the monster keeps bothering you, tell yourself, "I don't like this. Now I'm going to wake up." With practice, you'll be able to wake yourself up out of any nightmare.

Here are some concrete ways to encourage your child to share, understand, and take power over his dreams.

▶ Share your own dreams.

▶ Encourage the keeping of a dream journal (see "The Dream Journal" in Chapter 2, pages 28–29). Your child may be able to use such a diary to ponder the meaning of a series of dreams that occur during a particular time of his life.

"When you have dreams all together in a group, you can see how they relate to each other," says Jonni Kincher, author and developer of psychology materials for children. "Sometimes you learn what your certain symbol is. When you look back, in light of new dreams, the old ones tend to make a lot more sense."

Kincher suggests children ask themselves these questions when searching for patterns in their dreams: How many dreams go from good to bad? From bad to good? How many star you as the hero? As the victim? Which images repeat or reappear in disguised form? How do they change? (For example: Going from big to small, young to old, or real to artificial.)

▶ Your child might benefit from the experience of using clay and other materials to "make" his dreams. Kincher suggests that kids create bumper stickers, cartoons, even limericks that have to do with their dreams. "The more different things you do," she explains, "the more you fool around with one dream, the more things pop out, and the more associations are made."

Dreams can provide inspiration for original art of various kinds. My husband is a poet who sometimes writes in the morning as soon as he wakes up. His dreams are often rich with poetic imagery, and sometimes he dreams actual lines of poetry.

▶ You might ask your child to draw his dream for you. By putting it on paper, in effect taking control of it and placing it outside himself, he may find that upsetting feelings are resolved (or that happy feelings are deepened or clarified). If your child draws a nightmare, you might ask a few questions about the drawing to help him get over his fear or resolve the problem presented by the dream. For example, ask him what he'd do to help the person in the picture (even if he *is* the person), or how he might make the situation less scary. What would the monster or nightmare image say if it could speak? What would your child say to the monster?

▶ To help your child remember his dreams, suggest that he remind himself to remember them just before he goes to bed.

▶ Children's dreams often have common themes. Animals with sharp teeth are sometimes associated with dreams of anger. Frustration in trying to do something often indicates difficulty in communicating. Sensing something terrifying or dangerous may mean the child feels insecure or threatened.

Can your child make a stab at interpreting any of his own dream themes?

# Is Your Child a Type T?

Several psychologists have come up with questionnaires to determine whether someone is a "sensation seeker." Another label for this is a "Type T" personality (thrill seeker). Studies have found that more males than females fall into this category, and that males are more susceptible to boredom. Highest rates for thrill seeking for both males and females are found in the 16–24 age range, after which they gradually drop off.

Thrill seeking—risk taking—doesn't have to mean taking dangerous chances. As Arlene Erlbach explains in *Worth the Risk: True Stories About Risk Takers Plus How You Can Be One, Too* (Resources, page 198), "When you take a positive risk, you're trying something new to help yourself, others, or the world." A positive risk, notes Erlbach, is a chance to explore your abilities, interests, talents, and dreams. Risk taking can open you up to fresh ideas and experiences—perhaps trying something new, or striving to reach a goal.

Is your child inclined to take healthy risks? Find out by trying the following:

- Brainstorm with your child some possible thrill-seeking activities. Older kids may come up with some rather dangerous or unsavory endeavors. In the spirit of brainstorming, of course, you'd accept all as possibilities, and then use the conversation as a springboard to talking about healthy versus dangerous or antisocial risks. Discuss the fact that thrill seekers can learn to channel their interests in productive ways—making discoveries, perhaps, or finding gratification in high-energy careers.

    Discuss people's possible motivations for seeking thrills or taking risks—positive or negative—such as excitement, defiance, self-respect, self-discovery, escape, boredom, self-destructive tendencies, or revenge. Can your child think of an example of each? Ask questions like these: What would you do if you had a million dollars? Which do you prefer, old friends or new friends? Are you adventurous about trying new foods? Would you ever try skydiving? If you had the best job in the world, what would it be? What risks would you be willing to take to reach an important goal?

- One of humankind's oldest desires has been to alter consciousness, or to feel "high." The bad news, of course, is that this has led to the abuse of alcohol and other drugs. The good news is that there are actually quite a few ways to alter one's consciousness without using harmful substances.

    In *Highs! Over 150 Ways to Feel Really, REALLY Good . . . Without Alcohol or Other Drugs* (Resources, page 197), Alex Packer suggests ways to achieve what he calls "serenity highs," "physical and sensuous highs," and "social, spiritual, and creative highs." Serenity highs may come from deep breathing exercises, meditation, intense focus on an object, or self-hypnosis. Physical and sensuous highs may result from sports or exercise, riding a roller coaster, watching a metronome, meditating on a mandala, or aromatherapy. Social, spiritual, and creative highs may be achieved through hiking, contemplating water (relaxing by a river, watching the ocean, meditating on a waterfall), drawing or painting, studying philosophy, or doing community service. Other ways that have been suggested throughout history are to run, fast, or chant. Writers can get high—even young writers—by focusing intently on what they're writing so that time dissolves (see "Time Awareness," page 192).

Work with your child to develop a personal list of healthy ways to feel "high." Examples suitable to young people include:

- exercising, which has been shown to raise levels of endorphins (brain proteins that are natural mood-boosters)

- participating in sports and games, which are mentally and physically exciting

- listening to music, making music, dancing

- laughing

- accomplishing something, such as completing a story, running for a school office, painting a picture, or even cleaning up a messy room

- meditating, which is an age-old method of relaxing the body and focusing the mind

# Memory Mysteries

*Steve walked in the door, dropping his keys on the dining room table, his books on the kitchen table on his way to the refrigerator, and his shoes in the living room next to the phone. The next morning he spent precious minutes searching for his shoes, books, and keys, and was late for class.*

*Renee, an artist, had only visited Steve's home once, many months before. Yet she could describe in detail each room's layout, including the fabric and color of each piece of furniture. When she asked Steve to close his eyes and describe what she was wearing at that moment, Steve could only venture a guess: "Something bluish?"*

Steve and Renee are examples of how individuals vary in their memory abilities, but the processes of memory work the same in everyone. Depending on how long you want to remember something, your brain stores information in three different ways, or stages. Share these with your child.

The first stage is called "sensory register." Usually your eyes hold onto an image for only a fraction of a second before it's replaced by another image.

Sensory-register memory fades quickly unless it's transferred to the next stage, called "short-term memory," or STM. When Steve dropped his keys on the table, he saw what he was doing but didn't think about it. The image of keys in that particular location never even made it from his sensory register into his short-term memory.

STM is an active part of memory. What you choose to keep in STM depends on what matters to you. Short-term memories usually disappear within 15–20 seconds unless you consciously attend to them because you feel they're important. Apparently, Steve wasn't particularly interested in keeping track of his belongings by remembering where he put them—or in what Renee was wearing.

The third stage, called "long-term memory" or LTM, is practically limitless. It can hold as many as one quadrillion separate bits of information. The longer you think about something, the longer it stays in STM and the greater its chances of moving to LTM. Renee, apparently, had thought enough about Steve's home to hold details in her long-term memory—perhaps because she's an artist and is especially sensitive to her surroundings.

Teach your child to use mnemonics (from the Greek *mnemon,* to remember). A mnemonic is any technique that helps you remember things better, usually by forming a strong association. It could be anything from a rhyme ("Thirty days hath September . . .") to a strong visual image (such as associating someone named Mrs. Reddin with the color red, imagining her in a red shirt) to putting a rubber band on your wrist. The best mnemonics are the ones you make up yourself—otherwise, you may find yourself struggling to remember your mnemonic!

Here are some ways to test and strengthen your child's memory abilities.

- Both you and your child can do this at the same time: Try to draw from memory as many details as possible of what's on each side of a penny (or another common coin).

   Most people can recall only a few of the penny's features. Though we handle pennies nearly every day, their details aren't significant enough for us to commit them to memory. Try this exercise again after allowing a few minutes to study a penny.

- Fill a tray with ten to twenty small, common, related items, such as baby care products, kitchen utensils, or assorted pieces of hardware. Show the tray to your child for one minute and then put it out of sight. Ask your child how many items she can recall. (Either she can write them down, or you can write them down as she calls them out to you.) Afterward, check the tray to see how many items she named correctly.

   Many people who try this activity don't do very well. With practice and a few tricks, however, memory can be improved.

   Fill a tray again. This time, suggest to your child that she think through the way the items are used, placing them in some sort of order in her mind. Since she only has a minute, she'll have to think very quickly.

For example: "You open the diaper pin, take off the baby's diaper, apply baby powder while holding a rattle to distract the baby, wash your hands with the soap, put the bib on the baby, and then feed the baby using the spoon."

Your child's performance should be much improved, partly due to the effort of focusing her mind.

▶ Teach your child the "Method of Loci," a way to commit a list of unrelated items to memory. (*Loci* means "places" in Latin.) Basically, you connect the items you want to remember with familiar locations, following a predetermined order (such as clockwise).

*Example:* Imagine each item on a list of unrelated household objects as being in a particular spot within a room: the glass is on the shelf as you enter, the broom stands next to the shelf, the book is on the TV, and so on. Mentally take a trip around the room to visit each item.

Once you've explained the Method of Loci, give your child a list of unrelated items to commit to memory.

▶ Teach your child how to make associations that will help him remember things.

*Example:* When you meet a new person and want to remember his or her name, think up something funny or bizarre to associate with it. Say your son wants to remember the name of his new coach, Jimmy Ruder. He might associate his coach with the phrase, "He's ruder than the old coach."

Mr. Lafflin likes to laugh!

▶ Tell your child about *déjà vu*, the feeling we all get sometimes that we've been in a particular place or situation before, even though we know we haven't. Scientists don't know for sure why this is such a common experience, but several theories have been suggested. Perhaps a situation feels familiar because it triggers memories of an experience that evoked similar feelings. Or maybe déjà vu has something to do with a slight lag time between the processing mechanisms of two parts of the brain.

Has your child ever experienced déjà vu?

## Play Your Way to Insight

Put Monopoly away for now—kinder, gentler feelings have invaded the game room. Professionally designed psychological games aren't meant to replace therapists, but to extend their work into the home or classroom. So even if your child is the most normal, well-adjusted child on the block, he'll still gain new insights—and perhaps a more cooperative attitude—by occasionally playing psychological games. The following games are available from Childswork/Childsplay, or you can design your own using a similar format:

- **The Angry Monster Machine.** Is it better to express anger with loud, possibly hurtful exclamations ("I hate you!"), or to hold those angry feelings inside and hope they go away? Neither. When five- to ten-year-olds play this game with an adult, they learn better ways to deal with anger. Players fashion monsters from Play Doh (included) and then transport their monsters around the board on little plastic trucks. When players reach a Transforming Machine, they complete a sentence like, "What really makes me angry when I'm at school is _____" ("when the teacher blames me for something I didn't do," "when I lose my homework," "when Joey bumps my chair"). They then revamp their monsters after choosing a Transformer Card that suggests alternate ways to deal with anger ("talk it out," "turn your monster into a mouse"). The first player to transform all four monsters is the winner.

  This game shows kids such anger-management techniques as talking your anger out, taking five deep breaths, turning on music, getting advice, and making a lot of noise in a place where you won't bother anyone.

- **My Two Homes.** When six- to twelve-year-olds play this game with their parents (or other adults), they work their way around the colorful board between Mom's house and Dad's house, receiving safe opportunities to express emotions and learn more about the reality of divorce.

  If a child rolls the dice and lands on Mom's house square, she picks a card from the pile there (either a Situational Card or a Factual Card). Sample situation: "Carol has nightmares about her house burning down and being all alone. She doesn't know whether she can count on her mom or dad if her dreams come true. What can she do to feel better?" A factual question: "Most people who get divorced will get back together again. True or false?" Plastic chips are awarded for answering factual questions correctly (answers are in the leader's guide that comes with the game) and for giving any response to situations. No one is required to answer.

- **You & Me.** This game teaches six- to ten-year-olds important, day-to-day social skills, including helping others, sharing, being polite, understanding another person's point of view, and being a friend. As players move around the colorful board, they draw pictures, answer questions, or act out charades about common social situations, receiving plastic chips for their efforts. When players earn twenty-five chips, they can be rewarded with special "social events" recommended in the instructions, such as sharing a snack, listening to or reading a story together, or going on an outing.

- **The Dinosaur's Journey to High Self-Esteem.** It doesn't hurt to be wary of materials—whether for children or adults—that are too self-consciously intent on raising self-esteem. This game for five- to twelve-year-olds manages to bypass the simplistic and tackle the important thoughts, feelings, and values that lead to a positive self-concept.

  After players choose their dinosaur markers, they toss the dice to see whether they will land on the Cave of Acceptance, the Land of Courage, or the Valley of Values. As they move around the board, they draw from one of three decks of cards that ask questions or describe situations related to personality growth. For example, "What is the worst name that anyone could call you?" "Name the sport or activity that you are best at." "You heard a smaller child crying all alone on the playground, but you didn't go to see what was wrong. Go back 3 spaces." No one loses, since it doesn't matter who comes in first—only that each player eventually crosses the finish line.

To order these games or to request a catalog, call Childswork/Childsplay at 1-800-962-1141 or check the Web site: *www.childswork.com.*

# Psychological Pursuits

Here are some additional ways to give your child a flavor of the world of psychology.

- **Time Awareness.** Hold a watch and ask your child to sit quietly and let you know when she thinks one minute has gone by; five minutes; ten minutes. Find out how her accuracy is affected when you ask her to gauge the same amounts of time while she's drawing a picture of the most fun day she can remember.

▶ **Flow.** As I discussed in the introduction to this book, psychologists who have studied the phenomenon of "flow" have found that when you're deeply engaged in some activity—when all your attention is on the task with none left over to feel distracted or anxious—time seems to stop or simply become irrelevant. When I interviewed novelists and poets about how they accomplished their creative work, the vast majority said they entered the timeless place of flow when they were writing—at least sometimes. (See *Writing in Flow: Keys to Enhanced Creativity* in Resources, page 198.)

When does time drag for your child? When does it move too quickly?

▶ **Attention.** Here's an experiment psychologists have used to demonstrate that each half of the brain draws on reserves to allow people to pay attention.

Have your child sit at a table and tap his right index finger steadily. Now ask him to start talking to you. As he speaks, his tapping will slow. Now ask him to switch hands, tapping with his left index finger while speaking aloud. His tapping won't slow.

Why? Because both the right hand and the speech function are controlled by the brain's left hemisphere. Using both at once drains attention from the same side of the brain. Most (but not all) left-handers have the same left-hemisphere dominance for language as do right-handers. Try this experiment on several right-handers and left-handers and compare results.

▶ **Inkblots.** In the Rorschach test, a person looks at inkblots printed on cards and tells what he or she "sees" in them. Clinicians then use the answers to analyze a client's mental state. Though this test is considered by many psychologists to be too subjective to be reliable, it can make for a fun and interesting home activity.

Have your child make her own "inkblot" cards, following these simple steps:

1. Drip some paint or ink in the center of a piece of paper.

2. Fold the paper exactly in half, lay it on a table, and press down on it so the paint spreads out in a random pattern.

3. Open the paper and let it dry.

4. Repeat until you have as many inkblots as you want.

Ask family and friends to take turns telling what they see in the blots. Aim for creative responses and the fun of the unexpected, without bothering about any deeper meanings.

▶ **Emotions.** To enhance your child's ability to express feelings and articulate emotions, work with him to enrich his vocabulary of feeling words.

List words describing various feelings (excited, nervous, thrilled, bored) and go over them with your child. Talk about the kinds of situations that might lead to each of the different emotions. (You're about to leave for the zoo, your dog died, or your best friend won the gymnastics meet and you placed fourth.) Try to figure out what's common to all the times your child feels a certain way.

With a young child, stick to the more basic emotions—happy, sad, angry, afraid—and have him act them out. Or he can draw, sing, or dance them.

▶ **ESP.** Just for fun, introduce the notion of psychic abilities and extrasensory perception (ESP). Hold a deck of cards and turn them over one at a time while your child guesses what the next card will be. (You could limit the guesses to "red" or "black" to improve your child's chances.) Then switch so your child turns over the cards and you do the guessing. Keep track of correct guesses. Some researchers have done similar experiments, in hopes of finding a higher-than-chance number of correct guesses—which might indicate that something "extra" is in operation.

▶ **What Psychologists Do.** If there's a psychologist, counselor, or family therapist among your acquaintances, see if it's possible for your older child to interview him or her. Some questions might be: How do you find out what a person's problem is? Do you give psychological tests? Do you do research? How do you learn about someone's personality? What kinds of questions do you ask people? Do you tell them what you think of their answers? Do you give advice?

▶ **Relationships.** The next time you're in a supermarket, department store, or bank with your older child, pay attention to the psychological dynamics of the people around you. Later on, talk about what you saw.

*Examples:* Who was bossing someone else around? Who was being bossed? Was one person being critical of another? Did people seem to behave differently with their families and friends than they did with customers or store employees?

▶ **Pop Psychology.** Write pretend questions to your child, as though she's an advice columnist. Your child then responds in writing. Later, collect all the questions and answers and put them together into a booklet. You could also do this orally, with your child pretending to be a radio advisor.

*Examples:* "My kid never does her chores without my nagging her. What should I do?" "My friend lies a lot. Should I trust him?"

▶ **Positive Psychology.** A field known as "positive psychology" focuses on what makes people happy and resilient and on how to encourage optimism—as opposed to treating psychological distress once it occurs. Most people enjoy spending time with those who can look on the bright side of situations. You can help your child become someone who isn't thrown by life's little inconveniences and has a generally bright personal outlook.

*Example:* Have a "Positive Week." Every time a negative thought enters your mind, turn it around to a positive one.

The first day I tried this, it rained on my daily walk. Normally, these would have been my thoughts: "My hair is going to flop, my tennis shoes will take hours to dry, and I'm going to have to change my clothes when I get home." But during my Positive Week, my thoughts went like this instead: "This rain is wonderful, flowers will grow, people won't have to water their lawns, the air feels cleaner, and I'm experiencing nature in a gentle way." And I actually felt good.

What does your child think brings happiness? (*Hint:* It's been scientifically proven that more money isn't the key for most people.)

# Special Effects

Find ways for you and your child to demonstrate these "special effects," each of which has important implications in psychology.

1. **The Hawthorne Effect.** When researchers at a factory in Hawthorne, Illinois, studied how light affects workers, they found that no matter how the lighting was changed, the workers were always more productive than they were before the change.

   Just knowing that someone is watching seems to change people's behavior. Think of situations when your child or you were being watched. How did this affect your behavior? For example, when your child was a toddler, were you more patient with his demands in the supermarket if you knew you were being observed by other shoppers? When your child takes a test in school or does chores under your supervision, are the results better than, worse than, or the same as when he performs the exact same work unobserved?

2. **The Placebo Effect.** It's been shown many times that a "medicine" containing no active ingredients, only sugar, will often have some effect on a person's medical complaint—*if* the person believes it's real medicine. In some cases, a placebo can even help as much as actual medication.

   At home, you can see the Placebo Effect in the remarkable healing powers of a parent's kiss or when a child feels better after putting a bandage on a cut. Can you and your child think of other examples?

3. **The Rosenthal Effect.** This is also called the Pygmalion Effect or the "self-fulfilling prophecy." Many experiments have shown that the experimenter's expectations can powerfully affect the results.

   *Example:* In a famous study, teachers were told that one group of students had scored high on an I.Q. test, while a second group had scored "average." The teachers saw the first group as happier, more interesting, and more curious than the second group, when in fact students had been put into each group randomly. The study also showed that the children perceived to be "smarter" gained more points, on average, when they took the I.Q. test again than did their "average" classmates.

   Teach your child a difficult new task. Act as if you assume she'll learn it easily. What happens?

# Resources

*All My Feelings at Home: Ellie's Day* by Susan Conlin and Levine Friedman (Seattle: Parenting Press, 1989). Ages 4–8. An introductory book for young children about feelings—what they are and how to express them.

*The Beast in You: Activities & Questions to Explore Evolution* by Marc McCutcheon (Charlotte, VT: Williamson Publishing, 1999). Ages 8–12. Kids look to their own bodies for clues to the human animal's past. Includes discussion of Charles Darwin's theories and the creationism controversy. This book is a good adjunct to any exploration of human behavior and why we are the way we are.

*Becoming Me: An Autobiography for the Reader to Complete,* edited by Linda Beattie (Kalama, WA: Kopacetic Ink, 1998). Ages 6 and up. This 126-page workbook invites readers to reflect, answer questions, complete sentences ("I get mad when . . ."), and draw responses that illustrate who they are. Designed to help young people feel good about themselves and the particulars of their own personal life journey.

*The Book of You: The Science and Fun! of Why You Look, Feel, and Act the Way You Do* by Sylvia Funston (New York: HarperCollins, 2000). Ages 8–12. From your fingerprints to the patterns in the irises of your eyes to the way you smell, there's nobody exactly like you. But what makes you *you*? Is it your genes or your dreams or the day you were born? This good-natured grab bag of fun facts and activities will help young readers get to know themselves better.

*The Brain Explorer,* edited by Pat Murphy and the Exploratorium (New York: Henry Holt, 1999). Ages 8–12. Written by the staff of the famous Exploratorium Museum in San Francisco, this adventure in the brain presents dozens of brainteasers, riddles, problems, puzzles, optical illusions, word games, number games, and more.

*The Brain: Our Nervous System* by Seymour Simon (New York: Mulberry Books, 1999). Ages 8 and up. Colorfully illustrated and written by the author of many science books for children, this is a good introduction to the body's most important organ for determining who we are and why we behave as we do.

*The Brain Pack: An Interactive, Three-Dimensional Exploration of the Mysteries of the Mind* by Ron Van der Meer and Ad Dudink (Philadelphia: Running Press, 1996). Ages 8–12. Packed with more information than a three-pound brain may be able to store at once, *The Brain Pack* leads you through basic brain anatomy, beginning with a life-sized pop-up of the inner human head. You'll also learn about emotions, the senses, intelligence, memory, and more. Hands-on features such as the Primary Emotions Wheel, pull-out flaps, and pop-up charts are entertaining, as are the fact-or-fiction games, memory exercises, I.Q. tests, and pull-out pamphlets. In a tray in the back of the book, you'll find a fifteen-minute audiocassette tour of the brain and a deck of cards that playfully tests your psychic abilities.

*Dreaming Your Real Self: A Personal Approach to Dream Interpretation* by Joan Mazza (New York: Perigee, 1998). For adults to read so they can better help children reflect on what might be going on in dreams. Features helpful techniques and a non-dogmatic approach to interpretation. Mazza is also the author of *Dream Back Your Life: A Practical Guide to Dreams, Daydreams, and Fantasies.*

*Highs! Over 150 Ways to Feel Really , REALLY Good . . . Without Alcohol or Other Drugs* by Alex J. Packer, Ph.D. (Minneapolis: Free Spirit Publishing, 2000). Ages 13 and up. Describes safe, creative ways to find peace, pleasure, excitement, and insight including highs related to sports and exercise, the senses, nature, family, creativity, and more.

**How Do You Feel Today?** P.O. Box 1085, Agoura, California 91301; (818) 706-2288; *www.how doyoufeeltoday.com.* This company produces a variety of posters, each playfully illustrating an emotion (for instance, feeling aggressive, disbelieving, hurt, paranoid, smug, and withdrawn). Therapists and teachers use these posters to open up communication with children about feelings, but they're also excellent tools for vocabulary building and discussion at home. Available in regular or laminated versions.

*I'm Frustrated (Dealing with Feelings)* by Elizabeth Crary (Seattle: Parenting Press, 1992). Ages 4–8. This interactive book helps young children learn to handle difficult feelings in productive ways. A frustrating situation is described, and then the reader chooses one of several possible ways to react. Turning to a particular page shows what might happen if that reaction was chosen and gives additional choices.

*It's All in Your Head: A Guide to Understanding Your Brain and Boosting Your Brain Power* by Susan L. Barrett (Minneapolis: Free Spirit Publishing, 1992). Ages 9–12. Explains how we think, learn, and remember, as well as how to be more creative. Explores what genius is, whether we can learn in our sleep, and whether there's anything to ESP.

*Looking at the Body* by David Suzuki (New York: John Wiley & Sons, 1991). Ages 8–12. A kid's-eye scientific look at the body, including sections on the brain, nerves, and communication. Includes many simple, illustrative activities.

**Neuroscience Resources for Kids: Sleep and Dreaming Experiments,** *faculty.washington.edu/ chudler/chsleep.html.* This site includes activities such as "Sleep Journals," "Be an REM Detective," and "Drop Off or Drift Off?" Excellent selection of sleep- and dream-related links. Also see Neuroscience Resources for Kids: Explore the Brain and Spinal Cord, *faculty.washington.edu/chudler/introb.html.* This site leads to numerous interesting pages for budding psychology students.

*On Monday When It Rained* by Cherryl Kachenmeister (Boston: Houghton Mifflin, 1989). Ages 4–8. Using text and expressive photographs, this simple book describes a variety of situations and the resulting emotions felt by a young boy, including embarrassment, pride, excitement, and anger.

*Psychology for Kids: 40 Fun Tests That Help You Learn About Yourself* by Jonni Kincher (Minneapolis: Free Spirit Publishing, 1990), for ages 10 and up, and *Psychology for Kids II: 40 Fun Experiments That Help You Learn About Others* (Free Spirit Publishing, 1998), for ages 12 and up. Are you an extrovert or an introvert? An optimist or a pessimist? Are you creative? What body language do you speak? The tests and experiments in these books, based on psychological theories and research, empower children to learn more about themselves and others. The second book, for older readers, tackles such topics as gender differences, learning, perception, and logic.

*Sleep Is for Everyone* by Paul Showers (New York: Harper Trophy, 1997). Ages 3–6. A classic book for young children, newly reissued and illustrated. Find out what happens when animals and people sleep and what happens when they don't sleep enough.

*Stick Up For Yourself! Every Kid's Guide to Personal Power and Positive Self-Esteem* by Gershen Kaufman, Ph.D., Lev Raphael, Ph.D., and Pamela Espeland (Minneapolis: Free Spirit Publishing, 1999). Ages 8–12. This book shows young people how to make choices, be assertive about their needs, and feel better about themselves. It includes a sizable section on developing a feelings vocabulary.

*T.A. for Kids and Grown-Ups, Too: How to Feel OK About Yourself and Other People* by Alvyn and Margaret Freed (Carson, CA: Jalmar Press, 1977). All ages. Also by the authors: *T.A. for Tots* and *T.A. for Teens.* A child-friendly explanation of Transactional Analysis (TA), which is based on the theory (more fun than it sounds) that we all have parent, adult, and child ego states.

*Worth the Risk: True Stories About Risk Takers Plus How You Can Be One, Too* by Arlene Erlbach (Minneapolis: Free Spirit Publishing, 1999). Ages 10–15. Twenty young people tell their own true stories about risks they chose to take—and what happened. Also includes chapters to help readers understand healthy vs. foolish risks, choosing risks to take, and more.

*Writing in Flow: Keys to Enhanced Creativity* by Susan K. Perry (Cincinnati: Writer's Digest Books, 1999). An exploration of the phenomenon of "flow"—when time seems to stop because you're so focused on what you're doing—from how to get there while writing, to what it feels like, to how to make it happen when you're feeling blocked. Based on interviews with many top novelists and poets, this book is accessible to young adults interested in writing and in learning how their favorite authors work. See excerpts at *www.bunnyape.com/writinginflow.htm.*

# CHAPTER 14

# REAL LITERATURE: FAMOUS AUTHORS' BOOKS FOR KIDS

**A**n exciting and often-overlooked way to expose your children to first-rate reading is by introducing them to children's books written by famous authors of adult works. When you choose stories and poems for children by celebrated writers, you know at the outset that they'll be written well. Since these authors' tales and verses were often first loved by their own children, other young readers are likely to find them appealing, too. These authors have learned the knack of not talking down to their audience. In fact, like all good children's literature, the books described in this chapter are also stimulating for teens and adult readers.

Besides the value and appeal of the works themselves, there are at least two more good reasons to track down many of the books listed here. These books are a fine way for your child to get to know prominent authors early, in an accessible way, without the difficulty of tackling full-length adult works. And later, when your child chooses to read—or is required to read for school—the adult works of these authors, writers like Tolstoy, Clifton, and Hawthorne, will seem a little like old friends.

# Ways to Bring Literature to Life

As you share good books with your child, consider trying some of the following ways to enrich the reading experience:

- Design a reading nook. Collaborate with your child on choosing materials—a rug, pictures or a poster for the wall, inexpensive shelving, a lamp—that will make this place truly conducive to reading and thinking. You might bring up the idea of ergonomics and how important it is to have good posture when reading for a long period of time. (Thus, a fairly good chair is a better addition than a large, floppy pillow, though it's nice to have both options.) Choose a quiet place, if possible. You might also set aside a reading time for the whole family so that the living room, for instance, becomes "the reading nook" between 7:00 and 8:00 every evening.

- Encourage your child to begin a reading journal in which he keeps track of books he reads and his reactions to each. Such a journal could also list new words learned from each book (or a few chosen from each), with short definitions to help cement the learning. Your child might like to get creative with his responses to literature—writing letters, parodies, and alternate endings, or providing his own illustrations. But be sure to keep it fun and voluntary.

- Suggest that your child write to a favorite author. Many authors have Web pages or can be written to in care of the publisher (look for the address on the back of the title page). Some authors get very few personal letters and answer them all, while others get a great many letters and must resort to answering only a few or sending a form response. In either case, allow several weeks, at least, to get an answer.

- Your child might enjoy writing a letter to a character in a book. From a "so sorry you lost your dog" message to one that invites a character to become a friend, your child can feel free to use her imagination in these creative interactions.

- Start a family book club to encourage discussion and more sophisticated thinking about literature. Good children's literature can often be enjoyed by all members of the family. I've heard of book groups composed of women in their seventies who read and enjoyed the Harry Potter series.

▶ Help your child act out a scene from a favorite book, as though it were a play. Some children will enjoy choreographing a dance that illustrates some scene they liked or found moving. Or how about making simple puppets and presenting the story as a puppet show?

▶ One familiar way of reenacting a beloved story is to make a shoe-box diorama of a setting or scene, perhaps creating tiny characters out of clay or other materials.

▶ Some children enjoy imitating an author's distinctive style in writing of their own. To help your child do this, suggest that he think about what makes this particular author unique. Is it the author's use of short sentences and lots of dialogue? Is it her absurd sense of humor? Is it her use of talking animals or of imaginary or mythical creatures?

▶ Is a picture always worth a thousand words? Have your child take both sides of the argument by finding, first, a book illustration that communicates a wealth of detail and nuance. Then have her find a passage in a book that expresses what she thinks no picture possibly could. When are pictures more expressive than words, and vice versa? Think about the inner world of characters and the ways a good author or illustrator can show various perspectives either in a few words or a single picture.

▶ Suggest that your child collect figures of speech and wordplay from the books he's reading. Eventually, once he's accustomed to expressions like "raining cats and dogs," he'll develop the sophistication to understand and appreciate more complex metaphors. For instance, in Saki's *The Story-Teller* (see page 210), the lady of the house who ineffectually confronts a new governess is compared to "a general of ancient warfaring days." In the next paragraph, she's said to have "regained none of her lost ground." Only a child who is familiar and comfortable with the many ways language can be played with will be able to grasp this extended metaphor.

▶ Encourage your child to research an author's life or to seek information on unfamiliar words, places, historical events, and ideas found in books. Without making a huge "educational" lesson out of it, get across the idea of how much fun it can be to learn more about the author or background of a good book.

▶ Many children's books are fables of one kind or another—that is, stories with morals. After reading such a fable, your child might like to make up, with your help, her own short fable (two or three paragraphs) based on some event in her life. It helps if the event involved someone whose behavior was greedy, lazy, untruthful, or imperfect in some other way. Encourage your child to include lots of details about what happened— and, of course, the story must have a moral.

▸  After reading a rhyming book or a book of poetry for children, ask your child to try his hand at writing a poem in the same style (more or less). Some children respond well to being given a key word such as *puppy* or *cloud* and then being challenged to write, in five minutes, a poem using the word. Anything goes.

# Recommended Books

What follows is a list of books that you and your child will want to add to your shelf of favorites. Each was written by someone better known as a writer for adults—so many are really hidden treasures.

Books go in and out of print. In these listings, I've tried to note the publication dates of the most recent editions. You may find other versions available as well. Some of the recommended books are, at the time of this writing, out of print. I've included these (marked with an asterisk ✱) because they're high-quality resources well worth a little detective work. You might also find that some of them have been republished.

You can check the current edition of *Books in Print* or *Children's Books in Print* at any library or bookstore. You can also look up any of your own favorite authors and see if they've written children's books. When searching for an out-of-print or hard-to-find title, start with your local library—you may find the book you want right on the shelf. If it's not there, ask the librarian for help. Public library systems are connected in many ways, and you'll most likely find your local librarian happy to track down books from other branches or systems. Many libraries will even search out and buy a copy of a hard-to-find book. Your family might also enjoy searching for these treasures yourselves, which you can do by visiting secondhand bookstores or Web sites like *www.abebooks.com,* an Internet-based book search service that was developed by used-book dealers.

The age ranges for these books are approximate, either suggested by the publisher or based on my own experience.

Angelou, Maya, *Kofi and His Magic* (New York: Knopf, 1996). Ages 4–9. This West African journey focuses both on a young boy's daily activities, such as weaving the Kente cloth, and on his imagination.

Angelou also wrote *My Painted House, My Friendly Chicken, and Me* and *Life Doesn't Frighten Me.*

* Barthelme, Donald, *The Slightly Irregular Fire Engine* (New York: Farrar, Straus and Giroux, 1971). Ages 5–11. In 1887, a plucky little girl investigates a mysterious Chinese house that suddenly appears in her backyard. Her escapades are illustrated by engravings of the time.

* Beattie, Ann, *Spectacles* (New York: Ariel, 1985). Ages 8–12. When an eight-year-old girl puts on her grumpy great-grandmother's glasses, she's magically able to see into the past. She begins to understand some of the old woman's frustrations.

* Benchley, Nathanial, *Feldman Fieldmouse: A Fable* (New York: Harper Trophy, 1971). Ages 7 and up. A philosophical talking mouse helps his nephew learn how to live a good life and fulfill his dreams.

Bradbury, Ray, *Switch On the Night* (New York: Knopf, 2000). Ages 4–8. This fable presents a boy who conquers his fear of the dark by imagining the flipping of a light switch as a way to illuminate the night.

* Buckley, William F., Jr., *The Temptation of Wilfred Malachey* (New York: Workman, 1985). Ages 10 and up. This modern morality tale features a main-frame computer that teaches a poor but aspiring student (who fancies himself a sort of Robin Hood) that computing can be more profitable than petty theft.

Capote, Truman, *A Christmas Memory* (New York: Knopf, 1996). All ages. A heartwarming memoir of Capote's own childhood in a rural Alabama household of the 1930s.

Capote also wrote *The Thanksgiving Visitor.*

Clavell, James, *Thrump-O-Moto* (New York: Delacorte, 1986). Ages 6 and up. This is a fantasy about a Japanese apprentice wizard who travels through time.

Clifton, Lucille, *The Boy Who Didn't Believe in Spring* (New York: Dutton, 1992). Ages 3–9. Two skeptical city boys set out to find spring, which they've heard is "just around the corner."

---

* The large asterisks on pages 203–215 indicate books that may be out of print.

———*The Lucky Stone* (New York: Yearling, 1986). Ages 8–12. A lucky stone provides good fortune for its various owners.

———*Some of the Days of Everett Anderson* (New York: Henry Holt, 1987). Ages 3–9. Each of six-year-old Everett's days of the week is described in a poem. Other Everett Anderson books include *Everett Anderson's 1-2-3, Everett Anderson's Christmas Coming,* and *Everett Anderson's Goodbye.*

Cummings, E. E., *Fairy Tales* (Orlando, FL: Harcourt, 1987). Ages 4–8. These four amusing and imaginative tales, written by the poet for his own small daughter, have titles like "The House That Ate Mosquito Pie" and "The Little Girl Named I."

Dickens, Charles, *The Magic Fish-Bone* (Orlando, FL: Harcourt, 2000). Ages 6 and up. The oldest girl of nineteen children is given magical powers and has to figure out how and when to use them.

Dorris, Michael, *Morning Girl* (New York: Disney Press, 2000). Ages 8–12. Morning Girl, who loves the day, and her younger brother, Star Boy, who loves the night, take turns describing their life on an island in pre-Columbian America. In Morning Girl's last narrative, she witnesses the arrival of the first Europeans to her world.

———*Guests* (New York: Hyperion, 1999). Ages 8–12. Dorris weaves moral themes into this beautifully written story of a young Native American boy.

Eco, Umberto, *The Bomb and the General* (Orlando, FL: Harcourt 1989). Ages 5–8. A plea for world peace, in which the atoms in atom bombs decide to exit the bombs so they fall harmlessly, putting a war-mongering general in his place (as a doorman).

———*The Three Astronauts* (Orlando, FL: Harcourt 1989). Ages 5–8. An American, a Russian, and a Chinese astronaut (along with a Martian) become friends once they realize that each is capable of loneliness and tears.

\* Fast, Howard, *The Magic Door* (New York: Avon Camelot, 1980). Ages 10–14. The story of a boy in a 1920s New York tenement who passes through a magical door into a lush past world.

Fleming, Ian, *Chitty Chitty Bang Bang* (New York: Bulls Eye Publishing, 1989). Ages 8 and up. Two children persuade their inventor father to buy and restore an old car, which turns out to have magical powers.

\* Gardner, John, *Dragon, Dragon, and Other Tales* (New York: Knopf, 1975). Ages 10 and up. A dragon terrorizes a kingdom by stealing spark plugs from people's cars, among other irritating antics, in this collection of decidedly untraditional fairy tales. In another tale, a cobbler's son disguises himself as a brush salesman to confront the dragon.

\* ——*Gudgekin the Thistle Girl* (New York: Knopf, 1976). Ages 10 and up. In an irreverent parody of fairy tales, Gardner invents a princess with spunk.

Gardner also wrote *A Child's Bestiary* and *The King of the Hummingbirds*.

\* Godden, Rumer, *The Old Woman Who Lived in a Vinegar Bottle* (New York: Viking, 1970). Ages 5 and up. A retelling of an English folk tale.

Gogol, Nikolai, *Sorotchintzy Fair* (Boston: David R. Godine, 1991). Ages 5 and up. An adaptation of a Russian tale about a young man who wins the hand of a young woman by using the villagers' superstitions against them.

Hall, Donald, *The Man Who Lived Alone* (Boston: David R. Godine, 1998). Ages 5–9. Hall tells in simple words the life story of a self-sufficient man who chooses to live alone.

——*Lucy's Christmas* and *Lucy's Summer* (San Diego, CA: Browndeer Press, 1994 and 1995, respectively). Ages 5–8. In these picture books, Hall evokes the life of fictional Lucy Wells and her family in 1910 rural New Hampshire, imagining them living in the house that is now home to Hall himself.

——*Old Home Day* (San Diego, CA: Browndeer Press, 1996). Ages 4–8. This picture book traces the history of Blackwater Pond, a small New England settlement, from its geological formation to a vision of its coming bicentennial celebration.

——*The Ox-Cart Man* (New York: Viking, 1980). Ages 6–12. In a lovely combination of text and illustrations (this book won the Caldecott Medal), Hall describes the daily life of an early-nineteenth century New England family through the changing seasons.

——*When Willard Met Babe Ruth* (San Diego, CA: Browndeer Press, 1996). Ages 5–12. Willard is twelve when this story begins. Readers will find lots of realistic details about America during the years 1917 to 1935.

Harjo, Joy, *The Good Luck Cat* (Orlando, FL: Harcourt, 2000). Ages 3–7. In this picture book, poet Harjo writes about Woogie, a cat with amazing luck and more than the usual number of lives.

Harrison, Jim, *The Boy Who Ran to the Woods* (New York: Atlantic Monthly Press, 2000). Ages 8 and up. This is an autobiographical tale about a boy who loses his sight in one eye. The trauma leaves him angry and unruly until his father introduces him to the woods.

Hawthorne, Nathaniel, *A Wonder Book for Girls and Boys* (New York: Oxford, 1996). Ages 9 and up. A retelling of Greek myths for young people.
   Hawthorne's other book for children is *Tanglewood Tales.*

\* Helprin, Mark, *Swan Lake* (Boston: Houghton Mifflin, 1989). Ages 7 and up. An elaborate narrative serves as a background for the characters in the ballet "Swan Lake."
   ——*A City in Winter* (New York: Viking, 1996). Ages 7 and up. The little girl in *Swan Lake,* now a grown-up queen, recalls her life and how she got her throne back.

Herriot, James, *Only One Woof* (New York: St. Martin's Press, 1993). Ages 6 and up. A silent sheepdog accompanies his master at his chores, never barking until he sees his brother for the first time since they were separated as pups.
   Among the other Herriot tales suitable for children are *Moses the Kitten* and *The Christmas Day Kitten.*

\* Hoban, Russell, *How Tom Beat Captain Najork and His Hired Sportsmen* (New York: Puffin, 1978). Ages 5 and up. Young readers will delight in the understated British humor of this story. A strong point is made for the value of playing as an aid to creativity.
\* ——*The Flight of Bembel Rudzuk* (New York: Putnam, 1982). Ages 4–7. In this funny picture book, young wizard Bembel Rudzuk creates a "squidgerino squelcher" (using three jars of monster powder), which annoys the princess (his mother, who wonders who is going to clean up the mess).
   ——*The Marzipan Pig* (New York: Farrar, Straus and Giroux, 1991). Ages 6–10. A touching story that begins with a marzipan pig who gathers dust behind a sofa until eaten by a mouse. The chain of events that follows is sure to delight.
\* ——*The Stone Doll of Sister Brute* (London: Pan Books, 1968). Ages 4 and up. The uproarious (yet poignant) tale of a small, furry creature who has nothing to love and who eventually uses a stone as a doll. Finally, she does find love in her own family, but it's a mixed blessing.
   More Hoban books for kids include *The Mouse and His Child, Harvey's Hideout, Jim Hedgehog's Supernatural Christmas,* and *Jim Hedgehog and the Lonesome Tower.*

Hoffman, Alice, *Horsefly* (New York: Hyperion, 2000). Ages 5–8. A timid girl overcomes her fear of horses when a newborn foal is placed in her care.

Another Hoffman book for children is *Firefly.*

Hughes, Langston, *Black Misery* (New York: Oxford University Press, 2000). All ages. In simple but stark and hard-hitting language, Hughes writes about prejudice from a young child's viewpoint.

——*Popo and Fifina* (New York: Oxford University Press, 1993). Ages 7–10. Hughes wrote this tale of two Haitian children with poet Arna Bontemps.

——*The Sweet and Sour Animal Book* (New York: Oxford University Press, 1997). Ages 3–7. Simple, amusing poems for young children about real and made-up animals, engagingly illustrated with photographs of clay creatures made by art students.

Other Hughes poetry books for kids include *The Book of Rhymes, The Pasteboard Bandit,* and *The Dream Keeper and Other Poems.*

Hughes, Ted, *Tales of the Early World* (New York: Farrar, Straus and Giroux, 1987). All ages. These ten imaginative creation tales are filled with unusual and amusing characters.

Hughes wrote many other children's books, including *How the Whale Became, The Iron Giant: A Story in Five Nights* (from which the fine animated film, *The Iron Giant* was made), and *Nessie the Mannerless Monster.*

Huxley, Aldous, *The Crows of Pearblossom* (New York: Amereon, 1973). Ages 4 and up. In this simple and amusing tale, a hungry snake keeps eating Mrs. Crow's newly laid eggs, until Mr. Crow and his friend Old Man Owl fool the snake into eating some real-looking clay eggs. Mrs. Crow, described as rather helpless, isn't treated very respectfully by her husband. Huxley, who wrote this story in 1944, was, of course, a product of his culture; parent-child discussion of such stereotyping of women can be worthwhile.

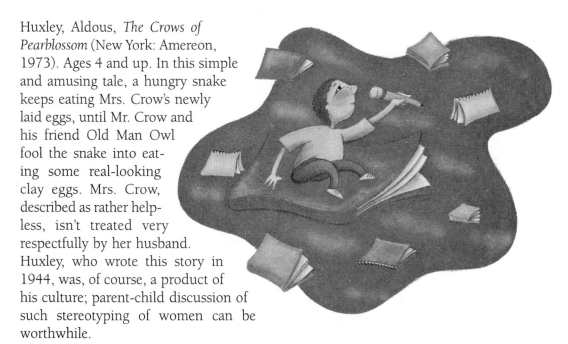

\* Ionesco, Eugene, *Story Number 3* (New York: Harlin Quist, 1971). Ages 3–5. In this simple, magical tale, little Josette visits her papa in bed one morning and asks for a story. They then take an imaginary airplane ride above the city.

Ionesco also wrote *Story Number 1* and *Story Number 2,* where we're first introduced to Josette. In *Story Number 4,* Josette plays hide-and-seek with Papa.

Jarrell, Randall, *The Animal Family* (New York: HarperCollins, 1997). Ages 8 and up. This is a moving fantasy of how a solitary man finds a family—consisting of a mermaid, a bear, a lynx, and a little boy. The language is poetic and the characters kind and understanding toward each other, despite their differences. This Newbery Honor Book was Jarrell's last work before his death.

——*The Bat-Poet* (New York: Harper Trophy, 1996). Ages 8 and up. A beautifully written and touching allegory of a poetry-writing bat who can't sleep during the day. When the bat poet's peers make fun of his creative images, he simply stops sharing them. He fares little better with a mockingbird, who, though he admires the bat's poem, analyzes its rhyme scheme instead of feeling its emotion. Finally the bat poet finds an appreciative audience and is able to unleash more of his imagination. Young readers will see the value of being true to one's nature and may also get an increased appreciation for poetic imagery and the difficulties of the artist's life.

——*Snow-White and the Seven Dwarfs* (New York: Farrar, Straus and Giroux, 1987). Ages 5 and up. Jarrell translated this version from the German, saying he tried to make it as much like the original story as he could.

Jarrell also wrote *The Gingerbread Rabbit* and *Fly by Night.*

\* Joyce, James, *The Cat and the Devil* (New York: Schocken, 1981). Ages 6 and up. This simple story is actually a letter Joyce wrote to his grandson Stephen in 1936. (A crucial few lines are in French.)

Kazantzakis, Nikos, *At the Palaces of Knossos* (Athens, OH: Ohio University Press, 1988). Ages 12 and up. This is an adventure story with characters out of classical Greek mythology. A historical chronology at the end helps readers put events into perspective.

Keneally, Thomas, *Ned Kelly and the City of the Bees* (Boston: David R. Godine, 1995). Ages 7–12. This is a first-person, inside-a-beehive adventure, written for Keneally's daughters.

\* Kennedy, William, and Brendan Kennedy, *Charlie Malarkey and the Belly Button Machine* (New York: Atlantic Monthly Press, 1986). Ages 4–8. William Kennedy began writing this amusing bedtime story with his son when Brendan was four.

Kesey, Ken, *Little Tricker the Squirrel Meets Big Double the Bear* (New York: Puffin, 1992). Ages 6 and up. Kesey retells a story his grandmother told him about a quick-thinking squirrel that outwits a big, hungry bear. This is an especially good read-aloud book.

King, Stephen, *The Eyes of the Dragon: A Story* (New York: New American Library, 1994). Ages 8 and up. King wrote this adventure/fantasy/fairy tale—complete with dragons, princes, and magic—for his thirteen-year-old daughter because she had no interest in his popular horror stories.

* Kinnell, Galway, *How the Alligator Missed Breakfast* (Boston: Houghton Mifflin, 1982). Ages 4 and up. This brightly illustrated book contains some delightfully absurd characters and situations: a rabbit who tries to fly and then writes a book about it, a strolling bathtub, an alligator who swallows a car, and a porcupine whose haircut makes him look like a hat.

Koontz, Dean R., *Santa's Twin* (New York: HarperPrism, 1996). Ages 8–12. As told in verse, two girls set out to save Santa from his mischievous twin, Bob, who has not only stolen Santa's sleigh but has stuffed Santa's toy bag with mud pies and broccoli.

Kotzwinkle, William, *Trouble in Bugland: A Collection of Inspector Mantis Mysteries* (Boston: David R. Godine, 1986). Ages 10 and up. This is a collection of clever takeoffs on the Sherlock Holmes mysteries.
——*Hearts of Wood & Other Timeless Tales* (Boston: David R. Godine, 1986). All ages. Five fairy tales about such wonders as carousel horses that come alive and a butterfly catcher who dreams he's a butterfly.

Le Guin, Ursula K., *Catwings* and *Catwings Return* (New York: Orchard, 1990 and 1999, respectively). Ages 5–10. Four winged kittens fly away from the dangers of the city only to find adventures they hadn't expected. The feline characters are provided with realistic histories and human-like emotions. Le Guin also wrote other Catwings tales, including *Jane On Her Own* and *Wonderful Alexander and the Catwings*.
——*Very Far Away from Anywhere Else* (New York: Atheneum, 1976). Ages 12 and up. This story centers on a seventeen-year-old intellectual who longs for and finally finds someone who understands him.
——*A Visit from Dr. Katz* (New York: Atheneum, 1988). Ages 5–8. A tale of two cats who help cure their young female owner of the flu by curling up on her tummy.

✳ Mamet, David, *Warm and Cold* (New York: Grove Press, 1989). Ages 4–7. This is a very brief, evocative tale of a man traveling by train in winter, away from those he loves.

Mamet also wrote *Three Children's Plays*.

✳ Maurois, Andre, *Fattypuffs and Thinifers* (New York: Knopf, 1989). All ages. Two boys find themselves on opposite sides of a negotiating table because the nations of the Fattypuffs and the Thinifers want to fight about their differences.

McEwan, Ian, *The Daydreamer* (New York: Bantam, 2000). Ages 8 and up. A ten-year-old boy daydreams about fantastic events in this wryly amusing tale about the imagination and growing up.

O'Rourke, Frank, *Burton and Stanley* (New York: Sunburst, 1996). Ages 10 and up. Two droll African storks are transported to America's heartland by a freakish ill wind. They communicate in Morse code with a railroad depot agent, who becomes determined to help them return to their Kenyan home before winter, hunters, or wildlife agents prevail.

Oz, Amos, *Soumchi* (Orlando, FL: Harcourt, 1995). Ages 12 and up. The misadventures of an eleven-year-old boy growing up in British-occupied Jerusalem.

Rushdie, Salman, *Haroun and the Sea of Stories* (New York: Viking, 1990). Ages 8 and up. This rather complicated fantasy adventure, which began as a bedtime story for Rushdie's son, concerns a son's attempt to rescue his father and return to him his "gift of gab." Younger readers will need help with the language.

Saki, *The Story-Teller* (Boston: David R. Godine, 1987). Ages 9 and up. All thirteen of these witty tales are about children. In each, the kids come off better than their petty and predictable elders.

Sandburg, Carl, *Rootabaga Stories, Part One* and *Rootabaga Stories, Part Two* (Orlando, Fl: Harcourt, 1988 and 1989, respectively). Ages 5 and up. The language in these stories is lyrical, the characters and story lines strange and fantastic. Readers will find such oddities as a broom handle that marries a rag doll, two skyscrapers who whisper together and decide to have a child (who turns out to be a train), and a jackrabbit who jumps so high he never comes down.

Saramago, Jose, *The Tale of the Unknown Island* (Orlando, FL: Harcourt, 2000). All ages. This is a wry and surreal fable about a determined man and the king's

211 adds a flowing note to

cleaning woman who prepare a boat to find an unknown island. Instead, they find themselves and love. The tale can be experienced on more than one level, and the unusual lack of "he said, she said" indicators adds a flowing note to the reading.

Singer, Isaac Bashevis, *Stories for Children* (New York: Farrar, Straus and Giroux, 1985). All ages. These thirty-six tales feature a variety of interesting characters including an absent-minded professor who forgets his own address, a Yiddish-speaking parakeet who plays unwitting matchmaker, and a wise rabbi who battles a wicked witch. In simple prose, Singer writes of magic, fools, love, and deceit.
——*The Golem* (New York: Farrar, Straus and Giroux, 1996). Ages 5 and up. Singer retells the tale of the golem, a clay giant who helps the Jews of Prague.
   Singer also wrote *The Power of Light: Eight Stories for Hanukkah* and *When Shlemiel Went to Warsaw and Other Stories.*

❋ Stafford, Jean, *Elephi: The Cat with a High I.Q.* (New York: Yearling, 1962). Ages 7 and up. A bored cat smuggles a small foreign car into his apartment so he can have a playmate.

Strand, Mark, *Rembrandt Takes a Walk* (New York: Crown Publishing, 1990). This is an amusing fantasy about a boy who visits his absent-minded, art-collecting uncle and finds he can remove food from famous paintings. When Rembrandt steps out of a painting, the boy takes him for a walk around town, where the famous painter is obsessed with drawing everything he sees. Vividly illustrated by artist Red Grooms.

Tan, Amy, *The Chinese Siamese Cat* (New York: Macmillan, 1994). Ages 4 and up. A colorful picture book that tells an amusing fable about the ancestry of some kittens.
——*The Moon Lady* (New York: Aladdin, 1995). Ages 5–9. A picture book about a long-ago autumn moon festival in China, through the eyes of a seven-year-old.

Thomas, Dylan, *A Child's Christmas in Wales* (Boston: David R. Godine, 1984). All ages. First published in 1954, this is probably Thomas's most famous childhood reminiscence. The language is musical and should be read aloud for optimum pleasure.

Thurber, James, *The 13 Clocks* (New York: Dell, 1992). Ages 8 and up. A complex, funny tale of a prince, a princess, and a wicked duke who's afraid of Now.
Thurber also wrote *Many Moons, The Wonderful O,* and *The Great Quillow.*

Tolkien, J. R. R., *The Hobbit* (Boston: Houghton Mifflin, 1999). Ages 7 and up. This fantasy adventure about the mythological kingdom of Middle Earth can be enjoyed both by older children and, as a read-aloud, by kids as young as seven. Tolkien continues the saga in the epic trilogy *Lord of the Rings.*
——*Roverandom* (Boston: Houghton Mifflin, 1999). Ages 9 and up. Tolkien wrote this fantasy to console his son for the loss of a tiny toy dog.
——*Smith of Wootton Major* (Boston: Houghton Mifflin, 1991). Ages 8 and up. A deftly written fantasy about the odd things that happen to a boy who eats a star at the Feast of Good Children.
Tolkien also wrote *Mr. Bliss, Farmer Giles of Ham,* and *The Adventures of Tom Bombadil* (poems).

Tolstoy, Leo, *The Lion and the Puppy and Other Stories for Children* (New York: Seaver Books, 1988). Ages 5 and up. Tolstoy wrote these tales for a primer used in a school he founded. His aim was to invent interesting stories that would teach right from wrong while conveying messages about freedom, courage, generosity, patience, and respect for nature. The title story is about a lion that learns to love a puppy that has been tossed to him as food. When the puppy dies, the lion dies of grief.
\* ——*The Fool* (New York: Schocken, 1981). Ages 5 and up. A retelling of a Russian folk tale, written in verse.
Tolstoy also wrote *Fables and Fairy Tales.*

\* Twain, Mark, *Poor Little Stephen Girard* (New York: Schocken, 1981). Ages 6 and up. A witty short story about a boy who hears of someone who became successful by collecting pins in front of a bank.
Other Twain stories for children include *A Cat-Tale,* written for his own daughters; *The Stolen White Elephant,* about a giant, white, Bible-eating elephant; and *Legend of Sagenfeld,* a fairy tale.

Verne, Jules, *Adventures of the Rat Family* (New York: Oxford University Press, 1993). Ages 7 and up. A droll literary fairy tale with lots of dialogue to keep the action moving and many intriguing words for younger readers to learn.

Walker, Alice, *To Hell with Dying* (Orlando, FL: Harcourt, 1993). Ages 9 and up. Told from an adult perspective, this reminiscence concerns old, alcoholic

Mr. Sweet, who is often on the brink of death. The children who are his friends save him with kisses, tickles, and love.

Walker also wrote *Finding the Green Stone*.

Wilbur, Richard, *Loudmouse* (Orlando, FL: Harcourt, 1982). Ages 6–10. The story of a mouse whose family's safety is endangered because he cannot speak softly.
——*The Disappearing Alphabet* (Orlando, FL: Harcourt, 1997). All ages. "If G did not exist, the color green/ Would have to vanish from the rural scene." And so on.
——*A Game of Catch* (Orlando, FL: Harcourt, 1994). Ages 4 and up. This picture book is about three boys, one of whom directs the others by telling them to do whatever it is they're already doing.
——*Opposites, More Opposites, and a Few Differences* (Orlando, FL: Harcourt, 2000). All ages. A collection of Wilbur's previous volumes of poems (*Opposites and More Opposites*), plus some additional poems. This book asks whether, for example, there's an opposite of "sheep" or of "SOS."
——*The Pig in the Spigot* (Orlando, FL: Harcourt, 2000). All ages. Funny poems about words within words (if you find a pig in your spigot, for instance, turn the spigot on full force to eject it).
——*Runaway Opposites* (Orlando, FL: Harcourt, 1995). All ages. This is a fancifully illustrated version of some of Wilbur's amusing "opposites."

Wilde, Oscar, *The Happy Prince and Other Stories* (Hertfordshire, England: Wordsworth, 1999). Ages 6 and up. This volume contains nine magical tales first told by Wilde to his own two sons. In "The Selfish Giant," a giant keeps children out of his garden, and spring doesn't come until he has a change of heart. In "The Star Child," a proud boy learns humility as he wanders through his medieval world.

Wilde also wrote *The Nightingale and the Rose*.

Wolitzer, Hilma, *Wish You Were Here* (New York: Farrar, Straus and Giroux, 1986). Ages 9–12. The characters here are absolutely believable, as are those in Wolitzer's other books for preteens, *Introducing Shirley Braverman* and *Out of Love*. She tackles the everyday, the dramatic, and the traumatic—divorce, death, war, shyness, loneliness—with skill, humor, and insight.

Woolf, Virginia, *The Widow and the Parrot* (Orlando, FL: Harcourt, 1988). Ages 9–12. This story, illustrated by Woolf's grandnephew, was written at the request of her nephews, Quentin and Julian Bell, for a family newspaper they put out regularly when they were young. They didn't like it; it wasn't as frivolous as they'd hoped.

# Rhymes for Young Readers

In addition to some of the books mentioned earlier that contain verse, here are some poetry books for children written by notable poets (or by novelists crossing over):

Brodsky, Joseph, *Discovery* (New York: Farrar, Straus and Giroux, 1999). All ages. A picture-book poem that celebrates America before and after it was "discovered," and the spirit of discovery itself.

Ciardi, John, *The Hopeful Trout and Other Limericks* (Boston: Houghton Mifflin, 1992). All ages. This volume includes forty preposterous limericks.
   More Ciardi for children: *I Met a Man, Fast and Slow,* and *Doodle Soup.*

\* Dickey, James, *Bronwen, the Traw, and the Shape-Shifter: A Poem in Four Parts* (Orlando, FL: Harcourt, 1986). Ages 5–10. A long, lyrical poem based on stories Dickey told his daughter when she was three and four.

Dickinson, Emily, *A Brighter Garden* (Philomel, 1990). All ages. Twenty-three illustrated poems that explore the seasons.
——*Dickinson: Poetry for Young People,* edited by Frances Schoonmaker Bolin (New York: Sterling, 1994). Ages 7–12. This is a collection of some of Dickinson's more famous yet accessible poems, including "Hope Is the Thing with Feathers." Difficult words are explained at the bottoms of pages.

Eliot, T. S., *Old Possum's Book of Practical Cats* (Orlando, FL: Harcourt, 1982). All ages. Kids will enjoy your reading aloud these appealing poems about the personalities and antics of particular cats (widely known due to the long-running musical based on this volume, *Cats*).
——*Growltiger's Last Stand and Other Poems* (New York: Farrar, Straus and Giroux, 1990). All ages. A picture-book version of three poems from *Old Possum's Book of Practical Cats.*

Field, Edward, *Magic Words* (Orlando, FL: Gulliver, 1998). Ages 4–9. Poems based on Inuit creation stories.

Frost, Robert, *You Come Too: Favorite Poems for Young Readers* (New York: Henry Holt, 1987). All ages. Frost himself selected these poems as especially suitable for young people. Many have to do, at least in part, with nature, such as "The Road Not Taken."

———*Poetry for Young People: Robert Frost,* edited by Gary D. Schmidt (New York: Sterling, 1994). Ages 7–12. Each of the poems in this collection is followed by a simple "explanation," provided by the editor.

Klein, A. M., *Doctor Dwarf & Other Poems for Children* (Kingston, ON: Quarry Press, 1989). All ages. Written for the poet's children, these poems concern Jewish history and stories.

Nash, Ogden, *Ogden Nash's Zoo* (New York: Stewart, Tabori & Chang, 1987). All ages. Funny verses about a variety of animals, some unique to Nash ("Long-winded storytellers flinch/If I bring up the three-toed grynch").

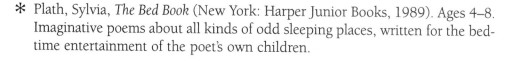

✳ Plath, Sylvia, *The Bed Book* (New York: Harper Junior Books, 1989). Ages 4–8. Imaginative poems about all kinds of odd sleeping places, written for the bedtime entertainment of the poet's own children.

Service, Robert W., *The Shooting of Dan McGrew* (Boston: David R. Godine, 1995). All ages. This classic read-aloud poem is set in the time of the Alaskan Gold Rush. Service was known as "Canada's Kipling," and the rhythms in this poem make it easy to see why.
  Service also wrote *The Cremation of Sam McGee.*

Stein, Gertrude, *The World Is Round* (San Francisco, CA: North Point Press, 1988). Ages 8 and up. Stein's only children's book, which features idiosyncratic punctuation and a childlike approach to reality, concerns nine-year-old Rose and her search for self.

Stevenson, Robert Louis, *My Shadow* (Boston: David R. Godine, 1989). Ages 2–5. Colorful illustrations turn this poem from Stevenson's *A Child's Garden of Verses* into a picture book.

Updike, John, *A Child's Calendar* (New York: Knopf, 1965). Ages 4 and up. Simple, rhyming poems about the months.
Updike also wrote *The Magic Flute, The Ring,* and *Bottom's Dream.*

# . . . and More

While you're searching out books, keep your eyes open for the following respected authors' contributions to children's literature:

Margaret Atwood, *Up in the Tree, Anna's Pet, For the Birds,* and *Princess Prunella and the Purple Peanut*

Clive Barker, *The Thief of Always*

Pearl S. Buck, *The Water-Buffalo Children* and *The Dragon Fish*

Peter Carey, *The Big Bazoohley*

Roddy Doyle, *The Giggler Treatment*

Louise Erdrich, *The Birchbark House*

William Faulkner, *The Wishing Tree*

Faye Gibbons, *Mountain Wedding*

Robert A. Heinlein, *Citizen of the Galaxy*

Garrison Keillor, *Cat, You Better Come Home*

Jonathan Kellerman, *Daddy, Can You Touch the Sky?*

Maxine Kumin, seventeen books for children plus several written with poet Anne Sexton

Alison Lurie, *Clever Gretchen & Other Forgotten Folk Tales, The Heavenly Zoo,* and *Fabulous Animals*

Lorrie Moore, *The Forgotten Helper*

Howard Norman, *The Girl Who Dreamed Only Geese*

Joyce Carol Oates, *Come Meet Muffin!*

Chaim Potok, *The Tree of Here*

Reynolds Price, *A Perfect Friend*

Francine Prose, *The Demons' Mistake: A Story from Chelm*

Anna Quindlen, *The Tree That Came to Stay*

Mordecai Richler, *Jacob Two-Two's First Spy* (and two previous adventures)

Theodore Roethke, *Party at the Zoo*

George Sand, *The Mysterious Tale of Gentle Jack and Lord Bumblebee*

May Sarton, *A Walk Through the Woods*

Lynne Sharon Schwartz, *The Four Questions*

Gary Soto, *Jesse, Baseball in April, Local News, Taking Sides,* and *Pacific Crossing*

Muriel Spark, *The Very Fine Clock*

Elizabeth Spires, *The Mouse of Amherst*

William Stafford, *The Animal That Drank Up Sound*

Frank R. Stockton, *The Griffin and the Minor Canon*

May Swenson, *Poems to Solve* and *More Poems to Solve*

Anne Tyler, *Tumble Tower*

Leon Uris, *Tales from Forever Island*

Voltaire, *The Dog and the Horse*

# Index

# About the Author

**Susan K. Perry, Ph.D.,** is a social psychologist and award-winning author. Her books include the bestseller *Writing in Flow: Keys to Enhanced Creativity; Catch the Spirit: Top Teen Volunteers Tell How They Made a Difference;* and *Fun Time, Family Time.* She has had more than 700 articles in national and regional publications, including *Child, Parenting, Seventeen, Woman's World, USA Today,* and the *Los Angeles Times.* She is Contributing Editor to *L.A. Parent* and *Valley* magazines, and Fun and Activities Expert at ParentCenter.com. She won a First Place Award for Service Articles from the American Society of Journalists and Authors, as well as a First Place Award of Excellence in the Parenting Publications of America annual competition.

Susan teaches psychology at Woodbury University and teaches writing at various university extension programs and online for Writer's Digest. She is also a one-on-one writing consultant. She obtained her doctorate in human development from The Fielding Institute. Earlier, she founded and directed an unusual and successful early childhood program called Discovery House School. She was also a teacher for the Gifted Children's Association of Los Angeles, for which she developed innovative courses in human relations, creativity, science, and reading.

She is the mother of two grown sons and lives in Los Angeles with her husband, poet Stephen Perry. Her Internet home is *www.bunnyape.com.*

# Other Great Books from Free Spirit

### You Know Your Child Is Gifted When...
*by Judy Galbraith, M.A., illustrated by Ken Vinton, M.A.*
This one-of-a-kind book makes it fun and easy to learn the basics about what makes gifted kids "tick" and how you can support their unique abilities. A light-hearted introduction to life with a young gifted child, it blends humorous cartoons and lively illustrations with solid information on giftedness—its characteristics, challenges, and joys. For parents and educators of gifted children in grades PreK–6. *$10.95; 128 pp.; softcover; illus.; 6" x 6"*

### What Young Children Need to Succeed
Working Together to Build Assets from Birth to Age 11
*by Jolene L. Roehlkepartain and Nancy Leffert, Ph.D.*
Based on groundbreaking research, this book helps adults create a firm foundation for children from day one. You'll find hundreds of practical, concrete ways to build 40 assets in four different age groups. Comprehensive, friendly, and easy-to-use, this book will make anyone an asset builder and a positive influence in children's lives. For parents, teachers, all other caring adults, and children. *$9.95; 320 pp.; softcover; illus.; 5¼" x 8"*

**Leader's Guide** *$19.95; 152 pp.; softcover; 8½" x 10⅞"*

### Growing Good Kids
28 Activities to Enhance Self-Awareness, Compassion, and Leadership
*by Deb Delisle and Jim Delisle, Ph.D.*
Created by teachers and classroom-tested, these fun and meaningful enrichment activities build children's skills in problem solving, decision making, cooperative learning, divergent thinking, and communication. For grades 4–8. *$21.95; 168 pp.; softcover; illus.; 8½" x 11"*

### The School-Savvy Parent
365 Insider Tips to Help You Help Your Child
*by Rosemarie Clark, M.Ed., Donna Hawkins, M.Ed., and Beth Vachon, M.Ed.*
Who knows the most about how to prepare your child for a happy, safe, successful school year? Teachers! Straight from the source, here are hundreds of positive, practical tips all parents can use to become active, informed supporters of their children's education. For parents of children ages 4–14. *$12.95; 208 pp.; softcover; illus.; 5" x 8"*

## Being Your Best
Character Building for Kids 7–10
*by Barbara A. Lewis*
Written for children ages 7–10, this book invites them to explore who they are and who they'd like to be. Even elementary school kids can learn about and build important character traits like caring, citizenship, respect, and more—traits that will help them grow into capable, moral teens and adults. For ages 7–10. *$14.95; 172 pp.; softcover; illus.; 7¼" x 9¼"*

**Leader's Guide** *$18.95; 144 pp.; softcover; 8½" x 11"*

## How to Help Your Child with Homework
Every Caring Parent's Guide to Encouraging Good Study Habits and Ending the Homework Wars (*Revised and Updated*)
*by Marguerite C. Radencich, Ph.D., and Jeanne Shay Schumm, Ph.D.*
Put an end to excuses and arguments while improving your child's school performance. Realistic strategies and proven techniques make homework hassle-free. Includes handouts, resources, and real-life examples. For parents of children ages 6–13. *$15.95; 208 pp.; softcover; 7¼" x 9¼"*

## The Reading Tutor's Handbook
A Commonsense Guide to Helping Students Read and Write
*by Jeanne Shay Schumm, Ph.D., and Gerald E. Schumm Jr., D. Min.*
Based on Jeanne Schumm's years of experience training volunteer tutors, this book is for anyone who wants to make a difference in a young person's life. Includes reproducibles. For grades 1–12. *$18.95; 152 pp.; softcover; 8½" x 11"*

## Bringing Out the Best
A Guide for Parents of Young Gifted Children
*Revised and Updated*
*by Jacqulyn Saunders with Pamela Espeland*
This popular handbook explains how to tell if your child is gifted, how to choose the right school, how to deal with teachers, and more. Includes activities to do together and tips for avoiding parent burnout. For parents of children ages 2–7. *$14.95; 240 pp.; softcover; B&W photos and illus., 7¼" x 9¼"*

To place an order or to request a free catalog of SELF–HELP FOR KIDS® materials, please write, call, email, or visit our Web site:

**Free Spirit Publishing Inc.**
**217 Fifth Avenue North • Suite 200 • Minneapolis, MN 55401-1299**
**toll-free 800.735.7323 • local 612.338.2068 • fax 612.337.5050**
**help4kids@freespirit.com • www.freespirit.com**